C000254550

Pharaoh Seti I

For Ingrid

Pharaoh Seti I

Father of Egyptian Greatness

Nicky Nielsen

PEN & SWORD
HISTORY

First published in Great Britain in 2018
by Pen & Sword History
An imprint of Pen & Sword Books Limited
47 Church Street
Barnsley
South Yorkshire
S70 2AS

Copyright © Nicky Nielsen 2018

ISBN 978 1 52673 957 5

The right of Nicky Nielsen to be identified as
Author of this Work has been asserted by him in accordance
with the Copyright, Designs and Patents Act 1988.

A CIP catalogue record for this book is
available from the British Library.

All rights reserved. No part of this book may be reproduced or
transmitted in any form or by any means, electronic or mechanical
including photocopying, recording or by any information storage and
retrieval system, without permission from the Publisher in writing.

Typeset in Ehrhardt
by Mac Style

Printed and bound in the UK
by TJ International Ltd, Padstow, Cornwall

Pen & Sword Books Limited incorporates the imprints of Atlas,
Archaeology, Aviation, Discovery, Family History, Fiction, History,
Maritime, Military, Military Classics, Politics, Select, Transport,
True Crime, Air World, Frontline Publishing, Leo Cooper,
Remember When, Seaforth Publishing, The Praetorian Press,
Wharncliffe Local History, Wharncliffe Transport,
Wharncliffe True Crime and White Owl.

For a complete list of Pen & Sword titles please contact
PEN & SWORD BOOKS LIMITED
47 Church Street, Barnsley, South Yorkshire, S70 2AS, England
E-mail: enquiries@pen-and-sword.co.uk
Website: www.pen-and-sword.co.uk

Contents

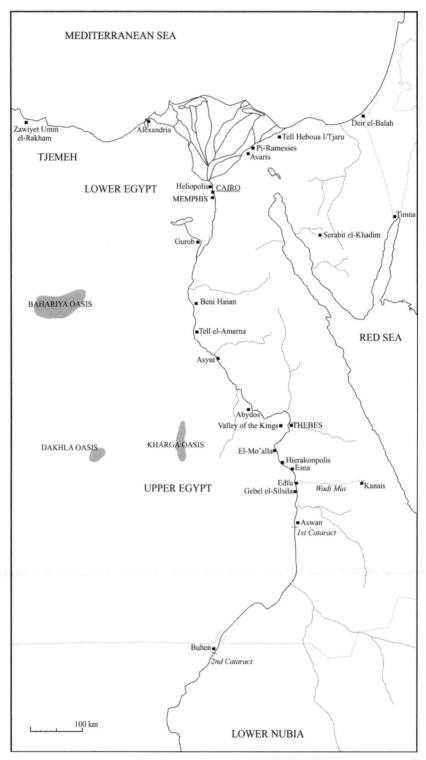

Map showing the major sites in Egypt during the reign of Seti I. (*Author*)

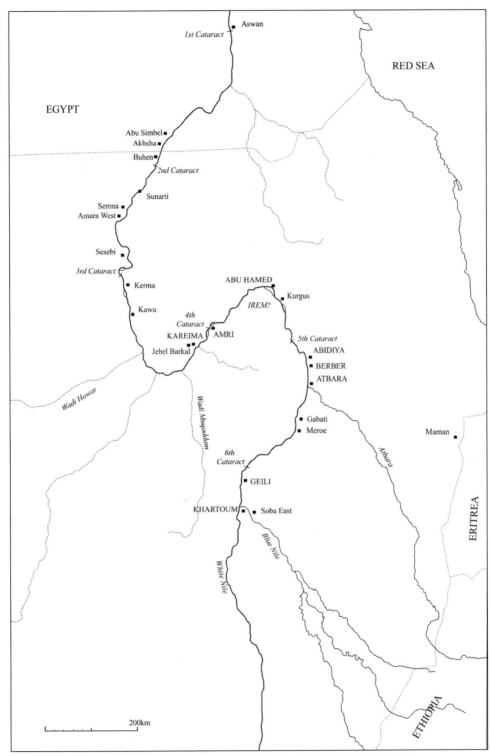

Map of Upper and Lower Nubia. (*Author*)

Map showing the principal locations and civilizations in the Near East during Seti's reign. (*Author*)

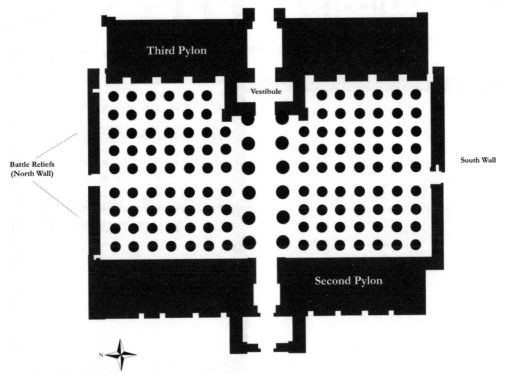

Plan of the Great Hypostyle Hall at the Karnak Temple in Luxor. (*Author*)

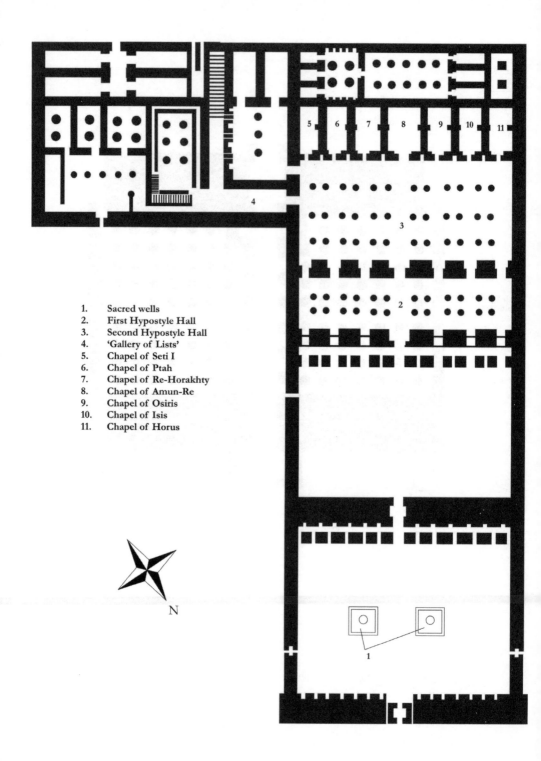

1. Sacred wells
2. First Hypostyle Hall
3. Second Hypostyle Hall
4. 'Gallery of Lists'
5. Chapel of Seti I
6. Chapel of Ptah
7. Chapel of Re-Horakhty
8. Chapel of Amun-Re
9. Chapel of Osiris
10. Chapel of Isis
11. Chapel of Horus

Plan of Seti I's temple at Abydos. (*Author*)

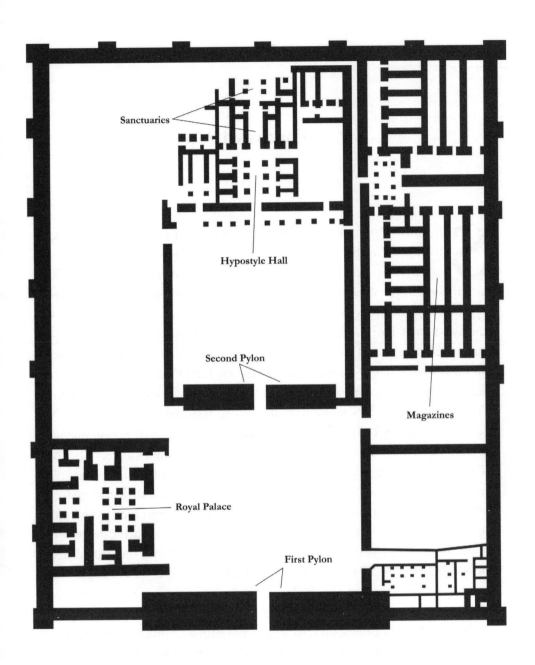

Sanctuaries

Hypostyle Hall

Second Pylon

Magazines

Royal Palace

First Pylon

N

Plan of Seti's mortuary temple at Qurna. (*Author*)

Foreword

Seti, son of Paramessu, was a remarkable man. His biography reads like a blueprint for the ideal dynastic king. Born the son of a soldier, Seti had royalty thrust upon him when his elderly father was unexpectedly gifted the throne of Egypt. After just two years working as vizier and co-regent alongside the renamed Ramesses I, Seti was himself crowned king of the Two Lands. He proved to be an ambitious and highly effective monarch: a successful warrior and an accomplished builder. Under his direct command, an aggressive series of military campaigns saw Egypt's borders secured and Egypt's military reputation, which had been somewhat tarnished during the Amarna Period and its immediate aftermath, restored to its former glory. Increased stability brought increasing wealth, which allowed Seti to finance a portfolio of ambitious construction projects throughout Egypt. The Temple of Re at Heliopolis, the Temple of Ptah at Memphis and the Temple of Amen at Karnak all benefited from his generosity. At the ancient cemetery site of Abydos, Seti built a unique monument: a subterranean cenotaph linked to an extensive temple whose seven sanctuaries were dedicated to the gods Osiris, Isis, Horus, Amen-Re, Re-Harakhty, Ptah and the deified Seti himself. On the west bank of the Nile, at Thebes, Seti erected a conspicuous memorial temple and, hidden in the nearby Valley of the Kings, he excavated the longest, deepest and most beautifully decorated of all the royal tombs.

After just over a decade on the throne, Seti, still a relatively young man by modern standards, died. As he had planned, his mummified body was buried in an elaborate alabaster sarcophagus in his extensive tomb. The rituals were performed, the tomb door was sealed and Seti's spirit journeyed into the west, where he transformed from a semi-divine being into a god. Today, Seti's mummy rests in Cairo Museum where his beautifully preserved head, brutally severed from his body by ancient tomb robbers, represents one of the finest examples of the dynastic embalmer's art.

I hope that this brief biography is enough to convince the reader that Seti I is a man entirely worthy of detailed study. Why, then, has he been overlooked by historians? The blame lies to a great extent with his son, the much larger-than-life Ramesses II. Ramesses followed his father onto the throne, and ruled Egypt for an almost unbelievable sixty-six years. This gave him sufficient time to impose his name on the Egyptian landscape by both building his own monuments and blatantly 'borrowing' the monuments and inscriptions of others. Ramesses cut his hieroglyphs larger and deeper than anyone else, so that by the time of his death his name was written large all over his land. A master of propaganda, he has been able to convince us that he, Ramesses, was and always would be Egypt's greatest king. With Ramesses usurping the historical limelight, Seti, the man who laid down the foundations for his son's reign, has been condemned to stand hidden in shadow.

So I am delighted that Nicky Nielsen has undertaken the task of restoring Seti to his rightful place as of one of Egypt's most successful kings. Setting Seti into his proper historical context, Dr Nielsen provides a scholarly, comprehensive and very readable guide through the intricacies of his family life, his reign and its immediate aftermath. His admiration for Seti and his achievements shines through his writing, making this book an essential read for anyone interested in the development of Egypt's dynastic age.

Dr Joyce Tyldesley (archaeologist, author and Senior Lecturer in Egyptology at Manchester University), October 2017

Acknowledgements

First and foremost, I would like to thank my parents Gitte and Leif for their encouragement during the writing process and for imbuing me with a love of history which would eventually become a career. I should also like to thank Philip Sidnell, commissioning editor at Pen & Sword for his help and interest; Dr Joyce Tyldesley for sharing with me some of her wealth of experience as an author and scholar; Dr Huw Twiston Davies for tolerating endless conversations about Seti and his reign with good grace; Dr Campbell Price, Dr Gina Criscenzo-Laycock and Dr Valentina Gasperini for their kind encouragement and crucially, Diana T. Nikolova for being with me every step of the way with unconditional support and love.

Chronology of Ancient Egyptian History

Predynastic Period	5300–3000 BC
Early Dynastic Period	3000–2686 BC
Dynasty 1	3000–2890 BC
Dynasty 2	2890–2686 BC
Old Kingdom	2686–2160 BC
Dynasty 3	2686–2613 BC
Dynasty 4	2613–2494 BC
Dynasty 5	2494–2345 BC
Dynasty 6	2345–2181 BC
Dynasty 7/8	2181–2160 BC
First Intermediate Period	2160–2055 BC
Dynasty 9/10	2160–2055 BC
Dynasty 11	2125–2055 BC (Contemporary with Dynasty 9/10)
Middle Kingdom	2055–1650 BC
Dynasty 11	2055–1985 BC
Dynasty 12	1985–1773 BC
Dynasty 13	1773–1650 BC
Dynasty 14	1773–1650 BC (Contemporary with Dynasty 13)
Second Intermediate Period	1650–1550 BC
Dynasty 15	1650–1550 BC
Dynasty 16	1650–1580 BC (Contemporary with Dynasty 15)
Dynasty 17	1580–1550 BC (Contemporary with Dynasty 15)

New Kingdom	1550–1077 BC
Dynasty 18	1550–1292 BC
Ahmose I	1549–1524 BC
Amenhotep I	1524–1503 BC
Thutmosis I	1503–1493 BC
Thutmosis II	1493–1479 BC
Thutmosis III	1479–1425 BC
Hatshepsut	1479–1458 BC
Amenhotep II	1425–1398 BC
Thutmosis IV	1398–1388 BC
Amenhotep III	1388–1350 BC
Akhenaten	1350–1334 BC
Smenkhare	1335–1334 BC
Neferneferuaten	1344–1332 BC
Tutankhamun	1332–1323 BC
Ay	1323–1319 BC
Horemheb	1319–1292 BC
Dynasty 19	1292–1189 BC
Ramesses I	1292–1290 BC
Seti I	1290–1279 BC
Ramesses II	1279–1213 BC
Merenptah	1213–1203 BC
Seti II	1203–1197 BC
Amenmesse	1201–1198 BC
Siptah	1197–1191 BC
Twosret	1191–1189 BC
Dynasty 20	1189–1077 BC
Setnakhte	1189–1186 BC
Ramesses III	1186–1155 BC
Ramesses IV	1155–1149 BC
Ramesses V	1149–1145 BC
Ramesses VI	1145–1137 BC
Ramesses VII	1136–1129 BC
Ramesses VIII	1130–1129 BC
Ramesses IX	1129–1111 BC

Ramesses X	1111–1107 BC
Ramesses XI	1107–1077 BC
Third Intermediate Period	1069–664 BC
Dynasty 21	1069–945 BC
Dynasty 22	945–715 BC
Dynasty 23	818–715 BC (Contemporary with Dynasty 22)
Dynasty 24	727–715 BC (Contemporary with Dynasties 23 and 25)
Dynasty 25	747–656 BC
Late Period	664–332 BC
Dynasty 26	664–525 BC
Dynasty 27	525–404 BC
Dynasty 28	404–399 BC
Dynasty 29	399–380 BC
Dynasty 30	380–343 BC
Dynasty 31	343–332 BC
Ptolemaic Period	332–30 BC
Macedonian Dynasty	332–305 BC
Ptolemaic Dynasty	305–30 BC
Roman Period	30 BC–AD 395

Author's Note

A great deal of public literature and documentaries – the good, the bad and the ugly – has been written and produced about aspects of ancient Egyptian history and culture. Given the sheer span of Pharaonic civilization, nearly 4,000 years, it is natural that certain periods and personalities have become focal points. Ramesses the Great, the archetypal pharaoh, is one of these, a role he has gained because of the length of his reign, his bombastic nature and the sheer scale of the many temples and monuments built during his reign, as well as perceived link to the Biblical narrative (largely a creation of Hollywood). Other rulers, like the female Pharaoh Hatshepsut, have grown in the public perception, due in her case to the tireless work of advocates within the Egyptological community rightly determined not to allow such a significant ruler to remain in the obscurity into which she had been pushed by her descendants. Other pharaohs, like Tutankhamun, are not famed or remembered in particular for any deeds or actions they took in life, but in his case rather because of the 'Egyptomania' created by the discovery of his tomb in 1922, an event which fired the collective imagination of much of the planet. The Egyptian Pharaoh Seti I, father of Ramesses the Great, has very rarely held a place in the sun. At most, his reign has been considered purely an antecedent to Ramesses, deserving of little more than a footnote, a passing paragraph in the far more magnificent tale of his son. This book is an attempt to remedy this unjust treatment of a fascinating king, and to cast Seti as a leading player in his own right, not merely a walk-on part on someone else's stage.

Seti was born as the son of a high-ranking military officer near the small outpost of Avaris in the north-eastern Nile Delta. He grew into manhood at the border fortress of Tjaru, surrounded by rough infantrymen, camp followers and exotic-looking Nubian and Libyan scouts and auxiliary troops. The soggy loam of the Delta and the swirling sands on the desert edge must have seemed a far cry from the calcite-tiled halls of power in Thebes and Memphis. But Seti rose in the hierarchy, along with his father. When the last king of the 18th Dynasty, Horemheb, died without a male heir, Seti's father, Paramessu, was crowned as king. He took the name Ramesses I and founded the Ramesside Dynasty. But he ruled for less than two years, and on his death, he left his young son in charge of an ailing superpower, riven by dynastic squabbles, chaotic successions and poorly conceived foreign policies.

This book will examine Seti's life and the actions he took to restore Egyptian military, cultural and economic power as he perceived it. It will discuss his active foreign policy, his itinerant style of governance and the overwhelming building projects he initiated throughout the Two Lands of Egypt. But Seti, despite being a supreme monarch, did not govern the country alone. It is also necessary to also dwell on the people – from the private soldiers in his army to the courtiers who advised him – whose labour and lives were given to achieve Seti's aims.

The book has been written with the interested public in mind. It is not a piece of original research, and lies quite far from the areas of research and types of writing I customarily engage in. Some colleagues will probably accuse me of simplifications; on the other hand, other readers may feel that I am too vague, and too comfortable hiding behind different theories and hypotheses, in lieu of being definitive. The truth is that we can rarely be absolutely certain of anything when we investigate ancient civilizations. Ignoring the inherent ambiguity caused by the fragmentary state of the evidence would be dishonest, as would inventing emotions and character traits for which there is no evidence at all. Writing this book has been a chance to try to understand not just the role and influence of Seti's reign, but more importantly perhaps, the historical antecedents which allowed for his existence. I have tried to write without undue nostalgia and without overstretching the existing evidence. The decision of whether I have succeeded or failed is ultimately up to the reader.

Chapter 1

Setting the Stage[1]

A visitor to Cairo's fabled Tahrir Square cannot fail to notice the bulk of The Museum of Egyptian Antiquities. Within its bright red walls, this neoclassical masterpiece has housed the world's largest collection of ancient Egyptian artefacts since 1902. While it was built by the French architect Marcel Dourgnon (1858–1911), the museum was originally the brainchild of his compatriot, François Auguste Ferdinand Mariette (1821–1881).[2] Mariette worked as an archaeologist in Egypt for most of his life, and rose to become Director of Antiquities in Cairo, spurning academic positions in Europe with the words: 'I would die or go mad if I did not return to Egypt immediately!' As he grew older, he became convinced that the customary division of finds after an excavation – European and American excavators would collect some of the better antiquities for their own museums back home – was deeply problematic. Attempting to protect Egypt's heritage, Mariette founded The Museum of Egyptian Antiquities in a former magazine in the Bulaq neighbourhood of Cairo in 1858, aiming to create a permanent home for the excavated antiquities and limit the number that were making their way out of Egypt to museums or private collectors. Due to flooding and other damage, the growing collection of museum pieces was moved, first to a former royal palace near the Giza Pyramids and then, in the early years of the twentieth century, to its current purpose-built home in Tahrir Square.

As you make your way through the bustle of the square towards the museum, accompanied by the blaring of car horns, you first arrive in the peculiarly peaceful sculpture garden which fronts the museum entrance. Some of the largest pieces of temple relief, sarcophagi and statues ever taken from Egypt's soil can be found here. Here too is the ostentatious sarcophagus which contains the remains of Mariette himself – a final reward for his service to the antiquities housed all around him.

One of the most visited exhibits accommodated within the museum's high-ceilinged, echoing halls is the Royal Mummy Room. Inside this dimly lit space lie some of the greatest kings and queens of ancient Egypt, most of them astoundingly well-preserved thanks to the embalmer's art. Here rests the body of Ramesses the Great, with tufts of auburn hair still curled at his temples, and his toe- and fingernails still clearly visible. Next to him, the mutilated corpse of the Second Intermediate Period Theban King Seqenenre-Tao, who met his death in battle, the injuries from an axe blow to his skull and several stab wounds still horrifically discernible.

Among the most well-preserved mummies in this august company is that of a middle-aged man with a prominent hooked nose, who lies with closed eyes, a slight smile playing around his lips. He appears – despite his shrunken form – to be sleeping peacefully. This is the body of King Seti I, the second ruler of the 19th Dynasty, the father of Ramesses the Great, and the *de facto* founder of the Ramesside Period. Born as a noble, but not a royal, Seti was not intended for kingship. But kingship was thrust upon him through an unusual combination of circumstances. As one of the Great Kings of the Late Bronze Age Near East, Seti used his time on the Horus Throne of the Living to reinvigorate Egypt's foreign policy, society and religious life after years of uncertain royal succession and internal strife. It was Seti's son, Ramesses II, whom history remembers as 'the Great', but it was Seti's reign which gave him the opportunities to earn his moniker.

* * *

Two great tributaries rise in Africa, one in the Great Lakes region and the other in Lake Tana in Ethiopia. These two waterways, the White and the Blue Nile, merge near the modern city of Khartoum in the Sudan before flowing north towards the Mediterranean. At times the river glides serenely past tilled fields, hemmed in by flat-topped foothills of sandstone or limestone, and at others the edge of desert plateaus constrict it on both sides, rendering the land barren and hostile. It forces its way through five granite cataracts before emerging onto the most abundantly fertile regions of its passage; the Nile Valley of Upper Egypt and the Delta of Lower Egypt. As a result of the differences in history and environment, the land which pharaoh ruled was always considered a union of these two lands, Upper and Lower Egypt. Before the construction of the Aswan High Dam, the river reached these lands heavily laden with silt, which it would deposit during its annual inundation. It was around this yearly occurrence, more than any solar events, that the ancient Egyptians constructed their calendar and measured their time.

The ancient Egyptian year was, unlike the Gregorian year, divided into three seasons: *Akhet* (Season of Inundation), *Peret* (Season of Growth) and *Shemu* (Season of Harvest). Each of the three seasons was in turn subdivided into four months, usually counted as 1st, 2nd, 3rd and 4th, each being thirty days long, giving an annual total of 360 days. The five additional days, known as epagomenal days, were added to compensate for the difference between the days listed in the civil calendar and the astronomical year. Each of the twelve months was divided into three weeks, each being ten days in length. Unlike many current calendars, the ancient Egyptian did not count the passing years by ascribing to each a number starting from a significant point in time, like the birth of Jesus Christ in the Gregorian calendar or the emigration of the Prophet Muhammad from Mecca to Medina in the Hijri. Instead, they counted the regnal years of the ruling pharaoh and began again when a new pharaoh rose to power. A full date would therefore be provided in the following manner, this particular example being from the fictional *Story of Sinuhe* which is set during the reign of Amenemhat I:

Regnal Year 30, Month 3 of *Akhet* (Inundation), Day 7

The date given then is the seventh day in the third of four months of the first season of the thirtieth regnal year of Amenemhat I. In modern terms, this date would fall in early August 1956 BC.

If a modern traveller could have followed the flow of the river in the time of Seti's ascension, they would have passed by small villages; in the Nile Valley set close to the banks of the river, and in the Delta built on small hillocks to prevent flooding during the inundation.[3] The farmers would have been working the soil of their fields with wooden hoes, sowing emmer wheat and barley by hand and leading flocks of animals – cattle, goats and sheep – across the mud to trample the grain into the ground. The wealth of Egypt was in its fertile earth; a gift – as the Classical author Herodotus of Halicarnassus noted – of the Nile. In every village, bakers spent their time huddled around small domed ovens, making bread by slapping a flat circle of dough on their red-hot clay interior, and catching the finished flatbread before it fell into the flames. This method of baking was in many ways comparable to the baking of tandoori naan across much of the Near East, India and China today. Larger loaves of bread were baked in ceramic moulds, and for special feasts and celebrations, bread was baked in the shape of animals and sweetened with figs and dates, or flavoured with spices such as coarsely crushed coriander seeds. Beer was brewed nearby, for it utilized the same basic raw ingredient cereals although bread was mostly made from emmer wheat and beer from barley. Ancient Egyptian beer had little in common with modern ales and stouts; rather it was brewed from cooked grain and malt, fermented in the sun, and equivalent in taste to modern wort.

Fishing boats made from bound reeds would have crowded the river, catching catfish and Nile perch with lines and nets, and hunting hippopotami with large bone harpoons, a dangerous task considering the temperament of these monstrous aquatic mammals. The slow rhythm of the bucolic scene would be interspersed with activity surrounding the major settlements: Elephantine lying on the doorstep to Nubia; Thebes, the town of Amun and the burial site of the New Kingdom pharaohs; Memphis, the city of the white walls, the traditional capital of Egypt since the Early Dynastic Period. The landing areas and harbours would have been bustling with workers carrying amphora of wine and olive oil, ingots of copper, planks of cedar wood traded from Byblos on the Canaanite coast, foreign captives and all manner of mammals, birds and fish, some preserved by drying or brining, others walking unknowingly to the slaughterhouses in the courtyards of villas and palaces.[4]

The focal point of these cities were the temple districts, large stone structures standing out in a sea of mud-brick houses, their undulating *temenos* walls signifying the divine waters of creation and the inner shrines with golden idols of the local god closed to all but pharaoh himself and the

High Priest appointed in his absence. Sculptors and artists worked in the temples, carving statues and relief from blocks of limestone, sandstone, granite, diorite and alabaster birthed from the rock face in quarries across the eastern desert and along Egypt's southern border. Expeditions sent out by the temples and by royal decree would return with gold from mines in Wadi Hammamat and Wadi Allaqi cast into crude rings for ease of transportation, and turquoise from the mines at Serabit el-Khadim in south-western Sinai.

Much of the metal and precious stones was transformed into images of the gods or jewellery worn by the royal family and their entourage. Some would undoubtedly be traded by the merchants working for the temple institutions, along with the surplus produce of temple lands. Royal scribes, commanders of the army, priests and all manner of officials would have thronged the palaces built near the temple districts, or else taken their ease within the shady tranquillity of their own villas, managing their private fortunes as well as working on the myriad tasks required for the central administration to function. A description of such an elite mansion from Papyrus British Museum 9994 dating to the 20th Dynasty gives a clear impression of their wealth and splendour:

'Raia has built a beautiful mansion [...] It is constructed like a work of eternity. It is planted with trees on all sides. A channel was dug in front of it [...] One is gay at its door and drunk in its halls. Handsome doorposts of limestone carved and chiselled. Beautiful doors, freshly carved. Walls inlaid with lapis lazuli. Its barns are supplied with grain, are bursting with abundance. Fowl yard and aviary are filled with geese; byres filled with cattle.'[5]

At the head of this throng of courtiers and wealthy nobles stood the viziers, one for Upper and one for Lower Egypt based in Thebes and Memphis. In theory, pharaoh ruled supreme over all these people, from the viziers and troop commanders in the cities to the farmers and bakers in their villages.

* * *

The Pharaonic civilization dominated Egypt from the Early Dynastic Period (*c.* 3000 BC) until the defeat of Cleopatra and Mark Antony at the hands of the later Emperor Augustus in 30 BC. Egyptologists sub-divide this extensive period of time firstly into 'kingdoms' (Old Kingdom, Middle Kingdom and New Kingdom), interspersed with periods of either unrest or significant decentralization and weakening of royal power known as 'intermediate periods' (First Intermediate Period, Second Intermediate Period and Third Intermediate Period). The most basic division (aside from the reign of individual kings) is the division of Pharaonic history into thirty-two 'dynasties', denoting specific ruling houses or families, often hailing from a specific geographical region. The 19th Dynasty for instance, was founded by Ramesses I, a non-royal military officer who most likely came from the north-eastern Delta region. This division of Egyptian history into dynasties is not a chronological tool invented by modern scholars. Rather, it dates back to the enigmatic historian Manetho.[6]

Living during the reign of the early Ptolemaic rulers who had risen to power in Egypt during the third century BC following Alexander the Great's conquest of the country in 332 BC, Manetho was an Egyptian priest from the Delta city of Sebennytos. He was a native Egyptian, but wrote several important works on Egyptian history in Greek, most likely on the orders of the new Greek-speaking Ptolemaic rulers who wanted to know the history of the country they now controlled. Manetho obliged and, using written sources held in Egyptian temples which have since been lost to history, he composed the *Aegyptiaca*, a comprehensive overview of the reigns of many Egyptian pharaohs.

Manetho began his recitation of royal reigns with the divine rulers of Egypt, and claimed that during the first 13,900 years of Egyptian history, the country was ruled by various gods, followed by five millennia of rule by demi-gods and finally an additional five millennia where the country was ruled by the Spirits of the Dead. After this (somewhat unlikely) list, Manetho discusses the human rulers of the country, whom he sub-divided into 'dynasties' using the Greek term δυναστεία. Manetho's dynastic division is still broadly maintained in common usage to this day, although several alterations and additions have been made, notably the introduction of Dynasty 0, a dynasty comprised of very early rulers of Egypt whom Manetho does not mention but whose existence has been verified predominantly by archaeological excavation of their tombs.

While Manetho's broad chronological divisions have been retained in modern Egyptology, there are significant problems with the historicity of his work and its transmission. The most serious of these issues is the fact that no intact copy of the *Aegyptiaca* has survived. Instead, references and quotations from this work have been preserved only in the writings of later authors, such as the Jewish historian Josephus (AD 37–100), the Roman author Sextus Julius Africanos (AD 160–240) and the Byzantine historian George Syncellus (eighth century AD). These authors biased Manetho's writings by their own interpretations and the selections they made among his work.

This long gap between the supposed composition of the work in the third century BC and the first mention of its existence more than 300 years later by Josephus also raise significant doubts about the historicity of Manetho himself, and suggests that while he may have composed some type of historical text, the actual authors of the *Aegyptiaca* post-date him. This theory is also supported by the existence of at least three clearly different versions of the text quoted by various later authors.

In compiling his original manuscript, Manetho (or other authors whose names have not survived) undoubtedly used existing records in the form of king lists.[7] Such compilations of Egyptian rulers had been in existence at least since the Early Dynastic Period.[8] During the 5th Dynasty, a more comprehensive king list – known as the Palermo Stone – was carved which, apart from listing kings of Egypt from the 1st to the 5th Dynasty, also included reference to notable events during the reigns of individual kings, such as the raids against Nubia by the 3rd Dynasty King Snefru as well as extensive records of the height of the annual Nile inundation, along with tax records and details of religious activity and building projects. The term 'Palermo Stone' is only partially truthful, as the original stela upon which this information was inscribed is in fact broken into seven fragments, only the largest of which is housed in the Regional Archaeological Museum Antonio Salinas in the Sicilian city of Palermo. Smaller pieces are kept in Cairo and the Petrie Museum of Archaeology in London. The original location of the stone is unknown, although it may have originated from the Memphite area, from where it was most likely uncovered during elicit excavations in the

1850s and sold to the Sicilian lawyer Ferdinand Guidano, who donated it to the museum.

No comprehensive king list has yet been discovered from the Middle Kingdom, although the Mit Rahina inscription dated to the reign of Amenemhat II preserves similar lists of military activity, tributes paid to the Egyptian state as well as rewards given to soldiers and courtiers, albeit only during the reign of Amenemhat II himself. Only with the advent of the 18th and 19th Dynasties are more extensive king lists preserved in the historical record. The first of these is the Karnak King List[9] carved in the Festival Hall of Thutmosis III at the Karnak Temple during the reign of this monarch and currently held in the Louvre Museum in Paris (E. 13481). By comparison to the Palermo Stone and also later king lists, it presents a heavily edited or abbreviated version of Egyptian history listing only sixty-one rulers from Snefru of the 4th Dynasty to Thutmosis III himself. It leaves out most of the rulers of the 13th Dynasty, along with several rulers of the New Kingdom, including Thutmosis III's own stepmother, Hatshepsut, who ruled as pharaoh before he came of age. By comparison, through archaeological exploration, and from the king lists of the 19th Dynasty, modern Egyptologists count as many as 200 rulers who either ruled alone or shared power during the period between Snefru and Thutmosis III. Along with the heavy-handed historical revisionism, the list is also damaged and many of the names are unreadable.

An additional two king lists are known from the reign of the 19th Dynasty ruler Ramesses II, son of Seti I. One of these, called the Saqqara King List, was found in the mid-nineteenth century in the tomb of the Overseer of Works Tjuneroy at Saqqara.[10] Similarly to the Karnak King List of Thutmosis III, it presents a heavily abbreviated version of the Egyptian royal chronology, listing only fifty-eight rulers from the 1st Dynasty to the reign of Ramesses II. As was customary on 19th Dynasty king lists, the rule of Akhenaten and the other Amarna Period rulers is simply expunged from history as an unworthy interim, as is the rule of the female Pharaoh Hatshepsut and the Hyksos rulers of the Second Intermediate Period. Far more extensive and useful is the Turin Canon,[11] which also dates to the reign of Ramesses II. It is a unique document and seemingly preserves the names of well over 200 individual rulers from the 1st Dynasty to the reign of Ramesses II.

Written in red and black ink on papyrus, the document was procured by the notable Italian explorer Bernadino Drovetti (1776–1852) in the early nineteenth century at Luxor, from whom it was purchased by the Egyptian Museum in Turin. Like Manetho, the list begins with a series of mythical and divine rulers of Egypt before listing the reigns of human rulers. Sadly, the papyrus is in a poor state of preservation and has crumbled into hundreds of pieces. Careful restoration work in recent years by the Danish Egyptologist Kim Ryholt has allowed the reconstruction of several hitherto unknown rulers, in particular of the Second Intermediate Period. Despite its damaged state, the Turin Canon remains a crucial piece of evidence. It is administrative in nature and as such preserves a far more objective and complete list of Egyptian rulers than any of the more formal inscribed king lists at Karnak, Saqqara and Abydos.

Formal king lists served primarily a political purpose. They helped to legitimize the ruler who ordered them carved by placing him in an allegedly unbroken framework of semi-divine rulers harking back to a mythical past where the gods themselves ruled the land. The exclusion of rulers who, in various ways, were perceived to have failed to govern correctly or – in the case of the Hyksos – were in effect foreign invaders or occupiers of Egyptian land, served both as a *damnatio memoriae* – to obliterate their existence from the historical record and from the public memory – but also helped to reinforce the state ideology that the Egyptian monarchy drew its legitimacy on a divinely ordained continuity and stability above all else.

* * *

Semi-permanent human habitation of the Nile Valley likely dates back at least as far as the Lower Palaeolithic Period, when bands of *Homo erectus* produced stone tools – in particular hand axes in the Acheulean tradition – found across sites in Middle Egypt, in particular around Abydos. Depositional processes, in particular drastic changes to the landscape itself over the last 250,000 years, have scattered many of these tools and objects far from their original contexts, leaving archaeologists unable to make sound judgements concerning which objects belong in which assemblages, and in general providing a fragmentary picture of the very earliest signs of human habitation in the Nile Valley.

With the arrival of the Holocene Wet Phase (*c.* 9,000 BC), human habitation spread from the confines of the fertile Nile Valley into the western desert, which at the time more resembled a sub-Saharan African steppe or savannah than the desolate sandy wastes of the modern day. Some of these new settlers built their home south-west of the modern city of Aswan in the western desert of Sudan at a region known as Nabta Playa.[12] From around 9,000 BC until the site was abandoned around the 4th Millennium BC, only interrupted by occasional periods of drought, humans inhabited the area, leaving behind rich assemblages of archaeological remains. Stone tools provide scholars with a sequence showing the development of their skill and techniques through the ages; botanical remains show that the inhabitants subsisted primarily on wild grasses and grains, supplemented by proteins from the many animals – buffaloes, gazelles and giraffes – that inhabited their milieu. Gradually, however, the weather patterns altered and the desert became increasingly arid, forcing the inhabitants to migrate into the Nile Valley. Here, those of their ancestors who had opted to remain behind rather than move to the savannah 5,000 years before had established their own cultures, which contained the early seeds of the Pharaonic civilization.

In Upper Egypt, this culture became known as the Naqada Culture, named after the site of Naqada near the modern city of Qift. Originally named by the British archaeologist Flinders Petrie,[13] it is subdivided into three chronological phases Naqada I (Amratian Culture, 4,400–3,500 BC), Naqada II (Gerzeh Culture, 3,500–3,200 BC) and Naqada III (Semainean, Protodynastic Period or Dynasty 0, 3,200–3,000 BC) which cover the period from roughly 4,400 BC to the foundation of the Egyptian state around 3,200 BC. The foundation or unification of the Egyptian state was caused by an increase in wealth and subsequent growth of strong elites at the Predynastic centre of Thinis in Middle Egypt. Eventually a strong ruler emerged from this area, unified all of Upper Egypt under his leadership and launched a series of campaigns against the various cultures which dominated Lower Egypt, such as the Buto and Ma'adi Cultures, and eventually brought the whole Nile Valley under his control. The name of this ruler was Narmer, although later Classical sources, including Manetho, name him Menes.

The Narmer Palette, one of the most notable artefacts from his reign, appear to show his triumph over the inhabitants of the Nile Delta and contain some of the earliest examples of royal Egyptian iconography, such as the depiction of pharaoh smiting a bound and kneeling enemy, which became tropes of ancient Egyptian art until the Roman Period nearly 3,500 years later. Little else is known about Narmer's reign, although according to later Classical sources, he may have been responsible for the foundation of the city of Memphis, locating his new capital at the intersection of the Nile Valley with the Nile Delta, a strategically crucial position to occupy which would have allowed him to respond quickly to unrest in either of his newly unified kingdoms, although this claim may be fictitious with power remaining centred around the city of Thinis.

The following two dynasties (the 1st and 2nd) – which are grouped together by Egyptologists as the Early Dynastic Period[14] – are among the most enigmatic and poorly understood periods of Egyptian history. The Egyptian written language, hieroglyphs, had not yet developed much beyond their original function as labels, and the lack of any significant grammatical structure naturally precluded the creation of the types of narrative and funerary texts which have helped to shape our understanding of the later parts of the Pharaonic civilization. From archaeological evidence, we know that the rulers of the Early Dynastic Period chose to be buried in elaborate tombs, located at Abydos in Middle Egypt. Unlike later times, human sacrifice accompanied these burials, with some, such as the tomb of the 1st Dynasty ruler Djer, surrounded by the auxiliary burials of several hundred retainers.

This period also led to the rise of what may have been the two earliest female rulers attested in human history. The first, Neithhotep, was long believed to be a male, based on the frequency with which her name appears in a royal *serekh* – a rectangular name border which generally denotes kingship – on various objects and inscriptions. More recent research suggests instead that Neithhotep may have been the wife of King Narmer, the first pharaoh of Egypt, and the mother of his son and successor, Hor-Aha. Given the sheer size of her tomb at Naqada and the rich burial goods with which she was interred, it is clear that she held a position of unusual power, and it is a likely interpretation that she served as regent and ruler in her own right after her husband's death, possibly holding the throne until her son reached maturity. A similar scenario was repeated at the death of Hor-Aha's grandson, King Djet, whose wife, Mereneith, also ruled as regent and pharaoh of Egypt on behalf of her son, the later King Den.

The rulers of the 2nd Dynasty are even more enigmatic than their predecessors of the 1st Dynasty, although the period seems to have been haunted by unrest, civil war and the fragmentation of the recently unified Egyptian state. Only one ruler is truly well known from this period, the final pharaoh of the dynasty, Khasekhemwy. Known from the Palermo Stone, Khasekhemwy may have been involved in a civil war triggered by his predecessor Seth-Peribsen, whom he defeated, and definitively ended the internal squabbles by reuniting the Two Lands of Upper and Lower Egypt through force of arms, prompting a period of unprecedented royal control and centralization which provided the foundations of the Old Kingdom, the Age of the Pyramids.

The Old Kingdom[15] was in many ways the first 'peak' of Egyptian civilization. The written language was expanded in scope and range, resulting in the creation of complex funerary texts, in particular for royal burials, but also the first private biographical accounts, in particular during the 5th and 6th Dynasties. Building on the legacy of the last ruler of the 2nd Dynasty, Khasekhemwy, the first ruler of the 3rd Dynasty, his son King Djoser, consolidated centralized royal power at Memphis and extended Egypt's sphere of influence by sending expeditions for minerals to Sinai and Nubia. Turning to one of his most senior ministers, Imhotep, whose roles were as far-ranging as Chancellor, High Priest of Heliopolis, Chief Builder and Chief Maker of Vases, he ordered the construction of one of the most significant burial monuments of the ancient world, the Saqqara Step Pyramid. Originally envisaged as a large *mastaba* – a rectangular mud-brick platform built over a tomb chamber, similar to those used by members of the court and the elite of the time – Imhotep and Djoser extended its scope by constructing a series of five smaller *mastabas* on top of the initial foundation, each one smaller than the previous, until the monument took the form of a step pyramid. Built from limestone, it constitutes the first monumental stone building in human history, and aside from the pyramid itself, the complex also included a maze of subterranean passages and burial chambers, and above-ground installations such as shrines, pavilions and colonnades used in the perpetuation of Djoser's mortuary cult.

The first ruler of the 4th Dynasty, Snefru, developed – with the aid of royal architects – the concept of a step pyramid into the more familiar shape of a smooth-sided pyramid. The experiment took three attempts, the first, the Meidum Pyramid, whose outer layers appear to have collapsed, followed by the Bent Pyramid which – as the name suggests – was initially built with a wrong side inclination of over 50 degrees. This was ratified to 43 degrees halfway through the project, giving the pyramid a lopsided or bent appearance. Snefru's final pyramid, the Red Pyramid at Dashur, was more successfully constructed, and it was in this monument that the king was laid to rest. Not to be outdone by Snefru's largesse, his successors Khufu, Chefren and Menkaure each built pyramids on the Giza Plateau, including the Great Pyramid of Khufu standing 147 metres tall, the last of the Seven Wonders of the Ancient World to remain intact to this day.

The vast expenditure on pyramid building of the 4th Dynasty was not matched by the rulers of the 5th Dynasty, whose funerary monuments are considerably smaller than Khufu's monstrous construction. Instead, complex funerary formula and rituals, known as the Pyramid Texts, were inscribed on the interior walls of their burial chambers and constitute perhaps the oldest religious texts in the world. They comprised primarily spells and utterances which were designed to allow the spirit of the deceased king to rise from the tomb and ascend to the sky to join with his fellow divinities after death. The afterlife described in these texts is inherently a royal afterlife, and only attainable for royalty. Courtiers and members of the elite obtained access to an afterlife through proximity to the king both in life and death, and as a result, private *mastaba* tombs cluster around the great pyramids of the Old Kingdom kings, as if jockeying for position and confidence, much as their owners would have done in life. This rigid centralization of both power and religion in the person of the king began to fade during the 6th Dynasty. Powerful regional rulers, known as nomarchs, gained greater autonomy and power, most likely due to the increasing complexity of ruling the country, which necessitated the dissemination of some previously centralized powers and privileges.

The period between the end of the Old Kingdom and the 11th Dynasty is known as the First Intermediate Period. Whereas the Old, Middle and New

Kingdoms are perceived as high-points of Egyptian civilization (and also periods of more intense centralization and royal power), the First, Second and Third Intermediate Period are marked by decentralization, the loss of royal power and the fragmentation of the unified state, either into its traditional elements of Upper and Lower Egypt or into smaller provincial centres.

The kings of the 7th and 8th Dynasty appear to have been unable to maintain control of the country and stop or reverse the decentralization begun during the 6th Dynasty. Several kings ruled during this period, but none of them for very long, the entire period lasting perhaps as little as twenty years – with seventeen different kings in all. This greatly weakened dynasty was eventually removed by the ascent of the rulers of the 9th and 10th Dynasties, who ruled from the city of Herakleopolis Magna, and were therefore known as the Herakleopolitan kings. However, like their predecessors, they were unable to retake full control of the country from powerful nomarchs based in particular in Middle Egypt and rival would-be royalty emerging in Thebes.

The relative insignificance of the king as a leader of the country during this period is expressed expertly in the biography of the nomarch Ankhtifi, who ruled the nomes of Edfu and Hierakonpolis and was buried near the modern village of el-Mo'alla. Ankhtifi was allied to the Herakleopolitan kings, and appears to have fought several wars against their rivals in Thebes, who had formed the 11th Dynasty. But even though Ankhtifi was technically in royal service, his biography has none of the fawning adoration of Old Kingdom private biographies which almost obsessively list the owner's proximity to the king, favours given by the king and specific instances of service to the king. Ankhtifi, by contrast, lists primarily his own achievements, and it is clear that he considers these achievements his alone, not to be shared with a pressured king on a far-away throne:

'I gave bread to the hungry, and clothing to the naked; I anointed those who had no oil; I gave sandals to him without any; I gave a wife to him who had no wife [...] I brought life to the provinces of Hierakonpolis and Edfu, Elephantine and Ombos.'[16]

Towards the end of the First Intermediate Period, a new royal house based in the southern city of Thebes eventually succeeded in scoring a series of decisive victories against the Herakleopolitan rulers in the north. After defeating his enemies within Egypt, the Theban King Mentuhotep II launched campaigns against Egypt's traditional enemies in Nubia and Libya, rekindling the dying flame of royal authority and effectively reuniting Egypt and laying the foundations for the Middle Kingdom.

A potentially dangerous situation occurred when Mentuhotep II's grandson, King Mentuhotep IV, died without an heir, but the succession crisis was averted when the dead king's vizier took the throne as Amenemhat I, founding the 12th Dynasty and moving the capital from Thebes to the newly founded settlement of Itj-Tawy, which was probably near modern-day Cairo, although its location has not yet been ascertained by archaeologists.

During the 12th Dynasty, Egyptian literature flourished, and a great deal of fictional compositions have survived to the present day, including *The Tale of Sinuhe*, which relates the adventures of a courtier who flees Egypt after the murder of Amenemhat I (a murder which may or may not have occurred in reality); *The Shipwrecked Sailor*, perhaps the earliest example of a *robinsonade*, which tells the story of a sailor marooned on a magical island inhabited only by a giant talking snake; but also more sombre compositions like *The Dialogue Between a Man and His Soul*, a deeply philosophical treatise wherein a man burdened by a heavy life disputes with his soul about the merits of the afterlife and the soul exhorts the man to appreciate life and not pursue the attractiveness of death.

The Middle Kingdom also saw Egypt's foreign policy altered from one based on occasional raids to secure financial gain in the form of loot, to a more regimented occupation of strategic areas to control mineral deposits and trade routes. Multiple forts were constructed along the Nile in Lower Nubia during the reigns of Senwosret I and Senwosret III in particular, while Amenemhat II pursued a more aggressive foreign policy in the Levant, and also expanded Egypt's trade with the Lebanese city-states.

With this expansion of Egypt's horizons, however, also came new enemies, in particular the Kingdom of Kush located in Upper Nubia and ruled from the city of Kerma below the Third Cataract. Eventually, when the power of the Egyptian kings began to wane during the 13th Dynasty, the Kushites jumped to fill the power vacuum, taking control of the Egyptian forts in Lower Nubia and pushing the Egyptian sphere of influence north to the

First Cataract below Aswan and entirely out of Nubian territory. Though the threat from the ascendant Kerma was no doubt palpable, a far more outlandish enemy had appeared in the late 12th Dynasty and effectively seized control of northern Egypt, forcibly shifting the Egyptian capital to the cities of Abydos and Thebes: the Hyksos.

The term 'Hyksos' comes from the ancient Egyptian words *heqa khasut*, meaning 'rulers of foreign lands'. While precise identification of their origins is still a subject of much debate, they most likely comprised tribes or groups of Semitic origin from the Levant. Already from the late 12th Dynasty and in particular during the 13th Dynasty onwards, Levantine influences began to appear in the archaeological record of the Eastern Nile Delta, suggesting a gradual influx of non-Egyptian cultural units, rather than an actual invasion. This is particularly visible at the site of Tell el-Dab'a,[17] also known by its ancient name, Avaris. The settlement was originally a planned Egyptian Middle Kingdom city which may have served as a posting station for expeditions to the copper deposits on Sinai or to the Levant. Throughout the 13th Dynasty, more and more typically Levantine traditions (such as donkey burials) and objects become apparent in the archaeological record as the Semitic population grew. By the end of the 13th Dynasty, these Levantine people felt strong enough to found their own royal line of succession, the 14th Dynasty.

The notion of the Hyksos as a brutalizing invasion force can be traced back to the Manetho, who claimed that:

> 'After they had subdued our rulers, they burnt down our cities, and destroyed the temples of the gods, and treated the inhabitants most cruelly; killing some and enslaving their wives and their children.'[18]

This hyperbolic description is not supported in the archaeological record, although the effective division of the Two Lands at the hands of Levantine foreigners no doubt left a permanent mark on the Egyptian national psyche. During the reign of Hatshepsut, several hundred years after the Hyksos had been removed from Egypt, they were still remembered and described as a manifestation of chaos in royal monumental accounts.

With the shift of Egyptian power from Abydos to Thebes and the rise of the 17th Dynasty, based in Thebes, war eventually erupted between the Egyptians and their Hyksos neighbours in the Delta. The cause of the war is unknown, although a literary story, *The Tale of Seqenenre and Apophis*, claims that the war began when the Theban King Seqenenre Tao received a letter from the Hyksos King Apophis wherein Apophis ordered Seqenenre to dispose of a Theban hippopotamus pool, because the braying of the beasts kept Apophis awake in his palace in Avaris. Considering that Avaris is more than 800km from Thebes, the letter was clearly meant as a metaphor; indeed it may simply have been a request that Seqenenre Tao pay tribute to the Hyksos to demonstrate his inferior position within Egypt, a demand which then provoked an armed Theban response. Seqenenre Tao led several skirmishes and raids against his northern enemy, and judging from the mutilated state of his mummy he may have died during one of them. His skull is marked by both stab-wounds from daggers and a killing blow from an axe.

Before his death, Seqenenre had, however, fathered two sons, Kamose and his younger brother Ahmose. As Kamose took his father's throne after Seqenenre's ignominious end, he received troubling news that the Hyksos were trying to form an alliance with the Kushite king at Kerma and coordinate an attack on the Theban enclave, effectively trapping the Egyptians between two fronts. Kamose summoned his councillors and, evidently frustrated by their pleas for him to maintain the uneasy peace with the Hyksos, he told them:

'I should like to know what serves this strength of mine, with a prince in Avaris and another in Kush and I sit united with an Asiatic and a Nubian, each in possession of his slice of Egypt, and I cannot pass by him as far as Memphis?'[19]

Kamose opted to fight his way out of the trap and launched an all-out attack on the Hyksos, although he seems to have focused primarily on seizing control of the country south of Memphis and does not appear to have reached Avaris itself. The campaign was successful, and the Hyksos were left badly bloodied by the loss of territory and also the plundering of their merchant ships which Kamose claims to have undertaken. The cause of Kamose's death is not known, and his mummy was destroyed shortly after its discovery, but it is possible that he – like his father before him – died in battle against the Hyksos, or suffered death from assassination.

With the war against the Hyksos still raging, the Theban throne was filled by Kamose's energetic younger brother, Ahmose. Ahmose did what his father and brother could not, and led the Theban army and navy in a frontal attack upon Avaris itself, first capturing the strategically vital settlement of Tjaru which lay on the edge of the eastern Delta. In doing so, he effectively blockaded trade and contact across the Sinai Peninsula in the Levant, leaving the Hyksos isolated in their capital. By the eighteenth year of his reign, after multiple assaults on Avaris, the city finally fell to Ahmose and his army, and the Hyksos were driven out of Egypt. Ahmose pursued them to their stronghold of Sharuhen in modern-day Gaza, besieged the settlement and conquered it after a protracted siege. Determined to create a buffer zone to prevent foreign enemies ever reaching Egyptian lands again, Ahmose campaigned as far north as Lebanon, and possibly to the banks of the Euphrates, although he did not consolidate this new territory, but merely demonstrated that Egypt was now in resurgence after the interim of the Second Intermediate Period. After quelling a rebellion led by an Egyptian rival to his throne in the later part of his reign, Ahmose campaigned in Nubia, retaking the Egyptian forts and fortifications in Lower Nubia from the Kingdom of Kush.

With the end of the Second Intermediate Period, another peak of Egyptian civilization dawned: the New Kingdom, comprising the 18th, 19th and 20th Dynasties. It was a time when foreign affairs and warfare more than anything helped to define the Egyptian civilization. The renascent Egypt exploded onto the world stage during the 18th Dynasty, and in matters of war, trade and diplomacy, Egypt became one of the key players in the ancient Near East and a dominant super-power.

Excursus: Source Material

The study of Seti's life and his impact on the development of Pharaonic Egypt comes under the remit of Egyptology. This discipline, which concerns the examination of ancient Egyptian culture, society, history, archaeology and language, is by no means a young or novel field of research. Interest in the Egyptian past and history can be traced back to the Ancient Egyptians themselves, who avidly visited and described the monuments of their ancestors. During the Ramesside period, this interest in the past glories amounted essentially to tourism, with officials from the nearby settlement of Memphis going on day trips taken to see Old Kingdom tombs at Saqqara and Giza, blazing a path which millions of tourists have taken since and continue to take to this day. Scholars rely predominantly on textual or archaeological sources to inform us about the ancient Egyptian culture, and this study of the life and times of Seti I is no different. It is therefore useful for readers unfamiliar with Egyptian civilization to understand how this source material – from humble potsherds littering a Delta field to inscribed narratives and depictions showing pharaoh triumphant in battle – has survived to be studied so many millennia after its creation.

With the triumph of Christianity throughout Egypt in the third century AD, the knowledge of how to read the hieroglyphic and hieratic scripts, and by extension how to use many of the historical sources preserved from earlier times, gradually faded from memory, with the last inscription written with hieroglyphic characters carved at the Temple of Philae in AD 394. Almost as soon as the knowledge was lost, scholars sought to recapture it, starting with Classical authors such as the Roman historian Ammianus Marcellinus (AD 330–395), who wrote a lengthy (and utterly erroneous) treatise on how to decipher Egyptian hieroglyphs. A hundred years later, the enigmatic scholar Horapollo (fifth century AD) contributed to the debate with his equally inaccurate 'dictionary' of hieroglyphs known as *Hieroglyphika*.[20] A copy of Horapollo's work was subsequently found on the Island of Andros in 1419 and brought to Florence by the monk Cristoforo Buondelmonti (1386–1430). Buondelmonti worked with the notable Florentine scholar Niccolo Niccoli (1364–1437), who was in his turn a close friend of the powerful politician Cosimo de' Medici (1389–1464). An avid humanist, Cosimo sponsored the copying and distribution of hundreds of Classical manuscripts among Renaissance scholars, and it was no doubt with Cosimo's help that the newly discovered *Hieroglyphika* became an immensely popular source of study among scholars in the late fifteenth century. However, by basing their own assumptions on Horapollo's incorrect conclusions, Renaissance scholars such as Athanasius Kircher (1601–1680) merely promulgated mistake upon mistake, and none of them succeeded in deciphering the elusive script.

It was not until a chance discovery near the Egyptian city of Rosetta on 15 July 1799 that the decipherment of hieroglyphs finally began in earnest.[21] While expanding the defences on Fort St Julien during the War of the Second Coalition between Great Britain and France, French soldiers uncovered a large slab of black stone. Lieutenant Pierre-François Bouchard (1771–1822) observed the excavation of the stone and, realizing that it was an ancient artefact of some significance, he informed his commanding officer, Colonel d'Hautpoul, of the discovery. The two men contacted the commander of the French battalions in Egypt, General Jacques-François de Menou (1750–1810).

During Napoleon's conquest of Egypt from 1799 to 1801, he had brought with him a corps of 'savants', scientific experts in various fields whom he had tasked with discovering as much as possible about the history, environment and geology of Egypt, and to this purpose Napoleon also founded the *Institut d'Égypte*, a scientific institute in Cairo. It was these French scholars who first realized that the inscriptions on the stone were in three different scripts. The top script was recognized as hieroglyphs, the third as Greek. The middle script was later shown to be demotic. It was also these scholars who first hypothesized that the content of the inscription was the same in all three languages, and that therefore the Rosetta Stone could provide the key to deciphering the hieroglyphic script.

However, British victory in the Second Battle of Aboukir and the subsequent landing of a British army in 1801 stopped the French investigation of the Rosetta Stone in its tracks. The conquering British army demanded the stone as a spoil of war. The besieged French garrison in Alexandria refused to surrender it and other antiquities, and the notes taken by their scholars. The British were adamant, however, to the point where General John Hely-Hutchinson (1757–1832) of the British Army refused to allow any food or goods to be sent into the city after its surrender until the stone and other materials were in British possession. The French high command finally agreed, and delivered the Rosetta Stone to General Hely-Hutchinson's men – although not before producing copies of the inscription which were duly sent home to Paris. The Rosetta Stone was sent to London in 1802 and presented to the British Museum by George III in June of that year, where it has remained ever since.

With the French retaining their transcriptions of the stone, the race was on to decipher the ancient Egyptian script. Some advances were made by the orientalist Baron A.I. Silvestre de Sacy (1758–1838) and the Swedish Diplomat J.H. Åkerblad (1763–1819). De Sacy was able to identify personal names in the demotic script, including that of Ptolemy, and Åkerblad identified various demotic grammatical elements. The biggest advances, and ultimately the key, came from the efforts of Thomas Young (1773–1829) and Jean-François Champollion (1790–1832). Young built on the suggestion of Abbé Jean-Jacques Barthélemy, that cartouches encircled royal names, and successfully identified the name Ptolemy in the hieroglyphic script via de Sacy's demotic discovery. As a result, Young could assign sound values to some of the hieroglyphic signs. He went on to correctly identify some groups of signs, such as those for 'king' and 'Egypt'. Ultimately, however, it was Champollion who proved that ancient Egyptian hieroglyphs comprised a system made of sound signs ('phonograms', like our alphabet) and sense signs ('ideograms', pictorial representations of objects) which were used in combination. Most importantly, he clarified that hieroglyphs conveyed a language and had a grammar, and were not, as previously believed, merely sets of magical symbols.[22]

After millennia of misunderstandings and downright fictional interpretations of the ancient Egyptian script, the scholars who today research ancient Egyptian society and history have an enviable corpus of textual sources at their disposal. These encompass literary narratives, bombastic monumental accounts of the king and his prowess in war, religious and philosophical treatises, laundry lists, tax accounts and private letters and testaments. In the midst of this apparent largesse, however, it is crucial to bear in mind that it is unclear how much of the original textual material has survived; certainly far more has been lost to the ravages of time than was ever recovered from the sands of Egypt, and as a result, the picture it now presents is fragmentary. Furthermore, tens of thousands of scraps of papyrus and ostraca, sculptural fragments and stela still lie unread in museums and in private collections, and more is found by archaeological missions with each passing year. It should also be noted that, like many ancient societies, the ability to read and write was intrinsically linked to the elite. The vast majority of the Egyptian population were illiterate, and it is unlikely that their stories, beliefs and legends are represented in the textual material which survives to this day.

Archaeological exploration allows modern scholars access to a different assemblage of source material to inform about ancient Egyptian history and society. While early archaeological exploration in Egypt amounted to little more than organized looting and tomb robbery, the nineteenth century saw the birth of a more scientific approach to archaeological exploration, championed to a great extent by the British archaeologist William Matthew Flinders Petrie (1853–1942).[23] Known affectionately as 'the man who discovered Egypt', Petrie grew up in Kent and was taught how to survey by his father, William Petrie, an electrical engineer. At an early age, Petrie turned to archaeology, lamenting at the tender age of eight about the rough excavation techniques used to unearth a Roman villa on the Isle of Wight.

After corresponding with the astronomer Charles Piazzi Smyth (1819– 1900), Petrie travelled to Egypt to undertake a survey of the Giza Pyramids over three years. After these initial forays in Egypt, Petrie began excavating on behalf of the newly formed Egypt Exploration Fund, replacing the Swiss archaeologist Edouard Naville (1844–1926) as the Fund's archaeologist in Egypt in 1884. For more than forty years, Petrie excavated all across Egypt, from Delta sites such as Tanis and Tell Nabasha to the settlements and cemeteries of Gurob and el-Lahun in the Fayum Oasis, and Koptos, Naqada and Tell el-Amarna in the Nile Valley. Petrie employed a more careful excavation method than his predecessors, using fewer – but better-trained – local workmen, running straight trenches rather than simply digging disorganized holes, and recording structures, finds and pottery to the best of his ability in journals and on tomb cards. While his methods are outdated and destructive by today's standards, Petrie nevertheless helped develop archaeological exploration in Egypt from opportunistic pillaging for financial gain to a careful scientific study of the past. Today, dozens of international and Egyptian missions are carefully at work, unearthing, recording and preserving Egypt's past.

Chapter 2

The Family Business

In late October 1886, a group of local farmers dug for treasure at the Middle Egyptian site of Tell el-Amarna. We can imagine them, working early in the morning and in the stillness of the evening to avoid the sweltering heat of the midday sun, swathed in robes, scarves across their faces to protect against the swirling dust and sand that covers this once-proud capital. History has not preserved the names of these *fellahin*, but they made a truly spectacular discovery. While working in the ruins of a large mud-brick complex which would later be known as the Hall of Records, they unearthed hundreds of clay tablets covered in the angular cuneiform script – the diplomatic *lingua Franca* (or indeed, *lingua Acadia*) of the Late Bronze Age world. Unaware of the true value of what they had found, the *fellahin* ferried the tablets across the river to the small village of Dar em-Moez, to a local antiquities dealer by the name of Elias.

He too was puzzled by the tablets, so he packed them in coarse linen bags and loaded them onto his donkey. Then he took them to the nearby town of Sohag, where he showed them to the superintendent of a French-owned flower mill, a certain Monsieur Frenay, who worked as an agent for the Louvre Museum and who was always on the lookout for new historical treasures for the museum's growing collection. After examining the haul, M. Frenay agreed to purchase some of the tablets and they ended their journey in the Louvre galleries in Paris.

When examined by French scholars, the tablets were wrongfully dismissed as fakes and returned to M. Frenay, who donated them to the French School in Cairo. The remaining tablets travelled to Luxor and fell into the hands of another antiquities dealer, Mohammad Mohassib, who successfully sold most of the collection to British and German agents.[1] By then, the true value of these tablets – later known simply as *The Amarna Letters* – had become known to the academic community. Five years later, in 1891–92, the famed British Egyptologist Sir Flinders Petrie found more fragments of these letters in the ruins of the Hall of Records.[2] By that time, the first transcriptions of the tablets had also begun to appear.

Over a century of dedicated scholarship has shown the Amarna Letters to be a unique collection of diplomatic correspondence written during the reigns of Amenhotep III, Akhenaten, Smenkhare and Tutankhamun. The majority of the surviving letters are written by vassals of the Egyptian state – local rulers of cities in modern-day Israel and Palestine such as Acre, Byblos and Jerusalem – and contain a plethora of requests for military or financial aid, complaints about rival rulers and lists of tribute sent to the Egyptian king. A smaller portion of the corpus, known as the 'Brother Correspondence', consist of more personal notes written to one another by the great kings of the Late Bronze Age, the rulers of Mitanni, Babylon, Assyria and Alashiya.[3] This assemblage of letters represents the physical manifestation of a complex poker game of international relations, which had been carefully cultivated by one of the most notable pharaohs of the 18th Dynasty: Amenhotep III. Very much the *Roi-Soleil* of Egypt, Amenhotep did not establish himself on the international scene in the Eastern Mediterranean through unending warfare and conquest – like his predecessor Thutmosis III. Instead, he maintained power through a system of inter-marriages and diplomatic gifts. While foreign rulers referred to him formally as 'my brother', it is clear that there was a hierarchy in these relationships – and that Amenhotep stood at its head.

Nowhere is this more clearly expressed than in his correspondence with the King of Babylon, Kadashman-Enlil. In an annoyed letter to Amenhotep, Kadashman-Enlil writes:

'my brother, when I wrote to you about marrying your daughter, in accordance with your practice of not giving a daughter, you wrote to me saying, "From time immemorial no daughter of the king of Egypt is given to anyone." Why not?'[4]

This was a particularly sore point for a proud King of Babylon, who had in fact given several of his own daughters to Amenhotep as wives. Nevertheless, the Egyptian pharaoh was steadfast in his refusal. An Egyptian princess marrying a foreign king could in extreme cases lead to a foreign ruler having a claim-by-birth to the throne of Egypt, and that could not be tolerated. Instead, King Kadashman-Enlil was reduced to (somewhat pathetically) asking Amenhotep to send any Egyptian noble woman who Kadashman-Enlil could then claim to his own courtiers was indeed a princess of Egypt. Other letters written to Amenhotep by foreign rulers detail the great wealth which was exchanged between them and the Great King, including silver, gold and furniture of exotic woods and ivory.[5]

In many ways, Amenhotep's Egypt was a golden period during the New Kingdom. After the traumatic experience of the Hyksos occupation during the Second Intermediate Period, Egypt emerged resplendent on the international stage. The early 18th Dynasty rulers, namely Ahmose I, Amenhotep I and Thutmosis I, busied themselves with re-establishing control of areas once dominated by Egypt. But they also sought to secure control of a 'buffer zone' of vassal states across Canaan to prevent any foreign armies from setting foot on Egyptian soil again.

This expansionist policy naturally brought the Egyptians into conflict with other states, both in the Near East and Nubia. Ahmose I focused primarily on Nubia after his expulsion of the Hyksos. He sailed south with his army and re-established Egyptian control of the massive river fortress at Buhen, installing a new commander by the name of Turi.[6] The Nubian kingdom of Kerma which had so threatened Egypt during the Second Intermediate Period was finally crushed by his grandson Thutmosis I, who recorded his victory in harrowing detail in the Tombos Stela:

'After he overthrew the chief of the Nubians, the despoiled Nubian belongs to his grip. After he had gathered the border markers of both sides, no escape existed among the evil-of-character; those who had come to support him not one thereof remained. As the Nubian *Iwntyw* have fallen to terror and are laid aside throughout their lands, their stench, it floods their *wadis*, their blood is like a rainstorm. The carrion-eating birds over it are numerous, those birds were picking and carrying the flesh to another (desert) place.'[7]

Conquests in the Near East followed during the reign of Thutmosis III, who successfully attacked and ravaged the Mitannian Empire, taking his army as far north as the Euphrates River in modern-day Iraq.[8] His son, Amenhotep II, consolidated his father's conquests, establishing a network of vassals whose fickle loyalties would both protect and frustrate the Egyptian state for several centuries.[9]

So this was the time into which Amenhotep III rose to the throne. Egypt's power had been reasserted, potential foreign challengers had been soundly defeated and extensive trade routes could now be established, bringing exotic goods to the Nile Valley from as far as Afghanistan and Sub-Saharan Africa. This wealth was channelled into an impressive building programme within Egypt, which would not be surpassed until the reigns of Seti I and Ramesses II, the latter of whom in particular did in fact usurp a great number of monuments and statues originally built by Amenhotep III. Among Amenhotep's most notable construction achievements was a vast pylon at the Karnak Temple and his own immense mortuary temple built on the West Bank of the Nile across from the modern city of Luxor, of which only a pair of giant statues – the so-called Memnon Colossi – remain.

Amenhotep also commissioned a great number of official scarabs, which carried texts detailing important events during his reign. Among these are the Marriage Scarabs, which testament his marriage to his Great Royal Wife, Queen Tiye, in Year 11 of his reign,[10] and also the Lion Hunt Scarabs, which document his successful hunt of over 100 lions in the desert. A further five scarabs, known together as the Gilukhepa Scarabs, record the arrival in Egypt of one of Amenhotep's foreign wives, Gilukhepa, the daughter of King Shuttarna of Mitanni, with a retinue of 317 female servants.[11]

Taken together, the written evidence from the reign of Amenhotep III, along with a wealth of archaeological evidence in the form of extraordinarily well-made objects, suggests a period of peace and prosperity in which Egypt's power was unchallenged and – by extension – the land itself was untroubled by internal strife.

However, this peaceful state of affairs came to an abrupt end. In Theban Tomb 92, belonging to Kheruef, a Steward of Amenhotep III's Great Royal Wife Queen Tiye,[12] are depictions that date towards the end of the thirty-eight-year reign of the king. In these depictions, the once powerful ruler is shown as frail and elderly – even ill. Several caches of black granite statues of the goddess Sekhmet, the goddess of both disease and healing, have been found in Luxor dating to the reign of Amenhotep III. Their presence has been explained as an offering to the goddess ordered by an increasingly infirm king.[13] Amenhotep eventually succumbed to his illness, dying in his middle age and leaving behind his wife, Queen Tiya, and his son, who took the throne under the name Amenhotep IV. History, however, would remember him under another name: Akhenaten.

* * *

It was early summer 1353 BC. Heat-haze flickered over the assembled courtiers who gazed on their pharaoh. He stood resplendent in a chariot covered with inlays of electrum. As he drove, armed mercenary troops dressed in the garish colours of their tribal dress flanked him on either side. Led by the king, the dazzling procession moved at a stately pace towards an unremarkable spot in the desert at modern-day Tell el-Amarna. According to a boundary stela cut in white limestone and set up at the limits of the new settlement, the king sacrificed a great number of cattle and fowl, as well as bread, beer, wine and incense to his god the Aten, the sun-disk. He then solemnly swore to continue his construction of a mighty city dedicated to the Aten, a temple – the 'House of the Aten' – and palaces and other mighty buildings.[14] Advocating the worship of the Aten above Egypt's traditional pantheon, Akhenaten wanted his new capital at Tell el-Amarna to be a physical manifestation of this religious change in direction. It is of course not known what the assembled courtiers thought of their new king's decision, but it is possible that some of them shuddered at the prospect of leaving their sprawling estates in Thebes and Memphis and following their messianic ruler into his new desert utopia.

While still a relatively new and untried king, Akhenaten had already caused some stir in Egyptian society. Early in his reign he had set up a shrine for the sun-disk, the Aten, within the large Karnak Temple in Thebes, traditionally dedicated to the Theban triad of Amun, his consort Mut and their son, Khonsu. He had also ordered the construction of monumental sandstone statues of his own image.[15] The latter decision was expected; his father, Amenhotep III, had famously constructed several such giant statues of himself all over Egypt. But Akhenaten's statues broke with tradition. In their depiction of the king, they merge male and female attributes, giving the ruler an otherworldly appearance that has even caused modern observers to claim that he was suffering from various illnesses and physical deformities.[16] This is not substantiated, and the statues should rather be viewed as one of many attempts made by Akhenaten to redefine royal monumental and religious tradition within the – admittedly somewhat hidebound – New Kingdom society.

The new king increasingly devoted himself to the worship of a single god, the Aten, spurning the traditional role of pharaoh as High Priest of Egypt's entire pantheon of gods and goddesses. He may have done this out of a genuine religious fervour, although there were also clear practical benefits. During the early and mid-18th Dynasty, the god Amun had appeared as the pre-eminent deity of kingship and victory. Worshipped at the Karnak Temple in modern Luxor, his importance grew exponentially as the Theban rulers of the Second Intermediate Period rose up against the Hyksos occupiers and commenced their conquests in the Near East and Nubia. Many of the spoils from these campaigns – both material wealth and prisoners-of-war – were donated to the Temple of Amun, along with vast donations of agricultural land. By the reign of Akhenaten, the priesthood of Amun at Karnak controlled enormous resources, potentially enough to challenge the supremacy of pharaoh. Akhenaten may have felt it proper to put the priesthood in their place by blatantly favouring another god over theirs.

Another aspect of the worship of Aten which must have appealed to Akhenaten was the complete omnipresence of the royal family. As Jacobus van Dijk has noted, during the Amarna Period, 'personal piety was now identical with total loyalty towards Akhenaten personally'.[17] This is particularly notable in the elite houses excavated at Akhenaten's capital of Tell el-Amarna, where the traditional household shrines dedicated to various local gods, or gods related to the home and protection of the family, were now replaced by shrines dedicated to Akhenaten himself and his family, although traditional gods, such as Bes, were still worshipped, even at Amarna.[18]

In founding his vast new capital at Tell el-Amarna, Akhenaten not only made himself a focal point for all divine worship, he also disbanded the priesthoods of other Egyptian gods, including Amun at Karnak. The long boulevards at Amarna were constructed for the purposes of public spectacle. Each morning when the king rode in his chariots from the palace to the Great Aten Temple to conduct offerings to the god under the open sky, the route would be lined with citizens and dignitaries. It was a daily affirmation of the semi-divinity of the ruler, as well as a demonstration of his military might, taking the form of regiments of Egyptian and foreign auxiliary troops running alongside him.

While it was occupied for less than half a century, Tell el-Amarna – the city Akhenaten built to honour his god and distance himself from the old gods of Thebes – has survived the ravages of time well. Due to meticulous scientific excavation, it has become an invaluable archaeological resource, to such an extent that much of our knowledge of Egyptian settlements is ultimately based on Tell el-Amarna. While the city's archaeological remains have informed modern researchers about ritual and everyday life in the capital, the Amarna Letters have simultaneously provided a tantalizing glimpse of Akhenaten's foreign policy.

The Amarna Letters are naturally a biased corpus – they contain primarily letters written to the Egyptian pharaoh and not his responses. Descriptions of the initial finding of the archive also suggest that many tablets were destroyed. This selective survival of material makes it more dangerous to rely exclusively on this assemblage when discussing Akhenaten's attitude to the surrounding world. It does, however, seem clear that Akhenaten did not have his father's exquisite flair for diplomacy. In a series of notorious letters sent to Akhenaten from King Tushrata of Mitanni, the Mitannian king complains bitterly that Akhenaten did not – as promised – send him statues of solid gold, but rather of gold-plated wood,[19] hardly the most surreptitious of diplomatic moves.

Over sixty letters in the archive are from Rib Addi, the Mayor of Byblos, who repeatedly pleads for Akhenaten to send him help in the form of an army to fight off his enemy, Aziru. Akhenaten did not despatch help and Rib Addi was eventually murdered by Aziru. Akhenaten responded by ordering Aziru to Egypt, where he detained him, but then mysteriously released him back to his people, who promptly deserted the Egyptians and joined the ascendant Hittite Empire.[20]

Akhenaten's relations with his vassals in Canaan, including Rib Addi, were overseen by a group of native Egyptian diplomats called 'commissioners' (*rabisu*) in the scholarly literature. The Egyptian titles held by these individuals are unknown, although many are thought to have held military offices, such as 'troop commander' and 'stable master'.[21] At an unspecified point in Akhenaten's reign, one of his vassals, Satatna, the Mayor of Akka (modern Acre in Israel), wrote the king a terse letter complaining that an Egyptian commissioner by the name of Sjuta 'turned against' him over a complex matter of a deserter whom Sjuta had refused to hand over to Satatna for punishment.[22] The resolution to this conflict is not known, but the commissioner Sjuta appears again in another letter, this one from Abdi-Heba, the Mayor of Jerusalem. In this letter, Abdi-Heba assures the Egyptian ruler of his loyalty and, in an extravagant demonstration, entrusts eighty prisoners-of-war and twenty-one (no doubt beautiful) women to Sjuta to bring back to pharaoh as tribute.[23] The name 'Sjuta' appears to be an attempted literal rendering of the Egyptian name Sjuty, which in itself is a variant form of the name Seti.[24]

Seti was not, at this time in Egyptian history, a common name, although it underlined the familial relations this commissioner had in the north-eastern Nile Delta and the cult Seth at Avaris. Given the quasi-military role of the commissioners, it is reasonable to assume that this Seti is identical to the troop commander Seti who appears on a fragment of a votive stela currently held in the Oriental Institute Museum in Chicago (OI 11456).[25] In this monument, Seti is mentioned alongside his son, the stable master Paramessu and his brother, the Fan-Bearer of the Retinue, Khaemwaset. At a later date, this same Seti appears on a statue deposited by his son within the temple enclosure at Karnak. On this statue, Seti is listed as both a 'judge' and 'troop commander'.[26]

This troop commander, judge and commissioner could not have known it as he was making his way back from Jerusalem with a caravan of prisoners-of-war and concubines – and he probably did not even know during his lifetime – but he was to be both the father of a king and the spiritual ancestor to one of the most notable royal dynasties Egypt had ever seen: the Ramessides.

* * *

It is generally accepted that Akhenaten died in Year 17 of his reign, even though the last inscription by this king and his enigmatic Great Royal Wife, Nefertiti, has been dated to Year 16.[27] What followed the reign of Akhenaten was a certain amount of confusion. Part of this confusion was caused by later Egyptian rulers, including Ramesses I and Seti I, who sought to destroy the memory of the – to them – heretic and oppressive Amarna rulers by defacing and destroying their monuments, and omitting Akhenaten and his immediate successors from official king lists. It seems clear, however, that Akhenaten was followed by Smenkhare, a perplexing monarch who ruled for less than a year, and Neferneferuaten, a female pharaoh who ruled for only two years. The precise identity of these two rulers is a hotly contested subject, with some Egyptologists suggesting that one or both of them were in fact to Akhenaten's Great Royal Wife, Nefertiti, continuing to rule from Tell el–Amarna after her husband's death.[28]

After Smenkhare and Neferneferuaten, a far more illustrious character took the throne of Egypt at the tender age of 10. Tutankhaten, the son of Akhenaten and one of the lesser royal wives, had been raised in Amarna, but upon his ascension (most likely aided, or perhaps impelled, by powerful members of the royal court such as the later Pharaohs Ay and Horemheb), he changed his name to Tutankhamun, married his sister, Ankhsunamun, and moved the royal capital away from Tell el–Amarna and back to Thebes. The young king's name change was significant; it represented a definitive break with the royal veneration of the Aten and in some ways a return to normality. Amun, Lord of Thebes, was again established as pre-eminent in the Egyptian pantheon and in the royal ideology. To monumentalize this theological and political shift, Tutankhamun ordered the creation of a Restoration Decree.[29] Written in the king's first regnal year on a large round-topped stela, the decree was originally set up in front of the Third Pylon at the Karnak Temple, well within the god Amun's domain:

'Now when His Majesty arose as king, the temples of the gods and goddesses, beginning from Elephantine [down] to the marshes of the Delta, [had] fallen into neglect, their shrines had fallen into desolation and become tracts overgrown with [///] plants, their sanctuaries were as if they had never been, their halls were a trodden path. The land was in confusion, the gods forsook this land'.[30]

The meaning of the decree is clear. Tutankhamun had risen as a saviour of Egypt, restoring the temples and the cults to their rightful places and, in doing so, securing the favour of the gods. Tutankhamun's attempts at restoration were by no means limited to such rhetorical blandishments. Among the most ambitious building projects of his reign was the completion of a large colonnade at the Luxor Temple, original begun by Amenhotep III.[31] Tutankhamun clearly desired to associate himself more closely with his distant ancestors than with his own father.

The actual significance of Tutankhamun's reign is debateable. Certainly it represented a break with the religious experimentation of Akhenaten's reign and a return to normality, but it did not in any way represent a political break with the ruling dynasty or the elite that had surrounded Akhenaten at Amarna. This break would not truly come until the reign of General Horemheb, who almost certainly had no direct bonds of kinship to the Thutmosoid line. There is no direct evidence of what societal role the ancestors of the future Seti I played during the reign of Tutankhamun. From the previously discussed fragmented stela OI 11456[32] dedicated to Seti I's grandfather, the commissioner and troop commander also named Seti, however, it is clear that his brother, Khaemwaset, was not only a member of the elite himself, as a Fan-Bearer of the Retinue, but also through the family connections of his wife, Taemwadjsy. This lady, about whom history preserves next to no information, was the sister of Amenhotep, called Huy, Tutankhamun's Viceroy of Kush. The Viceroy of Kush served as the direct representative of royal power in Nubia and therefore constituted the highest authority in that part of the world. It is difficult to imagine that the sister of such a powerful man would be married into a family which held low status, and on this basis alone it is clear that the two brothers, who would become the great-uncle and grandfather of Seti I, came from an elite family within Egyptian society.

During Tutankhamun's reign, two dignitaries rose to particular prominence: Ay, a former Fan-Bearer on the right side of the king during the reign of Akhenaten and possibly the brother of Akhenaten's mother, Queen Tiya;[33] and Horemheb, a military officer who – very much like the commissioner Seti – had served as an envoy to foreign lands and risen through the ranks to become commander-in-chief of the Egyptian army. It is likely that, due to Tutankhamun's tender years, it was Ay and Horemheb who effectively controlled the country. Towards the end of his reign, Tutankhamun designated Horemheb as the Deputy of the Lord of the Two Lands,[34] a title which generally meant that its holder would succeed to the throne in case of the king's untimely death without heirs. And Tutankhamun did indeed die young, at the age of 18 or 19, leaving no heirs to the throne. However, it was Ay who is shown leading the burial of the boy king in paintings within Tutankhamun's fabled tomb, and it was Ay who took the throne after his death as the new pharaoh. It appears as if Horemheb was somehow outmanoeuvred. This in itself is curious: how could an aged vizier have check-mated the commander-in-chief of the entire Egyptian army. Two possibilities present themselves; one is that Ankhsunamun, the widow of Tutankhamun, refused to marry Horemheb, who had been born a commoner. Another is that Horemheb was not in the country when Tutankhamun died, but away on campaign. This would have given Ay ample time to legitimize his own claim and sidestep Horemheb entirely.

Ay quickly married Tutankhamun's widow, Ankhsunamun, to legitimize his own claim to the throne, and during his relatively brief reign, he sought to continue the revitalization of the old cults begun by Tutankhamun. He also nominated his adopted son, Nakhtmin, to take the throne after him. However, with Ay's death, Horemheb refused to be circumvented again. Nakhtmin never inherited his father's throne, and instead Horemheb took power in what might have amounted to a military coup and the last of the blood relations to the 18th Dynasty rulers fell from power.

* * *

The Opet was an extravagant annual festival celebrating the Theban triad of Amun, Mut and Khonsu at Thebes. During the festival, the gods were carried from the inner shrines in the Karnak Temple on gilded barges to the Luxor Temple. Here, the ruling king was often re-crowned and his bond with Amun as the Lord of Victories and the pre-eminent god of kingship was reaffirmed. The first Opet Festival after the death of King Ay must have been even more extravagant and festive: at its climax the new king, Horemheb, would be crowned. As the general prepared to take this ultimate power for himself, he must have marvelled at how far he had come. Very little is known about Horemheb's parents, but it is likely that he was not a member of one of the great noble families of Egypt at all. Born in Herakleaopolis Magna near the entrance to the Fayum, Horemheb was a part of a burgeoning trend of military elites, which had begun to emerge during the early to mid-18th Dynasty.

In earlier periods the elite had unequivocally been scribes, and the scribal ideals of learning and wisdom were held in high regard. But due to the expansionist nature of the 18th Dynasty, certain soldiers within the standing army began to rise to prominence. On the battlefield it was easier for an individual to truly shine, regardless of what family he came from or what bureaucratic position his father and grandfather had held.

Accounts by soldiers such as Ahmose, son of Abana,[35] and Ahmose-Pen-Nekhbet,[36] who both fought in campaigns in the Near East and Nubia during the first half of the 18th Dynasty, show the amount of wealth a skilful (and presumably lucky) soldier could assemble: land, captives to work it, precious materials such as gold and silver, as well as valuable weapons taken from defeated enemies. This mounting wealth helped to cement these military men and their families as a force to rival the traditional scribal elite. By the reign of Ramesses II, the relationship between these two factions had deteriorated and scribal exercises from this period openly mock soldiers, listing the hardships of their life and – perhaps revealing some panic on the part of the authors – desperately urging pupils to abandon any thought of giving up their studies and joining the army.[37] It was more than anything this new climate of some limited social mobility in a traditionally rigid and inflexible hierarchy, which allowed a relatively lowly ranked soldier like Horemheb to rise to the highest office in the land.

The Egypt Horemheb inherited was a far cry from the prosperous and peaceful land it had been under Amenhotep III. Akhenaten's obsessive centralization of the administration and self-imposed isolation at Tell el-Amarna had taken its toll on Egypt's internal administration, as had the instability caused by several successive kings ruling only for brief periods of time. Thankfully for posterity, we have a fairly clear idea of Horemheb's priorities once his coronation was over. An extensive document, the Great Edict of Horemheb,[38] was set up in the Karnak Temple, carved into a large stone slab. The inscription purports to be a direct dictate from Horemheb himself to his scribes, wherein the king lays out a series of policies aimed at bringing some stability to the country. Chief among Horemheb's concerns was the apparent spread of corruption that had been caused by the centralization of the Amarna Period. The king's solution was simple and brutal: the Great Edict instructed that any officer of the army, or bureaucrat of the state, who dared to seize property to which he had no right was to have his nose amputated and afterwards be banished to the border fortress of Tjaru, presumably to serve as a common soldier. This would no doubt have amounted to an effective death sentence if passed against well-fed elderly administrators with sticky fingers.

This certainly seems a draconian punishment, but Horemheb may have felt that it was necessary in order to re-establish control of the country. As an old soldier himself, he undoubtedly also sought to strengthen the army by securing its provisions and properties. According to the Great Edict, Horemheb travelled throughout Egypt, energetically rebuilding temples which had fallen into disrepair, and undertaking new construction projects. Some of these projects, such as the building of several new pylons in the temple of Amun at Karnak, used the so-called *talatat* blocks, small limestone cubes originally used in the construction of shrines and temples dedicated to the Aten during the reign of Akhenaten.

Horemheb began the process of undoing and destroying the works of Akhenaten early in his reign. Tell el-Amarna was abandoned for good, temples built by Akhenaten were torn down and their building materials reused. The names of Akhenaten, Nefertiti and Ay were deliberately chiselled from monuments, and statues of the heretic pharaoh were destroyed. In the most obvious attempt to suppress even the memory of the Amarna Period, Horemheb officially claimed that his reign had begun at the death of Amenhotep III, thus essentially removing all the following rulers (including Akhenaten and Tutankhamun) from the official succession. The later Ramesside king lists continued this tradition and excluded the rulers of the Amarna Period. To further underline his return to the traditional worship of Amun of Karnak, Horemheb also had statues carved showing himself standing next to the god. Such statues – and many others during his reign – ended the artistic experimentation characteristic of the Amarna Period and returned to a more orthodox artistic canon.

Alongside these administrative and religious changes, Horemheb began making plans for his burial. He was not a young ruler and the task was therefore quite urgent. Before becoming king, Horemheb had organized the construction of a large limestone tomb at the Saqqara necropolis near modern-day Cairo.[39] The tomb is shaped like a typical New Kingdom temple. A visitor would first have come to two large mud-brick pylons which flanked the entrance to the tomb's superstructure. After passing through the pylons, one would have arrived at a series of courtyards and smaller storerooms. The courtyards were flanked with limestone relief showing triumphant scenes of Horemheb's military career; Horemheb being awarded with the Gold of Valour by Tutankhamun, soldiers in military encampment and rows of defeated enemies being brought back to Egypt in chains as captives.

A 10-metre-deep shaft in the inner courtyard gave access to the tomb's substructure consisting of several passages leading to one finished and one unfinished tomb chamber. The Saqqara tomb of Horemheb is one of the largest New Kingdom tombs in that vast necropolis, but despite its grandeur, it was the tomb of an 'ordinary' member of the elite, not of a king. Once crowned as pharaoh, Horemheb abandoned it in favour of a far grander burial in the Valley of the Kings.[40]

In order for this tomb to be constructed, Horemheb needed the workers from Deir el-Medina. This village, located on the West Bank of the Nile at Thebes, had been founded in the early 18th Dynasty to house the sculptors, artists and craftsmen who worked on carving and decorating the royal tombs in the Valley of the Kings. During his reign, Akhenaten had moved the community from their homes at Deir el-Medina to another small village close to Tell el-Amarna[41] so that they could work instead on constructing royal and elite tombs near his new capital. Horemheb moved the community back to Deir el-Medina and reorganized the village. Work soon began on a new tomb in the Valley of the Kings. This tomb, known as KV57 in Egyptological literature, was similar in overall design to earlier royal tombs. It consists of a long passageway and stairway leading to an ante-chamber and a pillared hall where the king's red quartzite sarcophagus was placed. The decoration in KV57 was, however, more complex than earlier tombs. Depictions of gods and scenes from funerary literature had customarily been painted on the plastered surfaces of the tomb chamber and passageways. By contrast, Horemheb ordered that the scenes be carved from the limestone rock in delicate raised relief before being painted. This new technique would be appropriated by some of Horemheb's successor, such as Seti I and Ramesses II, and used in the decoration of their own tombs in the Valley of the Kings.

As a king, one of Horemheb's most important tasks was securing a succession, preferably in the form of a son. This duty had become even more imperative by the confused succession following the death of Akhenaten. If Horemheb wished to truly remove the spectre of the Amarna Period, he would have to establish his own dynasty. In order to do so he needed a queen. Queens in ancient Egypt did not hold direct political power, nor did a direct translation for the modern term 'queen' exist.[42] These women were instead titled as *hemet nesut weret*, 'Great Royal Wife', and their primary duty was to provide as many heirs as possible to guarantee the succession. Horemheb was nearing middle age when he took power, and he had already been married once.

His first wife, Amenia, is almost exclusively known from her portrait in the form of a double statue owned by the British Museum,[43] and the marriage appears to have been childless. Amenia did not live to see her husband become king, but most likely died during the reign of King Ay and was buried in the one finished tomb chamber of Horemheb's tomb at Saqqara.[44] When the tomb was excavated by the Anglo-Dutch mission in the 1970s, a second set of female remains were found interred in the unfinished tomb chamber. Investigation suggested that these belonged to Horemheb's second wife, whom he married after becoming king. Her name was Mutnedjmet, and her marriage and later life appears a tragic tale. She was in her late twenties when she married the king, who was nearly twice her age. Her family ties are unknown, although she may have been a sister of the former queen, Nefertiti, and in this way helped Horemheb to legitimize his reign as pharaoh.

She retreated from public life only a few years after her marriage and died much earlier than expected in the 13th Year of Horeheb's reign. The discovery of her skeletal remains from the tomb at Saqqara provides clues to what ended her life prematurely. With her body was found a much smaller set of remains belonging either to an unborn foetus or a very young infant. It is likely that she either died giving birth to this child, or as a result of a serious miscarriage. Her skeleton in fact shows evidence of repeated miscarriages and difficult births. As no sons or daughters of Horemheb are known from any source material, it can be assumed that these children were either stillborn or died as infants. These repeated tragedies sapped the queen's strength and finally killed her, leaving Horemheb a childless widower.[45]

Her death must have been a major blow to Horemheb. Growing old now without an heir, any plans he may have had for a dynasty by blood were abandoned. Instead, Horemheb decided to provide the required stability by naming his successor before his death. To choose this successor, Horemheb looked to his closest ally, his vizier Paramessu.[46] This Paramessu was the same man whose father had been the commissioner and troop commander Seti during the reign of Akhenaten, and whose uncle had been the fan-bearer Khaemwaset. On the fractured limestone stela in the Oriental Institute Museum in Chicago discussed above, Paramessu is given only the military title 'stable master'. By the later reign of Horemheb, he had evidently risen well beyond these humble beginnings: on the 400 Year Stela,[47] which was set up during the reign of Ramesses II to commemorate the 400th anniversary of the construction of the temple of Seth at Avaris, Paramessu is listed as Horemheb's vizier, one of two first ministers at his court.

On the 400 Year Stela, he is also named 'His Majesty's Deputy in Upper and Lower Egypt' and 'Hereditary Prince in the Whole Land'. These titles are crucial as they mirror those which Horemheb himself had been given before he took power as pharaoh. They effectively singled out Paramessu as Horemheb's heir apparent. The attraction of Paramessu as a successor to Horemheb is obvious. Paramessu, like Horemheb, was a member of the military elite, having held military titles and being a descendant of a military family. During his long career he had held a number of significant military posts in Horemheb's administration before finally becoming vizier; he had been 'master of horse', a fortress commander, 'Charioteer of His Majesty' and 'General of the Lord of the Two Lands'. Like Horemheb, his family did not hail from the traditional Theban centre of power, but rather from the Eastern Nile Delta, probably near the settlement of Avaris. However, unlike Horemheb, Paramessu was both married and had at least one child, Seti, who was named after his grandfather.

This young man had already distinguished himself, despite his youth, and would undoubtedly have been well-known to the ageing Horemheb. He had, like his father, held a number of military titles such as 'fortress commander' and 'master of horse', alongside several religious titles, most notably High Priest of Seth.[48] Eventually, he was promoted by Horemheb to the same rank as his father, that of vizier. Paramessu and his son Seti in this way held the two highest offices in the land; one representing Horemheb as vizier in Memphis and the other in Thebes. By choosing Paramessu as his successor, Horemheb would not only guarantee a competent leader for the country, but also the foundations of a dynasty. The birth of Seti's first-born son, Ramesses, was yet another incentive for Horemheb to raise this family as his successors.

* * *

The precise length of Horemheb's reign remains a subject of scholarly debate, although the discovery of a vast assemblage of inscribed wine dockets in his tomb do not contain any regnal years beyond Year 14.[49] How Horemheb died is similarly unknown, and while human remains from several individuals were found in his sarcophagus upon its discovery in 1908, none of these have been successfully proven to belong to the king. Horemheb's reign had gone some way towards re-establishing the old ways, religiously and politically, after the relative chaos of the Amarna Period. Temples were once again being built to honour the entire pantheon of gods, the settlement of Tell el-Amarna lay abandoned and a significant restructuring of Egypt's military forces had given the new ruler the tools to reassert Egypt's dominance abroad.

After a long period of political and social upheavals, the new king Paramessu was no doubt eager to clearly define his reign as a new beginning. His first move to demonstrate this political break came in the form of his throne name. Once crowned, a king of Egypt would generally take five throne names. These names often contained clues towards the types of rulers they were determined to emulate and what policies they intended to enact. The five names of Paramessu can therefore provide us with vital clues to how he himself defined the terms of his kingship:

1. **Horus name**   Flourishing in Kingship
2. **Nebty name**   Ascending as King like Atum
3. **Golden Horus name**   Restoring Maat Throughout the Two Lands
4. **Prenomen**   Established by the Strength of Re
5. **Nomen**   Re has birthed him

The first two names allude to the divine right of Paramessu to rule as king, something he would undoubtedly have been keen to underline, considering his lack of connection by blood to previous dynasties. His third name not only invokes Maat – the symbol of justice and the correct order of the world – but also shows that the king intended to restore order after the chaotic aftermath of the Amarna Period. This name also resembles one of the throne names of Ahmose, the first king of the 18th Dynasty and shows Paramessu's desire to be considered the founder of a similarly powerful dynasty. While the prenomen or royal name chosen by Paramessu was *Menpehtyre*, he is today more commonly known by his nomen, or personal name, which in Egyptian is written as *Ra-me-su*, and anglicized as Ramesses I.

Ramesses I was not a young man when he took the throne and his reign was so short that only few textual records have survived to show how he began the task of establishing his own legacy. From a stela set up on the Sinai Peninsula in the first year of his reign[50] we know that he – most likely for political reasons – excluded references to Horemheb and took full responsibility for bringing order back to Egypt after the Amarna Period:

'Good god, son of Amun, born of Mut, Lady of Heaven, to be ruler of all that the sun's disc encircles; he who came forth from the body, citories being (already) decreed for him; who sets in order the Two Lands once again, and who has increased the festivals of the gods.'[51]

While this stela is largely rhetorical and contains limited information about actual policies, the reference to renewed religious festivals was no doubt included to further underline Ramesses as a definitive break with the general neglect of traditional rituals during the Amarna Period.

During the second year of his short reign, we are informed by a dedicatory stela set up in the Nubian fortress of Buhen[52] that Ramesses renewed the worship of the local god, Min–Amun, ordered a temple built in his honour and equipped it both with food offerings and with priests, slaves and no doubt land on which these slaves could work for the benefit of the temple. Another possible dedication stela from Karnak[53] suggests that Ramesses may also have donated land and wealth to Amun of Thebes. However, these sources do not contain the same level of policy detail as the Great Edict of Horemheb. Rather, the best documentation for this period of Egyptian history is in the form of a dedicatory stela set up at Abydos during the reign of Seti I, wherein he describes his own career during his father's reign.[54]

He claims to have witnessed the chaos of the Amarna Period, when there was 'strife and trouble abroad in the whole land' and where no one cared for the monuments of the gods or the tombs of their ancestors. Horemheb's reign is completely excluded from the description, which moves directly to the ascension of Ramesses I: 'So the Lord-of-All appointed my father as Ruler, to restore them to their places.'[55] According to this inscription, Seti was placed 'like a star' at the side of his father during his reign. It describes how the young prince regent was despatched by Ramesses I to the lands of Fenkhu to destroy the 'dissidents of the desert'. The precise location of Fenkhu is not known, although the term generally refers to all the Levantine people encountered by the ancient Egyptians. It is likely that this campaign was the antecedent to the military excursions undertaken as soon as Seti himself took the throne, against Bedouins on the Sinai Peninsula and city-states in Canaan and Lebanon.

* * *

But Seti's role during his father's reign was not merely administrative. More fundamentally, he was tasked with securing the foundations of the family dynasty. He had already married, and he may already have had a young son. Seti's wife, the future queen Tuya, is poorly represented in the contemporary sources, although this is not in itself unusual. As in many ancient societies, the lives and precise roles of women are usually poorly documented.[56] We know from a fragmentary inscribed stone from Medinet Habu, which dates to the reign of Tuya's son Ramesses II, that her parents were named Raia and Ruia. Raia was a Lieutenant of the Chariotry, and we may assume that he was a compatriot of both Horemheb and Ramesses I. It is tempting to assume that Tuya's marriage to Seti was one of political expediency and that Raia, as a lower-ranked military man from a less important family, used Tuya to secure his family's connection to the rising stars of Ramesses I and Seti. Marriages for love were far less common in ancient Egyptian society than they are in the modern Western World, and most marriages – at least within elite families – were organized to bring either political or economic benefits to both parties. Relationships based on love were known to the Egyptians, and dramaturgical love poetry was in vogue during the time of Seti and his immediate successors. But the source material is simply too poor to speculate whether Seti saw his new bride as a 'rising morning star' who captured his heart with her movements in the romantic manner described by a contemporary poem.[57]

After the marriage, Tuya gave birth to a daughter, Tia, during the reign of Horemheb, before her father-in-law was crowned as king. This young princess would later marry a royal scribe who – confusingly – had the same name as her: Tia.[58] He would later serve as a tutor to her younger brother. With the birth of her second child, Ramesses, Tuya's status as Great Royal Wife and future Mother of the King was cemented. While her public profile was withdrawn during the reign of her husband, she became a crucial public figure during the reign of her son, and may even have served him as an advisor and confidante.

Bearing in mind his growing list of descendants, the aging king Ramesses may have rested more easily, certain that his son had the support and the capability to continue his brief legacy and return order to Egypt. During the month of August in 1290 BC,[59] a message went out from the royal palace in Memphis: 'The Falcon is Flown to Heaven.' Ramesses was dead and the young Prince Seti was now ready to ascend the Horus Throne of the Living.

* * *

The heat in the Valley of the Kings even in early October would have been oppressive. The Valley, a natural bowl surrounded by tall limestone cliffs, can reach temperatures of well over 40 degrees centigrade. It was a trial for the procession winding its way through the gorges leading into the Valley itself. Heading the procession was Seti, the future pharaoh, already wearing the regalia of office; the blue *khepresh* crown, or 'war crown', favoured by New Kingdom pharaohs, a white linen kilt, the skin of a leopard draped around his shoulders and gilded sandals. With him came dignitaries and family members.[60] After the sweating courtiers came rows of solemn priests, their bald heads shining under a merciless sun. They burnt incense, chanted and shook copper sistrums. Mingling with the noise was the lamentations and wails of the female mourners who followed the funeral train, tearing at their clothes, beating and scratching their chest and smearing their hair and faces with ash. The centre of the procession was taken up by two large wooden sleighs, pulled by teams of oxen. On the first was the wooden anthropoid coffin containing the mummy of Ramesses I, on the second the king's canopic chest. Inside this chest were the four canopic jars containing the stomach, lungs, liver and intestines of the king, carefully preserved with natron.

After his death, Ramesses had been taken to the *Per Nefer*, the Good House, where the embalmers began work on his body,[61] with the mummification itself conducted in a temporary tent-like structure. After removing the brain by whisking it with a metal hook and allowing it to run out of the nose, the internal organs were removed to prevent them spoiling and separately preserved. The body was then covered with natron – a type of salt from Wadi Natrun in the eastern desert – and left for thirty days; the salt served to leech all the moisture from the body. After this, the chest and stomach cavities were filled with straw and wads of linen to preserve the natural contours of the body, before it was wrapped in linen bandages interspaced with protective amulets. In all, the process of mummification took seventy days and was intended to preserve the body against the ravages of time, thus guaranteeing the deceased ruler a safe and eternal afterlife with Osiris in the Underworld.

When the procession reached the newly finished tomb which would be the final resting place of Ramesses I,[62] the wooden coffin of the king was carried into the burial chamber, where it was placed upright so the deceased king could once again gaze upon his court. Seti approached his father's coffin and held a ceremonial adze to his lips. This ceremony, the Opening of the Mouth, awoke the deceased pharaoh and restored to him his powers of speech as well as his ability to receive offerings of food and drink. The ceremony also served a political purpose. As the deceased king was identified with Osiris, the Ruler of the Underworld, the person who opened his mouth took on the role of Horus, the champion of his father and the God of Kingship. By conducting this ceremony, Seti affirmed his right to rule as the personification of Horus, divine ruler of the Two Lands of Upper and Lower Egypt. When the ceremony was complete, the wooden coffin was carried to a large red quartzite sarcophagus and Ramesses was finally allowed to rest.

As Seti backed out of the tomb and saw it closed with a seal bearing his father's cartouche, he may have experienced a pang of regret. He had undoubtedly taken part in the burial of Horemheb, standing together with his father, and by comparison to Horemheb's lavish tomb, the tomb of his Ramesses was poor. His short reign meant that the workmen at Deir el-Medina had only had time to carve a short descending passageway and a burial chamber with three smaller antechambers. Unlike the delicate bas-reliefs which decorated the tomb of Horemheb, all the decorations in Ramesses' tomb were simply painted directly on the plaster. It may have been partly this paucity which would later inspire Seti to order the construction of one of the most beautifully decorated chapels from New Kingdom Egypt in honour of his father at the Middle Egyptian site of Abydos.

* * *

Despite the care taken by the Egyptian priests and workmen, the body of Ramesses I was not allowed to remain unmolested in his tomb. In 1817, the Italian collector and adventurer Giovanni Battista Belzoni (1778–1823) entered the tomb but found it empty. Its riches and the mummy of the king had vanished.

Unbeknownst to Belzoni, Egyptian priests had moved the mummy of Ramesses at the end of the first millenium BC, when tomb robbery and looting was widespread in the Theban Necropolis. They had reburied the king in another location, believing him safe. However, in the 1860s the Abd el-Rassul family had found the body of Ramesses I and had sold him to a private collector in the United States. Passing from collector to collector, the mummy eventually ended up in the Niagara Falls Museum in Canada. In the 1980s, Egyptologists hypothesized that the mummy was indeed Ramesses I, and a battery of scientific tests confirmed their speculation. In 1999, the mummy was sold to the Michael C. Carlos Museum in Atlanta, and in 2003 it was given as a gift to the people of Egypt by the city of Atlanta. In October 2003, Ramesses I's long journey back home ended to the sound of singing and a military marching band as his body was brought to rest in the renovated Luxor Museum.[63]

Excursus: On the Threshold

'It was he, indeed, who created my beauty; he made great my family in (people's) minds. He gave me his counsels as my safeguard, and his teaching was like a rampart in my heart.'[64]

Seti's route to power was in many ways both common and unorthodox. He was the son of a king, and as such, he represented the proper order of succession. But unlike most ancient Egyptian kings, he had not been born to rule; he had not even been born as a member of the royal family. His succession to the Horus Throne of the Living owed a tremendous amount to a highly unusual set of circumstances, whose antecedents can be traced all the way back to the beginning of the 18th Dynasty. The strong focus on Amun of Karnak by the Thutmosoid kings and the constant lavishing of wealth and land upon the Amun priesthood created a justification for Akhenaten to carry out his political and religious revolution, breaking for a time the power of Thebes and shifting the political capital to Tell el-Amarna.

The chaotic line of succession and weak rulers which followed his death provided the opportunity for a strong military leader to emerge, and emerge he did in the form of the general Horemheb. Horemheb could himself be viewed as more in line with the later 19th Dynasty and the Ramesside kings than the 18th Dynasty to which he belongs. He represented a bridge between the old and the new. He was clearly associated closely with the old Theban royal family, through his marriage to Nefertiti's sister but mainly by his strong association with Tutankhamun and Ay. Simultaneously, he represented the new breed of rulers to which Ramesses I and Seti I both belonged: members of the military elite who had risen to power, first within the ranks of the army before taking up administrative and religious posts.

Despite the efforts of both Horemheb and Ramesses I, the Egypt which Seti inherited was still weaker than it had been during the reigns of Thutmosis III and Amenhotep III. Horemheb's administrative overhaul of the interior policies of the country had been effective, as had the return to religious orthodoxy begun by Tutankhamun and championed by Horemheb and Ramesses I. But Egypt's foreign policy was still a major obstacle on the young king's road to success. In the north, the Hittite Kingdom was on the move, sensing potential weakness from the untried Egyptian monarch. Many of the former vassal states in Canaan and the Levant had quietly switched sides to join with Egypt's enemies. Even in Nubia, a province which had been effectively subdued and integrated since the fall of Kerma more than 200 years before, there were the faint stirrings of rebellion. The brief campaign undertaken against the Fenkhu during his father's reign had been little more than an experimental sortie by the young Seti. Now that he was solely in charge of the country and the army, he began making plans for how to reassert Egypt's dominance on the Near Eastern stage.

Chapter 3

Smiting Foreign Lands

Seti, the new king of Egypt, stood surveying his troops at the fortress of Tjaru in the late spring of 1289 BC. Soldiers hurried around him down the cramped streets between workshops, houses, magazines and granaries. They loaded mule trains with jars of olive oil and preserved meats, sacks of emmer wheat, barley and loaves of bread. Scribes sat by the entrance to the armouries supervising the distribution of weapons spears, axes, shields, bows and arrows to the thousands of infantrymen, most dressed only in a linen or leather kilt, the officers with armour made from leather and bronze. Disassembled chariots, transported on ox–carts, along with hundreds of horses were driven past the fort as the *Medjay* scouts prepared to leave well ahead of the army's vanguard. Seti's royal guards, with bronze spearheads and dagger blades engraved with their master's name and titles, closed ranks around the tall man with the dark auburn hair and the straight, sharply defined nose.

As he looked around at his troop commanders and standard bearers, the young king, not yet out of his twenties, must have felt a pang of realization, that had it not been for an unusual combination of circumstances, he would have been counted among those military officers, rather than commanding them. He had buried his father a mere eight months before, and spent the winter consolidating his powerbase in the courts of Memphis and Thebes. Now, as he set his army upon the road east across the parched terrain of northern Sinai, ready to face rebellious Bedouin and disloyal vassals, he may have felt that his life would have been easier if the burden of the highest command had not been placed upon his shoulders at all.

* * *

Egyptologists are both blessed and cursed when studying the military campaigns and foreign policy of Seti I. On one hand, an immensely valuable source of information exists in the so-called Karnak Battle Reliefs.[1] On the other hand, many of these reliefs are damaged, some are missing entirely and the ordering of the episodes and campaigns they describe remains a subject of intense debate.[2] Located on the exterior wall on both sides of the northern gateway, these reliefs consist of more than two dozen individual scenes, arranged in three horizontal registers. The upper register has been largely lost, and this has contributed to the lack of apparent unity in the individual scenes, which has exacerbated the inherent problems in establishing a coherent chronology of the events. The scenes themselves are finely carved using raised relief, and many show signs of slight alterations. It is unlikely that they were all carved contemporarily; rather they may have been created throughout Seti's reign.

Accompanying the reliefs is a series of texts, which describe the individual campaigns in somewhat grandiloquent terms.[3] The Battle Reliefs and their associated texts are not a clear-cut and unbiased historical record, and it would be a mistake to interpret them as such. They served a religious and political purpose; by showing Seti fighting against Egypt's enemies and returning to Thebes with spoil for Amun and his temple, the reliefs underlined Seti's right to rule. They are part of an artistic tradition showing the king of Egypt smiting foreign lands, which went back thousands of years to the very earliest foundations of Egyptian civilization. However, considered together with contemporary texts and archaeological data from the towns and cities Seti visited and conquered during his campaigns, as well as the forts he founded or expanded, the Karnak Battle Reliefs can nevertheless help to provide a comprehensive overview of how the young king set about restoring Egypt's imperial control.

* * *

The fortress of Tjaru, where Seti had assembled his army before setting off on his first military campaign as sole ruler of Egypt, had long served as the starting point on the Ways of Horus. The Ways of Horus was in essence a fortified highway running along the north coast of the Sinai Peninsula, connecting the eastern Nile Delta with the area of modern-day Palestine and Israel. Surveys by Ben Gourion University from 1972 to 1982 identified multiple New Kingdom sites, including fortified wells, production centres and larger forts.[4] Tjaru was well-known to Seti. Both he and his father had at some point in their careers been commanders of the fort; Seti may even have spent part of his childhood living within its walls.

The archaeological remains of this vast fortification were identified in the 1980s by archaeologists from the Ministry of State Antiquities, who conducted extensive excavations at the site for more than twenty years.[5] The excavations revealed a large mud-brick enclosure wall measuring 500m by 250m, guarded by towers with walls 13m thick. While Middle Kingdom material has been recovered from the area, the initial phase of fortified occupation was in the form of a Hyksos stronghold built during the Second Intermediate Period. During this time, the fortress included several granaries as well as domestic workshop structures. Following the expulsion of the Hyksos, the 18th Dynasty rulers reoccupied and expanded the site, with the most significant building phase dated to the reign of Thutmosis III, who added two large administrative buildings. After his father's death, Seti set out his own building programme for the fort, probably in preparation for his campaigns in the Near East. This programme saw the refortification and expansion of the fortress' mud-brick wall, and the rebuilding of one of the original Hyksos granaries as well as long rectangular magazines for the storage of equipment and weaponry. As Seti saw the daunting walls of Tjaru sink into the distance, his first target was the Shasu Bedouin of the Sinai Peninsula and Palestine. The purpose of attacking this loose confederation of nomadic pastoralists is not clear, although a text from the Karnak reliefs suggest that Seti was simply reacting to fermenting rebellion:

'Then one came to tell His Majesty: "The Shasu enemy, they are planning a revolt! Their chiefs are assembled in one place, upon the ridge of Kharu. They have fallen to confusion and trouble, one slays his ally. They ignore the laws of the Palace."'[6]

It is perhaps unlikely that the King of Egypt would under normal circumstance be too concerned with the internal tribal politics of the Shasu. However, the Ways of Horus did not simply serve as a military road. It was also a caravan trail and the way by which a great deal of Egypt's wealth in the form of tribute and trade entered the country. Any banditry on the part of the Shasu could potentially sever Egypt's link with the markets of the Near East, and also cut off the isolated strings of fortifications stretching across the northern coast of the Sinai Peninsula.

As a sedentary civilization, the Egyptian state traditionally viewed the transhumant pastoralists who occupied the fringes of its empire with deep suspicion, seeing these societies as representatives of instability and chaos. Pessimistic literature, such as *The Prophecies of Neferty*, written during the Middle Kingdom encapsulates this view. This text is in a sense a piece of historical fiction and royal propaganda, set during the reign of the Old Kingdom King Snefru, several hundred years before it was composed. In the tale, the Lector Priest Neferty makes a series of dire prophecies about the chaotic end of the Old Kingdom and the First Intermediate Period. A final prophecy predicts the rise of a king in the south by the name of Ameny (Amenemhat I) who would come to restore order to the land. One of the symptoms of the chaotic world described by Neferty is the arrival of nomadic communities within the Nile Valley:

'He gathered his thoughts on what would happen in the land, and called to mind the chaos in the east, the raids of the *Amu* with their strength when they disrupt the hearts of those at the harvest, as they take away the teams of oxen who were ploughing.'[7]

Later in the text, when Neferty describes the return of good law and order to the land after the ascension of Amenmehat I, he claims that:

'They will build the "Walls of the Ruler", Life, Prosperity and Health, and no Asiatic will go to Egypt, so that they can beg water to water their herds.'[8]

The text alludes to an issue historically present in many societies where nomadic and sedentary cultures come into contact. The basis of the nomadic economy, pastoralism and some limited agriculture, is vulnerable to climactic and environmental changes. In drier years, or during full-blown droughts, the already limited pasture and agricultural potential of the desert is lessened and the nomadic societies are driven to either barter access to sedentary grazing land, or seize the land by force. In extreme cases, nomadic communities may band together into tribal confederations in order to secure more land on which to subsist and pose a direct threat to sedentary communities. Such a situation occurred during the reign of Merenptah, when Libyan nomads invaded the Nile Valley with the aim – according to Egyptian texts – of 'fighting to fill their bellies'.

The suspicion with which the Egyptian state viewed the nomadic Shasu is even reflected in their name. The Egyptian verb '*Sjasu*' translates broadly as 'to wander' or 'those who move on foot', alluding to their itinerant lifestyle, a name which in turn is inspired by the Canaanite verb *sasa(h)*, 'to plunder'.[9] The battle between the Egyptian army and the Shasu is not described in detail in the Karnak Battle Reliefs. Rather, the text simply concludes that Seti 'fell on them like a mighty lion, turning them into corpses throughout their desert *wadis*, they were prostrated in their blood as if they had never existed'.[10] The fighting style and strategies of the Shasu are difficult to gauge. They were likely outnumbered by the Egyptians and their weapons of inferior quality. There is also no evidence that they owned or used horses in battle. Considering these disadvantages, the Shasu may have preferred to avoid facing the Egyptian army on an open field, relying instead on their knowledge of the desert environment. A contemporary text certainly alludes to the proclivity of the Shasu for ambushes and surprise attacks: 'The narrow pass is dangerous, with Shasu concealed beneath the bushes.'[11]

The Karnak Battle Reliefs convey the chaos of the eventual battle between Seti and the Shasu Bedouin. The Egyptian army is nowhere to be found; rather it is Seti alone – a giant figure standing in his chariot, firing arrows at his enemies – who is shown as the single victor of the battle. The Shasu are depicted as an unorganized rabble, fleeing towards a fortified city, desperate to avoid the charging king. Their weapons are comparatively primitive; semi-circular bronze-headed axes, of a type long obsolete in the Egyptian arsenal, and spears. They are dressed only in loincloths and wear no armour. One of the Shasu is shown in a tableau of death, an arrow lodged in his neck, falling forwards. Next to the city, another group of Shasu are feverishly breaking their weapons and flinging themselves on the ground in submission. After securing his victory, the captured Shasu were most likely sent back to Egypt with an escort. They would serve as tribute to Amun of Thebes and spend the rest of their lives working on one of the many estates owned by the Karnak Temple.

This campaign against the Shasu may have amounted to little more than a *razzia*, or raid for plunder and slaves, and it is unlikely that these nomads could have mounted a particularly formidable opposition to the young king. But his victory nevertheless secured the passage across northern Sinai and may have helped to curb any banditry – at least for a time. In order to further cement his control of the crucial Sinai crossing, Seti ordered the refortification and construction of several waystations and forts along the Ways of Horus. At Haruba, a large enclosure wall was repaired during his reign and several new granaries and storage magazines were constructed. At Deir el-Balah, a citadel was constructed in order to guard a small lake. These forts and their garrisons would both protect commerce and serve as stopping points for the Egyptian army when they crossed the parched terrain, guaranteeing a supply of food and water – alongside the supplies the army itself carried.

All in all, the campaign against the Shasu had been little more than a warm-up act. The enemies Seti faced in the Levant were unlikely to be as easily despatched. Towards the end of June 1289 BC, Seti and his army had crossed the Sinai Peninsula and the young king was ready to face the strife-ridden internal politics and powerful external forces at play in the Near East.[12]

* * *

After the easy victory over the Shasu in northern Sinai and southern Palestine, Seti and his army followed the coastal road, the *Via Marris*, into the Egyptian province of Djahy stretching from the port of Ashkelon in the south to the Lebanese city-states of Tyre, Sidon and Byblos in the north, all nominally under Egyptian control. Travelling along the *Via Marris*, the new king and his army would have encountered several major settlements whose rulers were Egyptian vassals, including Ashdod, Ashkelon and the town of Megiddo. The purpose of this northward march was not purely military; it was a *Tour de Triomphe*, a necessary obligation for the new king in order to ensure the loyalty of his foreign subjects. The surviving documentation does not detail precisely how this was achieved, although the Karnak Stela of Amenhotep II describes the type of political theatricals which accompanied a peripatetic Egyptian monarch:

'Month 2 of Akhet, Day 10: Turning southwards to Egypt. His Majesty proceeded upon horse to the town of Niy. Now those Asiatics of this town; the men together with the women were upon their wall adoring his Majesty. Their faces were lit because they stared upon the Great God [...] Month 2 of Sjemu, Day 20: Now he was in the camp, which was made for his Majesty at the town of Tjerekh. He caused that [the inhabitants] made an oath of allegiance.'[13]

One can imagine the crowds of spectators who rushed to the city walls to gaze in awe at the splendour of the Egyptian army marching below, the king leading the vanguard in a gilded chariot, surrounded by heavily armed bodyguards. Similarly to Amenhotep II, Seti may have demanded submission and oaths of allegiance from the chiefs of the cities, requesting them to join him in his camp and give tribute. According to the inscriptions at the Karnak Temple, Seti's unnamed fan-bearer spoke out in awe when he had seen the loyalty of these Asiatic chiefs: 'You are like Montu upon every foreign land! The chiefs of Retjenu behold you! Your renown is in their limbs!'[14]

However, in the midst of these protestations of loyalty and the bounty of tribute heaped upon the triumphant king, unwelcome news arrived at the royal camp on the 10th Day of the Third Month of Summer, almost a year after the death of Seti's father:

'On this day, one came to speak to his Majesty: "The wretched chief in the town of Hammath has gathered to him many people. He has conquered the town of Beth-Shan, joined by those from Pahyr. The chief of Rebi (Labwi) cannot come out."'[15]

Internal squabbling between the Levantine city-states and various ruling families was endemic. The 18th Dynasty Amarna Letters are filled with pleas for Egyptian military aid by local rulers to be used against rival city-states. Akhenaten appears to have ignored most of these, but Seti was not as complacent. The city of Beth-Shan had long been within the Egyptian sphere of influence, and Seti would not allow a vassal state to be unceremoniously attacked. Even if he may have been irked by the pointless distraction, his reaction was swift. He selected the First Division of Re, named 'Abounding in Valour', and despatched them inland to break the siege of Beth-Shan. Simultaneously, he sent the First Division of Amun against the city of Hammath, whose ruler had transgressed against him, and the First Division of Seth against the city of Yenoam, who may have been in allegiance with the ruler of Hammath. Seti himself continued along the coastal road towards the city-states on the Lebanese coast with the bulk of the army.

The battles at Beth Shan and Hammath are not recorded in the Karnak Reliefs, and are only briefly mentioned in the First Beth Shan Stela which – somewhat frustratingly – merely concludes that: 'Then in one day, they had fallen to the might of His Majesty.'[16] However, the Battle of Yenoam is depicted in greater detail at the Karnak Temple. From this relief it is clear that the Egyptians were facing a very different calibre of enemy from the Shasu. While the Canaanite foe is still depicted fleeing the field of battle in disarray, their equipment was clearly more technologically sophisticated; several warriors are shown on horseback and some carry large circular shields. Next to the chaotic battlefield, several Asiatics depicted stereotypically with pointed beards, shoulder-length hair and hairbands are hiding in a forest. On the parapets of the city of Yenoam, its citizens look on in apparent horror as their host is decimated by the Egyptian forces.

The detachments sent against Beth Shan were similarly successful. A large administrative building was constructed in Beth Shan, from which an Egyptian governor could control the local area.[17] Storerooms were also built, most likely to house supplies for the Egyptian imperial administration. Most notably, two large and finely cut stela were set up within this complex, commemorating Seti and his campaigns in the area during this first year of his reign.[18] But peace had hardly settled and the victorious troops returned, before another distraction arose. According the Second Beth Shan Stela, another messenger came to Seti, still *en route* to Lebanon, with bad news:

'[Then] one came to speak to His Majesty, Life-Prosperity-Health: "The Apiru of the Mountains of Yarumtu together with Tiyru tribe, they are mobilizing against the Asiatics of Ruma."'[19]

The Apiru had been a consistent thorn in Egypt's side since the Amarna Period. Like the Shasu, the Apiru were a nomadic community living throughout the Fertile Crescent. And like the Shasu, banditry appears to have been a profitable line of business for them. During the reign of Thutmosis III, Apiru warriors had attempted to steal horses from the Egyptian army,[20] and during the reign of Akhenaten, they had repeatedly attacked Rib Addi, the Mayor of Byblos and a vassal of Egypt. Now they were creating unrest during Seti's inspection tour of his provinces:

'Then His Majesty spoke: "What is on the mind of these wretched Asiatics in raising their weapons to bring turmoil again? They shall learn what they do not yet know!"'[21]

Seti's frustration is almost palpable. The allusion to the Apiru's ignorance of him is interesting. Seti was after all a new ruler, an unknown quantity. Perhaps the leaders of the Apiru wanted to test Seti, to assess his strength and gauge his response. If they had hoped for another detached ruler in the vein of Akhenaten, they were disappointed. As with the earlier disturbance caused by the ruler of Hammath, Seti simply sent a detachment of his army back along the coastal road to deal with the situation. After only two days, the Egyptian troops returned victorious, bringing prisoners and spoils of war for the king. With the province of Djahy resoundingly subdued, Seti could finally focus his attention entirely on the final stop on his inspection tour: the Lebanese city-states.

* * *

Seti wanted more than oaths of loyalty from the coastal cities of Lebanon. He desired a far more precious commodity: timber. *Cedrus libani*, or Lebanese cedar, is an evergreen coniferous tree which grew extensively across Lebanon, Palestine, Israel and Jordan during the Late Bronze Age. Often growing straight to a height of 30–40m, these trees were highly desirable for the construction of buildings and ships. Most native Egyptian trees, such as sycamores, mulberry trees and tamarisks, are shorter and have more crooked trunks, making the production of long, straight baulks and planks difficult. The cedar forests of Lebanon therefore represented an immense source of wealth, and not only to the Egyptians. As early as 2100 BC, the religious significance (and great value) of Lebanese cedar is described in *The Epic of Gilgamesh*. In Tablet V, the titular hero and his friend Enkidu go to the Mountain of Cedar and enter a great forest, where Enkidu vows to cut down the mightiest tree to make a door for a great temple of Enlil at Nippur. The two friends battle the guardian of the forest, the fearsome Humbaba, whom they eventually kill. Then they tie the felled cedars into a raft which carries them home.[22]

The famous myth finds an echo in multiple sources from the Bronze and Iron Age civilizations in the eastern Mediterranean. Reliefs from the Iron IIb Palace of Khorsabad depict the riverine or marine transport of timber logs strung after ships crewed by Phoenician sailors,[23] and in Kings 5:6, set during Iron Ib, King Solomon requests timber from his ally, Hiram of Tyre. After the trees have been felled, Hiram offers to 'float them [the timbers] in rafts by sea to the place you specify. There I will separate them and you can take them away.' In the Egyptian source material, Lebanese cedar appears as a luxury import from the Old Kingdom onwards. During the Middle Kingdom, the nomarch Khnumhotep II of Beni Hasan even boasts in his tomb biography that he used Lebanese cedar in the construction of his tomb, making 'a door of 6 cubits, consisting of pine of Nega [and] a double door of 5 cubits 2 palms being employed for the shrine of the sacred chamber which was within this tomb'.[24] During the New Kingdom, Thutmosis III recorded the receipt of Lebanese cedar from his vassals in Syria on the Gebel Barkal Stela: 'The princes of Retjenu dragged [timber] flagpoles with oxen to the harbour and they came with their tribute to the place where His Majesty was.'[25] A contemporary painting from the Tomb of Senneferi (TT99)[26] similarly shows a scene of Lebanese workers hauling cedar down from the forests to the coast, preparing to ship it to Egypt.

Arguably the most famous source for the trade of cedar between Lebanon and Egypt is *The Journeys of Wenamun*.[27] Set at the very end of the New

Kingdom when Egypt's international power was greatly diminished, the story tells of a Priest of Amun, Wenamun, who is sent to the Prince of Byblos to procure cedar wood for the construction of a sacred barge for the transport of the cult statue of Amun. After many misfortunes, Wenamun eventually secures the timber, but the papyrus on which the story is written breaks off before the conclusion to Wenamun's journey is reached.

Seti's interest in the submission of the Lebanese chiefs was therefore both political and economic. It is not clear which of the Lebanese city-states he visited, although a commemorative stela was set up during his reign in the town of Tyre. The Karnak Battle Reliefs show the moment the king accepts the submission from the chiefs of Lebanon in great detail. Seti himself, a giant figure towering over the scene, is faced by an Egyptian officer, the Royal Standard Bearer Mehy, and behind him kneel the chiefs of Lebanon, dressed in long robes, with hairbands and pointed beards. Behind them, other locals[28] are busily felling tall straight cedar trees to present as tribute to the king. The timber would later be used to manufacture a sacred barge and large flagpoles for the temple of Amun at Karnak.

With his tribute secured from the chiefs of Lebanon and the entire province of Djahy suitably supressed, Seti and his army began the journey back to Egypt. It is unclear whether they followed the coastal road back south, or whether the king went by ship to the Delta. However, by the end of the Fourth Month of Summer 1289 BC, Seti was back in Memphis, where he decreed the establishment of a sacred offering cult for Min-Amun at Buhen and endowed the temple, undoubtedly with some of his recently acquired spoils of war.[29] It seems likely that Seti then went directly from Memphis to the southern city of Thebes, where the lion's share of plunder and booty was donated to the Karnak Temple:

'His Majesty returned his heart joyful from his first campaign; his attack victorious against every foreign land. He plundered every rebellious foreign land by the power of his father Amun who commanded strength and victories for him.'[30]

Seti's baptism of fire, his first campaign as sole ruler of Upper and Lower Egypt, had ended. In many ways he had proved his worth; he had asserted his dominance over various vassal states through shows of force, which served to announce that the somewhat passive foreign policies of the late 18th Dynasty were a thing of the past. The initial inspection tour was followed by intense building activity; the construction of administrative headquarters for Egyptian soldiers and envoys in towns such as Beth Shan, as well as repairs and rebuilding of fortifications on the Ways of Horus.

However, viewed objectively, the military forces Seti had faced did not amount to a truly daunting adversary. Seti had himself only led a minor skirmish against ill-equipped nomads, while his forces had only engaged the armies of squabbling city-states and the Apiru raiders. It is not clear whether Seti engaged more organized enemies, such as the Kingdom of Amurru – a vassal to the powerful Hittite Empire – during his first campaign. He may, as Spalinger argued,[31] have advanced up the coast of Amurru and conducted limited campaigns in the area. An alternative view, presented by Murnane,[32] is that a peace treaty between Egypt and the Hittite Empire was still in effect and that Seti had little to gain from breaking it until securing a greater advantage – as indeed he appears to have done later in his reign.

Excursus: Seti's Army

While the king figures largely in the accounts of his campaigns, his central role begs the question: who were the men that marched alongside the young king, and who have so ungraciously been left out of the Karnak Battle Reliefs? The monumental and programmatic nature of most of the royal inscriptions from the Ramesside Period makes little or no reference to the structure of the Egyptian army – the primacy of the king is paramount in these depictions. However, administrative documents and private funerary monuments of the period provide a more balanced picture and can more profitably be used to answer the question of who fought in Seti's army.

Documentation which describes the Egyptian army prior to the New Kingdom is limited. During the Old Kingdom, the biography of Weni suggests that the army sent to campaign against Bedouin on the Sinai Peninsula was largely composed of mercenary or auxiliary troops from Nubia and Libya.[33] Similarly, texts such as the biography of Tjehemau at Abisko[34] suggests a strong Egyptian reliance on auxiliary troops, in particular from Upper and Lower Nubia. This reliance continued into the New Kingdom in the form of the *Medjay*, a Nubian tribe utilized as scouts. However, Egypt's increasing pursuit of an expansionist and aggressive foreign policy during the 18th Dynasty necessitated both a larger and better-equipped standing army which incorporated recent developments in weapons and armour, along with a much-expanded bureaucratic network for its management. The resurgence of a new military elite – which eventually paved the way for Horemheb and the Ramesside Dynasty – manifests itself in the disappearance of certain scribal and administrative titles during the 18th Dynasty and the appearance of new military titles, which were directly caused by new weapons technologies, such as stable master and charioteer. The army changed, with a greater focus on land-based units, such as chariotry and infantry, and less on riverine naval units. The national trauma caused by the Hyksos occupation of Lower Egypt brought about a marked change in Egypt's self-image, with a resulting aggressive foreign policy, deemed necessary to maintain the security and stability of Egypt. Within this climate, families whose members served various functions within the military began to emerge and grow in power and prosperity.

Conscription, forced or otherwise, is poorly attested in documentation from the Ramesside Period, and in the few cases where direct evidence can be found, members of the scribal class seem to have ardently challenged the army's growing authority. In Papyrus Bologna 1094,[35] a letter describes how three young priests were seized by officers from the army and forced to join up. An irate scribe of the armoury was despatched after the recruiting party to challenge the conscription. A similar situation is described in Papyrus Bologna 1086,[36] wherein a Syrian slave belonging to the Temple of Thoth in Memphis is seized by a high-ranking military officer, Khaemope, and forcibly conscripted. Again, the action is not unchallenged. A table scribe from the temple pursues Khaemope in the law courts of Memphis and eventually the entire debacle is blamed on an administrative error within the office of the vizier. Such documents can hardly be seen as demonstrating an ordered system of conscription – instead, they highlight failed attempts by the army to engage in one.

Instead, the army relied largely on new recruits from among the sons of already-serving soldiers. An 18th Dynasty official, Amenhotep son of Hapu, who served as the Royal Scribe of Recruits, eloquently refers to this practice:

'I recruited the youngsters of my lord, my reed pen counted them in their millions. I formed them into companies in the place of their fathers, a "staff of old age" as his beloved son.'[37]

A permanent standing army and a military class also brought with it inherent dangers. Idle soldiers can be perilous to the stability of the state, and the royal court had already seen the army, in the form of Horemheb, conduct what essentially amounted to a military coup. As such, both the military elite and the common soldiers were used in multiple roles during peacetime, both for economic and political reasons.

Because of the inherent bias in the written documentation towards the elite, we have more information about the type of administrative posts they filled within the army. The charioteers in particular are well-attested. Most of them served as Royal Envoys, and were responsible for diplomatic missions abroad. While some of their tasks may have been purely honorary or symbolic, the detailed description of duties undertaken abroad by the Charioteer and Royal Envoy Inuau during the reign of Ramesses II suggests that the majority were not. The need to train horses and practise the arts of chariot warfare is also evidenced by the discovery of stables and an exercise yard at Qantir-Piramesses,[38] and textual documentation, such as Pap. Anastasi III,[39] makes it clear that charioteers would have spent a great deal of their time practising with their weapons and vehicles and training their horses.

By contrast, common soldiers seem mostly to have been engaged in physical labour of various types. In Papyrus Turin B,[40] the governor of the town of Haunefer instructs an unnamed scribe to bring a large contingent of 600 infantrymen spread across three companies to the Karnak Temple in Thebes, where they were tasked with dragging three large stone blocks to the House of Mut, a smaller temple within the Karnak complex. A parallel set of circumstances is found in Papyrus Anastasi V,[41] which describes how a squadron of soldiers were used to convey three stelae to the Tomb of Ramesses II in the Valley of the Kings. A final example can be found in Papyrus Leiden 348,[42] which describes how Egyptian soldiers and Apiru prisoners-of-war were engaged in the transport of stone blocks for a temple pylon south of Memphis.

The majority of soldiers who campaigned with Seti would have been permanent members of the infantry and most likely had fathers, brothers or sons marching with them. In peacetime they served whatever manual roles the state required them to do in whatever geographical location, but when a campaign was ordered, they were mobilized and armed – most likely at the border fortress of Tjaru. Many of the officers who commanded them similarly came from military families, although their peacetime duties were far more diverse and more intrinsically linked to the centres of power in Memphis and Thebes. Many of the charioteers in particular may have had an intimate knowledge of the targets of Seti's campaigns through their travels as envoys, as would the king himself, whose father and grandfather had both undertaken similar missions. This knowledge of foreign lands and the details of Egypt's relationship with its neighbours – both historical and current – was crucial as Seti began planning a campaign which would bring Egypt into a direct collision with its most formidable enemy: the Hittite Empire in modern-day Turkey.

* * *

The Hittite Empire was a comparative newcomer to the political poker table of the ancient Near East. The Hittite civilization appeared around 2000 BC in modern-day Anatolia.[43] Until 1400 BC, the Hittites did not occupy themselves with Egypt, instead focusing on conquests in the south-east into Mesopotamia and interminable internal struggles for kingship. With the crowning of Tudhaliya I, the concept of Hittite kingship became more formalized, the king transforming from simply being a political leader to a semi-divinity similar to the Egyptian pharaoh. Conquests of Hurrian territory in Mitanni (already weakened by Egyptian campaigns in the area under Thutmosis III and Amenhotep II) soon followed, along with a southward expansion out of Anatolia towards Canaanite lands under nominal Egyptian control. The northernmost of these Egyptian provinces, Amurru (in modern-day Syria and Lebanon), was governed as vassalage of the Egyptian Empire during the Amarna Period. However, sensing growing weakness in Egypt, the vassal king of Amurru, Aziru, sought an alliance with

King Suppiluliuma I of the Hittites and defected along with his kingdom during the reign of Akhenaten.

A capable commander and ruler, Suppiluliuma I not only secured the province of Amurru from the Egyptians, but also continued his conquests of the petty kingdoms that had once constituted the Empire of Mitanni. The Egyptian response to Suppiluliuma's alarming expansionism seems to have been fairly mild. A retaliatory raid against the strategic city of Qadesh was launched, most likely during the reign of Tutankhamun, but was rebuffed by the Hittites, who took revenge for the slight by plundering Amki, a small area of Egyptian-controlled territory in southern Lebanon on the banks of the Litani River.

The continuing ascendency of the Hittites worried the Egyptians, who had chosen to provoke their enemy at the worst possible time. Tutankhamun had died unexpectedly shortly after the campaign against Qadesh and left no obvious successor in the form of a son. The strategically vital settlement of Carchemisch, an independent Hurrian kingdom, had fallen to Suppiluliuma after a short siege, and with its seizure, northern Syria and the mighty Euphrates River lay open to the Hittites. We can envisage the confusion at the Egyptian court: without a clear leader, factionalism would have become a damaging factor and surely only panic can explain the actions of Tutankhamun's widow, his sister Ankhesenamun.

She wrote and despatched a letter directly to Suppiluliuma, who was so astounded by its content that he exclaimed to his council that, 'such a thing has never happened to me in my entire life!':

> 'My husband has died, and I have no son. But they say, you have many
> sons. If you would send me one of your sons, then he would become
> my husband. I do not want to take a servant of mine and make him my
> husband. I am afraid!'[44]

The request was unprecedented. By marrying the widowed Egyptian queen, the chosen Hittite prince and his descendants would become kings of Egypt. Egypt would – in effect – become a vassal dominion of the Hittite Empire without a single sword-stroke. Suppiluliuma was naturally suspicious; the offer seemed too good to be true. He cautiously despatched his chamberlain to Egypt to verify the offer, and several months later the chamberlain returned with an Egyptian envoy by the name of Hani. The two men brought another letter from the queen wherein she restated her previous proposal. Suppiluliuma's suspicions were allayed and he ordered his son, Zannanza, to journey to Egypt and take up the double crown. A *de facto* Hittite Empire stretching from northern Turkey to Nubia seemed within his reach.

It is impossible to know precisely what happened next. The textual documentation only shows that Zannanza never lived to cross the Egyptian border, but died *en route*. Ay, Tutankhamun's vizier, was crowned as pharaoh instead and promptly married Ankhsunamun to legitimize his rule. Suppiluliuma was humiliated and understandably furious. He blamed the Egyptians, accusing them of murdering his son, and declared war:

> 'He smote the foot soldiers and the charioteers of the country of Egypt. The Hattian Storm-god, my lord, by his decision even then let my father prevail; he vanquished and smote the foot soldiers and the charioteers of the country of Egypt.'[45]

Little is known about this campaign, which must have taken place during the reign of either Ay or Horemheb. It is likely that the Hittites again launched attacks from their new bases at Qadesh and Amurru against Egyptian vassal states in Lebanon. Suppiluliuma certainly records taking Egyptian captives back to Hatti. It was, however, a pyrrhic victory. The captives were infected with a plague that ravaged Hatti for more than two decades and weakened the burgeoning empire. By the reign of Seti I, Suppiluliuma I had died and his grandson, Muwatallis II, ruled the Hittite Empire. Hatti remained a credible threat, and despite the presence of a possible peace treaty or ceasefire construed by Horemheb and Muwatallis' father, Mursilis, it was largely a matter of time before a transgression on either side would cause another war.

* * *

During the summer of 1287 BC, Prince Benteshina of Amurru received fearful news. The Egyptian King Seti I had arrived in his lands with a vast force of infantry and chariots and was demanding Benteshina's loyalty. The Kingdom of Amurru had been a Hittite vassal since the defection of King Aziru to King Suppiluliuma nearly half a century before. Benteshina was now facing an uncomfortable choice. Either he could remain loyal to the distant King Muwatallis of the Hittites and possibly see his kingdom ravaged by the Egyptians, or he could jump ship and swear loyalty to Seti – an action which would surely earn the enmity of the Hittites. A later treaty between the Hittite King Tudhilya IV and one of his vassals, Shaushgamuwa, records Prince Benteshina's decision:

'But when Muwatalli, the brother of the father of my Sun became king, the people of Amurru broke faith with him and this is what they had to say to him: "From free entities we became vassals. Now, however we are your vassals no longer!" And they entered into the following of the king of Egypt.'[46]

Shortly afterwards, back in the Hittite capital of Hattusas, Muwatallis received news of Benteshina's betrayal. But it was too late for him to react. Benteshina's defection had given Seti the strategic opportunity to take his army against the citadel of Qadesh on the Orontes River. With the city in Egyptian possession, the Hittite aspirations in Syria were curtailed and Egypt restored one of its major imperial possessions – the province of Amurru.

Inscriptions at the Karnak Temple give only a cursory overview of Seti's attack on the city of Qadesh and are limited to descriptions of the king as the slayer of tens of thousands, one who tramples the Asiatics and brings destruction to Qadesh and Amurru.[47] The accompanying reliefs show Seti in his chariot trampling a confused grouping of Hittite warriors, while others look on from the ramparts of Qadesh or run for cover in the nearby Labwi forest. The technological sophistication of Seti's enemies is evident – even in their defeat: horses and chariots are far more prevalent than in depictions of battles against the Shasu and the other Canaanite city-states.

While information about the specifics of the campaign is limited, archaeological evidence has confirmed Seti's conquest of Qadesh. A stela celebrating Seti's victory was found at Tell Nebi Mend – the modern designation for the ancient city itself.[48] The stela is poorly preserved, but it is nonetheless confirmation that Seti was in a position to order it raised on what had been Hittite-controlled territory. After Seti's death, Qadesh was retaken by King Muwatallis of the Hittites early in the reign of Ramesses II and the stela was taken down. It was, however, not defaced or destroyed, which, as Murnane notes,[49] is an interesting commentary on the fluidity of political alliances in the Late Bronze Age Near East. The rulers of Qadesh could not – at that time – have known if their city would soon again come under Egyptian domination, and chose to keep the stela intact so it could be quickly raised again to herald a change in political management. As the English rock band *The Who* noted in 1971: 'Meet the new boss / Same as the old boss.'

With two jewels in Egypt's imperial crown restored, Seti returned home with his army. It would be another four years before the eastern front troubled him again. In the meantime, he had designs that would take him to the western edge of Egypt's sphere of interest.

* * *

Of all Egypt's enemies, the pastoral nomads who inhabited the deserts west of the Nile Valley are the most enigmatic. They are generally called *Tjehenu* in Egyptian texts until the late Ramesside Period when other Libyan tribes, such as the *Meshwesh* and *Libu*, are mentioned. They inhabited an area called *Tjemeh*, which may have encompassed the eastern portion of the Qatara Depression and Egypt's northern Mediterranean coast. The near-invisibility of the Libyan nomads and their relationship with the Egyptian state in both textual and archaeological source material is caused by several factors.

Nomadic communities generally leave few archaeological traces, and the Libyans are no exception. They also used no written language amongst themselves, and so left no easily accessible body of administrative documents and literature which could have informed about their society and culture. This dearth has prompted an over-reliance on Egyptian source material – mostly textual and iconographic – to describe the Libyans. However, as the majority of these sources are in the form of royal monumental propaganda, their reliability is uncertain. To compound this issue, the actual amount of Egyptian sources which concern the Libyans is fairly limited, and the Egyptians themselves seem to have been relatively ignorant about Libyan society – or potentially, they simply did not care. A good example of this lack of detail is the so-called 'Execration Texts'. Execration texts are a specific type of document which usually comprise lists of enemies of the proper order of the world according to the Egyptian state. Once written out, the lists were symbolically destroyed in an execration ritual to nullify their harmful influence. The ritual itself is referenced on Papyrus Bremner-Rhind, a document dating to the Ptolemaic Period and currently held in the British Museum:

> 'You will depict every enemy of Re and every enemy of Pharaoh, dead or alive, and every proscribed deed he might dream of, the names of their father, their mother, and their children – every one of them – being written with fresh ink on a sheet of unused papyrus – and their own names being written on their chest, they themselves having been made of wax and bound with bonds of black thread; they will be spat on, they will be trodden with the left foot, they will be struck with a knife and a lance, and they will be thrown into the fire in a blacksmith's furnace.'[50]

One corpus of texts found at Saqqara was published in the 1920s by the eminent linguist Kurt Sethe and is known collectively as the 'Berlin Group'. Dated to the Middle Kingdom, the texts list roughly forty individual Nubian or Asiatic rulers and multiple foreign cities or districts that the Egyptians wished to harm with the execration ritual:

> 'The ruler of Sai, Seteqtenkekh, and all the stricken ones who are with him. The ruler of Websapet, Bakuayt called Tchay, born of Ihaas, born to Wenkat and all the stricken ones who are with him [...] The ruler of Iy-anq, Erum, and all the stricken ones who are with him [...] the ruler of Shutu, Zabulanu, and all the stricken ones who are with him [...] Their strong men, their messengers, their confederates, their allies, who will rebel, who will plot, who will fight, who will say that they will fight, who will say that they will rebel, in this entire land.'[51]

In some cases, such as the chief of Websapet, Bakuayt, the lists include entire genealogies and underline a sophisticated level of knowledge on the part of the Egyptians. The list of Libyan chiefs by contrast is both extraordinarily short and completely devoid of any detail about the names of chieftains, settlements or districts:

'The chiefs in Libya, all Libyans and their rulers. Their strong men, their messengers, their confederates, their allies, who will rebel, who will plot, who will fight, who will say that they will fight, who will say that they will rebel, in this entire land.'[52]

This list is so patently generic and so woefully bereft of any details that one wonders whether the Libyans were not simply included out of a sense of symmetry, rather than because they posed any kind of danger to the Egyptian state.

The lack of cogent information may not be entirely ascribable to sluggishness on the part of the Egyptian state, but rather to simple disinterest. Viewed dispassionately, the Libyan nomads represented only a limited threat to the Egyptian state, unlike the greater empires in the Levant and Nubia. Unlike Nubia, the Libyan Desert holds very few mineral deposits; and unlike Canaan and the Lebanese city-states, the Libyans had precious few luxuries and resources to trade. Put bluntly, the Libyans had nothing – for most of Pharaonic history – to interest the Egyptian state in the slightest.[53]

As a result, evidence for military campaigns against the Libyans from before the New Kingdom is limited. A fragmentary inscription from the reign of Mentuhotep IV suggests that he undertook a punitive raid against a Libyan chief.[54] According to the *Story of Sinuhe*, the 12th Dynasty ruler Senwosret I also led a campaign against the *Tjehenu*, although its scope is unknown.[55] Instead, as is so often the case with the unknown, the Libyans came to embody chaos. In Middle Kingdom pessimistic literature, such as the *Dialogue of Ipuwer and the Lord of All*,[56] 'Libyans watering their herds in the Delta' is employed as a metaphor for a world turned upside down and the triumph of disorder.

By the 18th Dynasty, the situation changed. The *Tjehenu* are still occasionally represented in the available source material, but now new tribes

– such as the *Meshwesh* – have appeared in Egyptian documentation.[57] Some hostility during this period is suggested by an inscription from Soleb dating to the reign of Amenhotep III, wherein the king claims to have seized *Tjehenu* Libyans in a raid and used the captives as a labour force.[58] The contact between the two cultures increased during the Ramesside Period until it culminated in several invasion attempts of Egypt by the 'new' Libyan tribes, the *Meshwesh* and the *Libu*, during the reigns of Merenptah and Ramesses III.

After his successes in the Levant, Seti launched a campaign against the *Tjehenu* Libyans, most likely around Year 6 of his reign in 1284 BC. The only record of this campaign is found in the Karnak Battle Reliefs, but the accompanying texts are both undated and also highly generic, with little actual information about what prompted the military action, and also what its scale and aims were. The text simply informs the reader that Seti trampled the distant foreign land of Libya and made a great slaughter among its people. The scale of this slaughter is called into question, however, by the admission later on in the text that the Libyans did not in fact face Seti in an open battle, but rather fled and '[spent] the day [of battle] in the caves, hidden away like foxes'.[59] Considering their lack of metal tools and weapons, of chariots and cavalry, the Libyan nomads appear to have made the wise decision of refusing to do open battle with the Egyptian ruler and his armies, and may instead have used their knowledge of the desert to hide and harass the Egyptian troops guerrilla-style.

The Karnak Battle Reliefs are not only silent on the conduct of the campaign, but more importantly on what instigated it. Murnane[60] interprets the campaign as the starting shot in a much longer conflict that would culminate with the invasions of Egypt during the late New Kingdom. Morris[61] interpreted the Karnak texts and reliefs as indicative of a Libyan invasion attempt of Egypt which Seti defeated. However, while pleasing as a logical narrative, both of these interpretations require the belief that the Egyptian state was aware that relations with Libya would deteriorate to the point of large-scale invasions attempts made against the Nile Valley more than sixty years before the first of these occurred.

Instead, the Libyan campaign should be viewed in the context of Seti's foreign policy: to re-establish and extend Egyptian imperial control on all three fronts, the Levant, Nubia and Libya. In the Levant, Seti's campaign not only returned previously lost Egyptian territory, but archaeological evidence from major settlements like Beth Shan also shows that the initial conquest was supplemented by the construction of infrastructure to house a beefed-up Egyptian administration, resulting in a more direct control over the vassal states. In Nubia, a province which had been firmly under Egyptian control for several hundred years, Seti constructed new fortified settlements at Amara West and Akhsha, cementing Egyptian dominance in the area. The Libyan campaign was no different. It represented an attempt to pacify the Marmarican coast and the Libyan tribes who inhabited the area to pave the way for the construction of several centres of Egyptian administration in the area. The construction of these centres was not undertaken in Seti's lifetime. Rather, it was his son, Ramesses II, who early in his reign capitalized on his father's preparatory work by constructing a line of fortified settlements stretching from the Delta along the coast to the modern town of Mersa Matrouh. Among these fortifications, only two – Kom Firin[62] and Zawiyet Umm el-Rakham – have been extensively excavated in recent times.

The most isolated of these forts, Zawiyet Umm el-Rakham,[63] is located nearly 320km from Alexandria and is an architectural copy of forts which Seti I built in Nubia, such as Amara West. It is composed of a large mud-brick enclosure wall, a limestone temple, magazines and domestic areas. The fortress was not only a military installation, but a functioning settlement in its own right, dependent both on cooperation with local tribes and local production of food and goods.[64] It is reasonable to assume that this level of self-sufficiency could not have been achieved without the pacifying actions taken by Seti in the area during Year 6 of his reign.

Viewed in isolation, Seti's change in focus from the growing threat of the Hittite Empire to the Libyan nomads occupying the very fringes of his empire may appear peculiar. However, if considered in concert with Seti's other ventures abroad, the Libyan campaign fits neatly within a defined foreign policy: first to re-establish control of the territory lost during the Amarna Period (primarily in the Levant), and secondly to create a more direct imperial administration in the Levant, Nubia and Libya, expanding Egypt's sphere of influence in all directions.

* * *

Even though Seti took time to campaign in Libya in Year 6 of his reign, developments in the Near East could not be ignored for long. In the year following his Libyan foray, Seti was back in Syria with his army and facing an old enemy: the Hittite Empire. It is curious perhaps that some time seems to have passed since Seti's blatant annexation of the Hittite province of Amuru and the vital city of Qadesh. One might have imagined that the Hittites would have reacted swiftly to the loss of their southern dominions, and struck back in force. Instead, the Karnak Battle Reliefs paint a different picture. The scene is a familiar one: the Egyptian king is in his chariot, trampling Hittite warriors. The enemy commander – shown standing in front of Seti's chariot – has been hit by several arrows fired by the king. This commander is unnamed, and the description of the battle is somewhat nonspecific. However, when Seti presents the prisoners from his campaign at the Karnak Temple to Amun, they are described as 'the great chiefs of despicable Retenu [Syria], whom his Majesty has brought off by his victories from the land of Hatti'.[65] This mention of Syria has led both Murnane[66] and Spalinger[67] to conclude that Seti did not in fact fight a Hittite army, but rather an army composed of Hittite vassals and levies from northern Syria. It is reasonable to assume that this army would have been led by the main figure of Hittite authority in the area, the viceroy of Carchemisch, Sarruma. Perhaps it is he who lost his life on the battlefield in front of Seti's chariot.[68]

Both the depictions and the accompanying texts in this scene are not helpful in the construction of a logical narrative. They are – like many royal monuments from Pharaonic Egypt – full of formulaic bombast and light on actual detail. Nor do the reliefs and inscriptions answer two central questions: why, having been slighted by Seti's capture of Amuru and Qadesh, did the Hittites not respond sooner; and why, when they eventually did, was their response so decidedly tepid, relying on vassal troops rather than the Hittite army itself?

The most reasonable explanation is that the Hittite Empire was distracted by political and military developments elsewhere. The break-up of the Mittanian Empire allowed the Hittites to secure vast territories in northern Mesopotamia, primarily the district of Hanigalbat.[69] However, this expansion brought the Hittites into contact with an ascendant force in the area – the Assyrian Empire. Assyria had grown out of the Sumerian

Empire and become a powerful state in its own right during the Late Bronze Age. Bordered by Babylon in the south, the Assyrians – like the Hittites – had designs on securing more territory and trade routes within the former Mittanian territory. This naturally brought the two countries into an extended conflict, and King Adad-Nirari I of Assyria forced the Hittite-held territory of Hanigalbat to switch its allegiance to him, also raiding the area to put down a rebellion against his authority during the same period when Seti was campaigning against the Hittites in northern Syria. Pressed on two fronts, King Muwatallis of the Hittites appears to have sent his main force to deal with the Assyrians, despatching a vassal army to face the Egyptian king.

Seti's second victory in northern Syria can then be explained more as the result of Muwatallis underestimating his Egyptian enemy, rather than by Seti's own strategic brilliance. But even though Seti returned home to Thebes loaded with captives and the spoils of war, the theatre of reciprocal warfare in northern Syria was far from over. After Seti's death, the city of Qadesh renounced its loyalty to Egypt and swore fealty again to the Hittites. This in turn prompted Seti's son, the young Ramesses II, to pursue an ill-advised campaign against the city.[70] The campaign nearly turned into a disaster when Ramesses underestimated King Muwatallis, who – perhaps learning from his previous mistake – had not despatched another vassal army, but rather the full military force of the Hittites and their allies. Only the timely arrival of Egyptian reinforcements prevented Muwatallis' troops from overrunning the Egyptian encampment on the plain below Qadesh and killing Ramesses. Instead, the battle ended in a grudging stalemate, but the campaign cost Egypt any hope of retaking the city of Qadesh and holding onto the province of Amuru, which reverted to Hittite control after the battle. In this way, Seti's hard work in northern Syria was undone by the folly of his son.

* * *

Of all the jewels in Egypt's imperial crown during the New Kingdom, Nubia was the least fractious, and also, in some ways, the most valuable. Nubia had played host to Egyptian raids or occupations from the very beginning of the Pharaonic civilization, with campaigns being launched to secure cattle, slaves and gold from the Old Kingdom onwards, in combination with more diplomatic trade missions, such as that undertaken by the 6th Dynasty official Harkuf to the court of the King of Yam in modern-day Sudan.[71] After the decentralized interlude of the First Intermediate Period, a more formal arrangement was sought. Initially this new arrangement manifested itself during the late 11th Dynasty in the construction of small drystone forts at strategic points, from where they could control valuable resources, such as the amethyst mines of Wadi el-Hudi.[72]

The advent of the 12th Dynasty and the ascension of powerful Middle Kingdom pharaohs saw a frenzied construction programne of vast mud-brick fortresses along the banks of the Nile in Lower Nubia. Some of these fortifications, in particular the great fort at Buhen, continued in use into the New Kingdom, and were still manned by Egyptian troops during the reign of Seti I and his dynastic successors. These forts functioned as traditional barriers or border posts, protecting Egypt's southern front from riverine expeditionary forces from the powerful kingdom of Kush which lay beneath the Third Cataract. But they also monitored activities among the pastoralist nomads who roamed the deserts around them and facilitated trade with exotic goods from Sub-Saharan Africa to the courts at Memphis and Thebes. A Middle Kingdom stela erected as a border post at the fortress of Semna, built immediately above the Third Cataract, records how this trade relationship was conducted:

'The Southern Boundary, made in Regnal Year 8 under the Majesty of the King of Upper and Lower Egypt, Senwosret III, who is given life forever and ever; to prevent any Nubian crossing it by water or by land, with a ship or any herds of the Nubians; except a Nubian who has come to do trade at Mirgissa or on a diplomatic mission. Every good thing shall be done with them, but without allowing a ship of the Nubians to pass by Semna going downstream, forever.'[73]

The text highlights how the border was not hermetically sealed to Nubians, but was left open to merchants and diplomats who could travel past the border fort at Semna and quarter at the fortress of Mirgissa closer to Egypt, where they could presumably barter their goods.

As the power of Egypt's Middle Kingdom waned, the fortresses fell under the command of the ruler of Kush, based in the city-state of Kerma. The resurgent Egypt of the New Kingdom retook the fortresses without much bloodshed, but remembered the fickle loyalty of their Nubian province. In response, 18th Dynasty rulers like Amenhotep III ordered the construction of vast temple towns throughout Nubia at Soleb, Wadi es-Sebua, Aniba and Sai.[74] These temple towns served as trade hubs, bases for gold mining and other quarrying expeditions, and also as points of cultural contact between Egypt and Nubia. The policy was overwhelmingly successful, and the indigenous culture in Upper and Lower Nubia – archaeologically identified as the C-Group during the Middle Kingdom and Second Intermediate Period – had all but vanished by the mid-New Kingdom.

By the time of Seti's ascension, serious military threats in the Nubian province were very much a thing of the past. Always eager to emulate Amenhotep III, Seti continued this ruler's policy in Nubia. At the fortress of Sesebi,[75] located near modern Delgo in Sudan, he repurposed a temple built early in the reign of Akhenaten and expanded the settlement and its fortifications. The discovery of large amounts of distinctive schist grindstones and spoil heaps of crushed gold-bearing quartz suggests that processing of the precious and sought-after mineral was conducted at the site.

But Seti was not content with merely repairing grand structures built on the orders of his predecessors. During his reign at least two new major fortified bases of operation in Nubia were built, one at Amara West,[76] which became the new administrative centre of Upper Nubia, and another at Aksha.[77] Amara West has been particularly well explored in recent years, archaeological excavations revealing that it comprised a sprawling settlement inside and surrounding a large mud-brick enclosure. Clear evidence of Nubian material culture and architecture inside the Egyptian settlement also suggests interrelations between the Egyptian administrators and settlers and their indigenous Nubian neighbours. Investigations of the nearby cemeteries have also provided a glimpse of the Egyptians stationed in the town, which included military officers, scribes, soldiers and their families. For Seti, Nubia embodied economic wealth, from its gold mines to the trade routes bringing ebony, ivory and other exotic goods to Egypt from further south in Africa. The importance of the region was such that no Egyptian pharaoh could tolerate rebellion or dissent.

But rebellion did come to Nubia during Seti's reign. After his adventures in the Near East and Libya, rumours of a small-scale insurgence at Irem reached the ears of the king as he held court in Thebes:

'One came and spoke to His Majesty: "Enemies in the foreign land of Irem have planned a revolt!"'[78]

The story of this rebellion and Seti's response to it has not been preserved on the walls of the Karnak Temple, like his campaigns against Amurru and Libya have. Instead, modern scholars know of the Irem rebellion from two stela set up at Amara West and Sai, most likely shortly after the rebellion was concluded.

As is customary with Egyptian monumental texts, it is difficult to discern practical considerations and military strategies in the stream of overwrought royal terminology. According to the stela from Amara West, Seti did not respond immediately to the growing rebellion: 'His Majesty waited to take action against them, to first hear their plans in their entirety.'[79] What might Seti have hoped to gain by his reticence? One explanation can be found by considering the location of the Irem rebels. Even though the geographical location of the land of Irem is still debated – with some scholars suggesting it should be found near Kawa, south of the Third Cataract,[80] while others have maintained that it was located further north and closer to the Kurkur Oasis[81] – the texts claim that the Irem rebels had set up their base of operations around several desert wells. While the precise aims of the rebellion are unclear, it is likely that they used this position to strike out at Egyptian settlements – and in particular against gold mining facilities – closer to the Nile. Without an immediate reaction from Egypt, the rebellion grew in scale, more rebels joining their comrades at the desert wells. Eventually, Seti responded.

'His Majesty spoke to all the noblemen, courtiers and followers: "What is wretched Irem that they should transgress in the time of My Majesty? It is my father, Amun-Re who will make them fall upon the sword of my Majesty! I caused every land to retreat before my Majesty!"'[82]

He despatched a large military force south to Nubia, most likely under the command of one of the two viceroys of Kush, a former general by the name of Amenemope,[83] who was also the son of Seti's vizier, Paser. It is also possible that Seti's own son and crown prince, the later Ramesses II, accompanied the army. The Egyptian army mustered on a fortified hill, positioning themselves between the Irem rebels in the desert and the River Nile. There they waited.

The Irem rebellion had soon grown so large that the water in the desert wells could no longer sustain the host. The Egyptian decision to remain in a fortified position rather than chase off into the desert, fighting on the enemy's terms, eventually forced the rebels to abandon their base of operations and strike out for the fertile river plain and the crucial water source of the Nile. Seti's initial hesitation was not born of cowardice or indecision. Rather, it appears to be a deliberate strategic move: the king had given his enemies enough rope with which to hang themselves. The Irem host was forced to move through the desert with limited resources and little or no water in a desperate attempt to secure access to the river. They arrived right under the noses of the Egyptian army comfortably encamped on high ground, no doubt both well-rested and well-watered. In a single decisive battle, the exhausted and dehydrated rebels were destroyed.[84]

After the battle, Seti's army took away 434 people including fifty-four young men. They also went into the desert and captured the five desert wells, along presumably with those rebels who had elected to remain behind rather than participate in the battle against the Egyptians. The captives from Irem were transferred to work on the properties owned by the various Egyptian temples in Nubia or royal estates throughout Egypt. Order was restored in Nubia, and the province would offer no more rebellion during Seti's reign.

Excursus: Conquering Every Foreign Land

As with many aspects of Seti's reign, his policy towards Egypt's neighbours was defined by a far more proactive approach than that of his Amarna Period predecessors. But despite this proactive attitude, there is none of the brash impetuousness that characterized the early forays of his young successor Ramesses II. 'Reaffirmation and reclamation' seems to have been the watchwords of Seti's actions in the early half of his reign: reaffirming Egyptian dominance over the Canaanite city-states and the Lebanese coast, and reclaiming the province of Amurru and the city of Qadesh. But Seti was not content with the (relatively speaking) simple act of conquest. On all fronts there is evidence of a deliberate long-term policy of consolidation, evidenced by the expansion of the imperial administration in the southern Levant, the construction of new fortified bases in Nubia and even the pacification of the Marmarican coast, which would pave the way for his son to extend Egyptian control of the *Tjehenu* Libyans to unparalleled levels with the construction of a chain of fortified settlements early in his reign.

The Karnak Battle Reliefs are undoubtedly a valuable source of information regarding Seti's foreign policy, even if their language and structure is extraordinarily programmatic in nature. There is, however, one crucial question which the reliefs do not satisfactorily answer: what was the role of the young prince Ramesses in his father's many campaigns? Considering the role that Seti played as commander-in-chief of Egypt's armies during the reign of Ramesses I, a similar role for his own son might have been envisaged. If this was the case, the reliefs are relatively silent on the matter. It is true that Ramesses appears in several of the reliefs and is named and given the titles 'Hereditary Prince, Eldest King's Son of his own body'. However, in most of these cases careful examination of the carvings have revealed that the figure Ramesses was simply carved on top of an earlier figure of an official, whose own titles have been nearly obscured by those of the prince. This modification seems to have been done after Seti's death, when Ramesses had become king.

The deleted official, whose name was Mehy and who held the high-ranking titles Troop Commander and Fan-bearer on the King's Right Side, appears with Seti in several different campaigns and clearly had a close relationship to the king. Sadly, he appears in no other official records, indeed his absence is so complete that some scholars have suggested that Ramesses – concerned about Mehy's closeness to his father – had him removed from all official records after Seti's death, and even ordered him executed. While this is without doubt a gripping narrative, there is not enough evidence to categorically suggest foul play. A more likely scenario is that Ramesses ordered the reliefs recarved to include his own person early in his reign as a

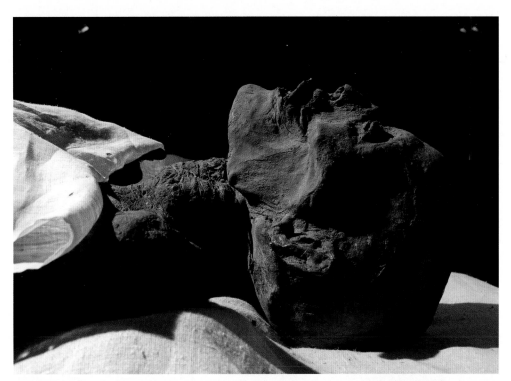

The mummified remains of Ramesses I on display in the Luxor Museum. (© *Alyssa Bivins*)

Seti in battle against the Shasu Bedouin on the Sinai Peninsula. (*Courtesy of www.meretsegerbooks.com*)

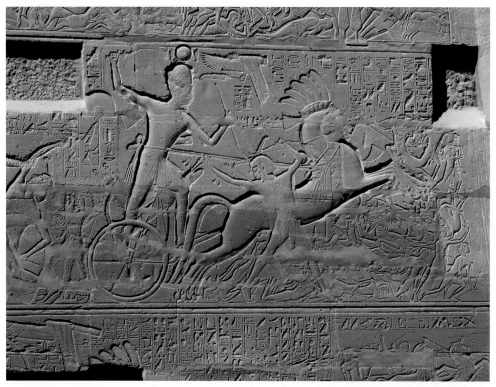

Seti slaying the Chief of Libya during his campaigns against the Tjehenu. (© *Steven Snape*)

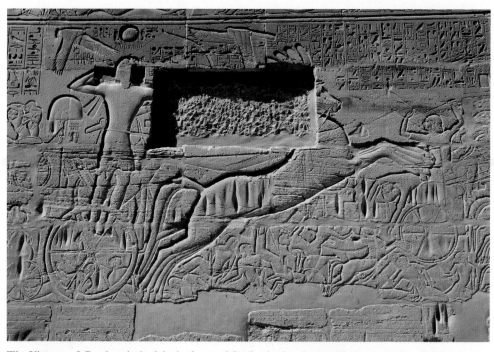

The Viceroy of Carchemisch slain in front of Seti's chariot during his battle against Hittite forces. (*Courtesy of www.meretsegerbooks.com*)

Cairo CG 751. Statue depicting Seti in the uniform of a Standard Bearer of the Egyptian army. (© *Hannah Pethen*)

Metropolitan Museum 22.2.21. Statue of Seti I with distinct traits which hark back to earlier depictions of the mid–18th Dynasty rulers Thutmosis III and Amenhotep III.

View of the Great Hypostyle Hall built during the reigns of Seti I and Ramesses II. (*Courtesy of www. meretsegerbooks.com*)

View of the Piazza del Popolo, Rome by Gaspar van Wittel (*c.* 1678) showing the Flaminian Obelisk and the surrounding square.

Scene from the Chapel of Ramesses I at Seti's Abydos Temple. (© *Raphael Epand*)

Fragment of relief from the Tomb of Seti I (KV17) currently located in the Neues Museum in Berlin.

Giovanni Battista Belzoni by William Brockedon (unknown date), currently kept by the National Portrait Gallery, London.

The mummified head of Seti I photographed in 1889 by the Egyptologist Emil Brugsch (1842–1930).

way of establishing his legitimacy to rule – and perhaps also to appear a more experienced military man than he truly was.[85]

While much of Seti's time and energy was undoubtedly taken up with campaigning and managing Egypt's burgeoning empire, it was not the only central duty he had as a monarch. An equally important task was to build, enlarge and endow temples and chapels throughout the Two Lands of Egypt.

Chapter 4

Houses of Life and Eternity

When Ramesses I died, ending his short reign, Seti – as prince regent and heir apparent – immediately ascended to the Horus Throne of the Living. His official coronation, however, could not be conducted until the embalming and burial rites of his predecessor were concluded. There are no sources which tell us specifically what tasks Seti faced during this potentially unstable interim period between ascension and coronation. He must have spent a great deal of his time solidifying his power base within the court and guarding against any whispers of usurpation or stirring of rebellion.

Among the most pressing concerns, however, was the choosing of his five royal names;[1] the names which – like all Egyptian pharaohs before him – were used both to express policy and to attempt to pre-emptively encapsulate the essence of a ruler's personal ambitions for his reign. The process of choosing the five names is somewhat obscure, although the Coronation Inscription of Hatsheptsut[2] from the mid-18th Dynasty does suggest that the actual formulation of the complex names was conducted by groups of lector-priests, no doubt under the watchful eye of the king. After the coronation, the five names were engraved on new and repurposed monuments throughout the land. A decree sent by Thutmosis I to Turi, his viceroy in Nubia, shows this promulgation of the royal names in action:

'My Majesty, life, prosperity, health, has appeared as the Dual King upon the Horus Throne of the Living, there has never been anyone like him. My titular is the following:

"**The Horus:** Victorious bull, beloved of Maat – **The Two Ladies:** The one who has appeared by means of the Uraeus, the one great-of-might – **The Golden Horus:** The one perfect of years, who has sustained minds – **The King of Upper and Lower Egypt: The Great one is the manifestation of the** *ka* **of Re – Son of Re:** Thutmosis, living forever and ever.""[3]

No doubt similar decrees were despatched to pharaoh's representative in the provinces within Egypt itself, and to those – like Viceroy Turi – who served the king in foreign lands.

Seti's five names are intensely political and they provide us with a rare glimpse into the mind of the young prince regent as he stood on the threshold of power. What were his ambitions and what type of ruler did he seek to become? The first hint is found in his second name, The Two Ladies. Within this lengthy titulary is the phrase *Wehem Mesut*, which literally

<u>Horus</u> The Strong Bull who appeared in Thebes and sustained the Two Lands

<u>The Two Ladies</u> Renewing births, the strong-armed one who has repelled the Nine Bows

<u>Horus of Gold</u> He who renews the crowns, he who subjugates the Nine Bows in all lands

<u>Prenomen</u> Established is the Truth of Ra

<u>Nomen</u> Seti, Beloved of Ptah

The five names of Seti I

translates as 'Repeater of Births'. This phrase had been used since the Middle Kingdom to denote a planned renaissance; a return to normality or prosperity after a perceived period of unrest or social upheaval. It was first used by Amenemhat I, the first pharaoh of the 12th Dynasty, to symbolize a definitive break with the decentralization of the First Intermediate Period and the return of unchallenged consolidated monarchical rule. A similar title was incorporated into the names of Tutankhamun, Horemheb and Seti's own father, Ramesses I, but unlike these three kings – cursed by short reigns and/or lack of progeny – Seti was the first ruler who delivered on the promise inherent in the name. His reign marked a definitive break with nearly every aspect of the Amarna and Post-Amarna Period, as well as forming the basis and consolidation of the Ramesside Period of the later 19th and 20th Dynasties.

Men-maat-ra   **Men-kheper-ra**   **Neb-maat-ra**

The prenomens of Seti I, Thutmosis III and Amenhotep III

In terms of inspiration and aims, Seti's prenomen provides an intriguing clue. Along with the king's personal name (his 'nomen'), the prenomen was far more widely used – and probably well-known within the population – than the entire titular. It was both engraved on monuments and used to decorate small everyday objects, such as vessels and jewellery. Seti chose as his prenomen the phrase 'Established is the Truth of Ra', which is pronounced in Egyptian as 'Men-maat-ra'. This phrase is a merger of two 18th Dynasty prenomens belonging respectively to Thutmosis III (Men-kheper-ra, 'Established is the Manifestation of Ra') and Amenhotep III (Neb-maat-ra, 'Lord of Truth is Ra'), taking the first part of the prenomen of Thutmosis III and joining it to the second part of that of Amenhotep III. The symbolism and intended message conveyed by this piece of amalgam is clear: Seti saw himself as the heir to the two greatest kings of the 18th Dynasty; Thutmosis, the Warrior, and Amenhotep, the Builder. Seti's exploits in the Levant, Libya and Nubia certainly earned him a place among the great warrior kings like

Thutmosis. But it was his apparent determination to outshine Amenhotep as a builder, endower and expander of temples throughout Egypt which more than anything defined much of his reign.

'Let it be made just like that of ancient times': Art and Artistry in the Time of Seti I

The innovative and aestheticizing art form championed by Akhenaten and described as 'Amarna' or 'Atenist' art in scholarly literature, rapidly began to fade after Akhenaten's reign, although some of its basic characteristics remained during the post-Amarna Period in the form of a more naturalistic expression of the royal form. Certain depictions of Ramesses I even retained these characteristics, such as a wooden figure of the king, which may originally have come from his tomb and is now housed in the British Museum.[4] In appearance it is difficult to distinguish from similar works of art attributed to the reign of Tutankhamun, and it suggests that even though the political influence of the Aten cult was well and truly ended by the advent of the 19th Dynasty, the art form it originally inspired still held some sway.

When Seti ascended the throne, the first item on his domestic agenda was to ensure that the damage he felt had been caused by the Amarna pharaohs was expunged from history. He conducted a campaign of restoration of temples and chapels which had either been vandalized or simply left to deteriorate during Akhenaten's reign, including the temple of Ptah at Memphis,[5] which he endowed with new limestone reliefs. These depictions, executed during the very earliest period of Seti's reign, are still firmly in the post-Amarna style of his father, but by the fourth year of his reign an evolution towards a more distinctive Ramesside style of relief carving is evident. Some scholars have – perhaps unfairly – compared this carving style unfavourably to the more virile and graceful reliefs depicting everyday life and historical scenes carved during the mid- to late 18th Dynasty, complaining that Seti's reliefs were too conservative and too static in their composition and expression.[6] It is clear from contemporary textual sources, and also from the reliefs themselves, that the art form Seti favoured was indeed in some ways conventional and represented a quest for a return to 'normality' after the experimentation of the Amarna Period. But any notion that there was no evolution, no innovation expressed during Seti's reign is a fallacy. Rather, the art of Seti I represented an interim period between the naturalism and innovation of the Atenism and Post-Amarna art forms and the dogmatism of the later 19th Dynasty. It was a period where experimentation met conservativism – expressed in a tendency towards archaism – but where no force held complete sway over the other, merging to produce some of the finest pieces of relief and sculpture of the New Kingdom.

Sculptural pieces in the round which depict Seti are comparatively rare, a dearth which has prompted scholars to focus their attentions on the copious reliefs carved during his reign. There are, however, two pieces of royal sculpture in particular which ably demonstrate the interplay between orthodoxy and innovation, along with the unusually high standard of craftsmanship which typified Seti's reign, and contrast so clearly with the sloppier work created during the reign of his son, Ramesses II, and his descendants.

Cairo CG 751[7] was found by the French Egyptologist Mariette at the Middle Egyptian site of Abydos and is currently held in the Museum of Egyptian Antiquities. The statue is carved from dark grey schist and shows the standing king holding a standard (now broken) in his left hand. After Seti's reign, this particular type of royal statue gained in popularity and many later Ramesside rulers chose to be depicted in a similar manner, as did members of the elite.[8] The innovative aspect of this particular depiction of Seti is his wig, composed of long lappets of wavy hair gathered into braids or tresses. This particular type of headgear was commonly associated with private members of the military elite during the 18th Dynasty,[9] and was not as a general rule used in depictions of royalty. Seti, however, appears to have retained a fondness for this type of wig, which he and his father had undoubtedly worn before their ascent to royalty after the reign of Horemheb. The reasons behind this preference are unclear, but it is tempting to speculate that this military-style wig represented a subtle nod by Seti towards his and his family's military past. The regnal year when the statue was carved has not been preserved, but the more mature Ramesside features – a slightly hooked nose, elliptical face and full cheeks – are generally considered hallmarks of the latter half of Seti's reign.

A granite statue of a kneeling Seti from the Metropolitan Museum of Art in New York,[10] by contrast, has distinctly archaistic characteristics. The king is depicted wearing the *nemes* headdress, and has a false beard strapped to his chin, his arms extended, supporting a laden offering table. The posture, garments and facial features of the statue bear undeniable similarities to 18th Dynasty royal statuary.[11] This desire for a return to traditional forms of statuary during Seti's reign is also clearly expressed in the Biography of Paser, who served as Seti's vizier in Thebes. The biography describes how Paser visited a sculptor's workshop, presumably at the Karnak Temple, and gave instructions to the artists:

'May Ptah favour you, O sculptor! Extremely good is this statue of the Lord which you have made. "Let it be made just like that of ancient times" - so it was said in the Palace.'[12]

In other words, Paser directly conveyed an order that was sent out from the Palace and from Seti himself; that the artists should take inspiration from the statues produced before the Amarna Period, and emulate the older style. This tendency towards archaism, coupled with an enduring proclivity for gentle innovation on the part of the artists, helped to define the mature Ramesside art form for several centuries.

* * *

The inhabitants of the Nile Valley during Seti's reign saw their world as one of duality. They were citizens of 'The Two Lands', one comprising the Nile Valley and the other the Nile Delta. But they also juxtaposed the fertility and abundance of the silt-laden river valley, which they called 'The Black Land' (*Kemet*), with the arid deserts that flanked their world, known as 'The Red Land' (*Ta Djeseret*). The desert provoked a fear of the unknown; it was a place of death, rather than of life, and was not ventured into lightly. But along with unknown terror, the desert wastes also held resources crucial to the elite – the king and the temples. Along the edges of the desert were outcroppings of limestone, sandstone, alabaster, granite and the manifold other types of stone, hard or soft, used to create architectural elements for temples, statues of gods and kings, and also private funerary objects, like stela and offering tables. Further afield, in the eastern desert and on the Sinai Peninsula, were precious minerals like gold, copper and turquoise, used both for trade and as diplomatic gifts, but also to manufacture tools and weapons or to adorn the images of gods. The variety of valuable minerals used in the decoration of divine images is described in the 12th Dynasty Stela of Ikhernofret from Abydos:

'I adorned for him [the god Osiris] his great barque for all eternity. I made for him a palanquin bearing the beauty of the foremost of the westerners, of gold, silver, lapis lazuli, bronze, Sesenedjem-wood and cedar of Lebanon [...] I bedecked the chest of the lord of Abydos with lapis lazuli and turquoise, electrum and every costly stone as decoration for the limbs of the god.'[13]

But the desert did not surrender its treasures easily. To maximize the quarrying and mining operations, it was generally the central authority in Memphis, namely the king or alternatively local nomarchs and governors who despatched expeditionary forces comprising scribes, overseers, masons, carriers and military personnel to bring back the desert's bounty. In some cases, when the required minerals were located deep in potentially hostile territory, attendant infrastructure was constructed to protect the expeditions. Seti's clear aim, apparent even in the early part of his reign, was not just to re-establish or repair existing temples and chapels. Rather, his throne name shows his desire to step into the shoes of Amenhotep III, one of the major builders of the New Kingdom. But such a grand ambition required a steady supply of raw materials.

* * *

The construction of a temple required both a softer stone, like limestone or sandstone, for the architectural elements – such as walls, columns, porticos and some statuary – and harder stone, like quartzite and – most importantly – the black Aswan granite used for obelisks and statues. Already in the second year of his reign, presumably following the swift Year 1 campaign against the

Shasu in Sinai and city states in the Levant, Seti turned his attention to the sandstone quarries at Gebel Silsila, located in southern Egypt, 60km north of the First Cataract at Aswan.[14] A massif of fine-grained and relatively durable sandstone lay exposed there, along the Nile, and this proximity of the raw material to the main transport artery in Egypt – along with the quality of the stone itself – had drawn the attention of the central state since the Old Kingdom, although major quarrying operations are not attested archaeologically until the Middle Kingdom. With the gradual shift from limestone to sandstone as the predominant building material for temples and other official structures during the New Kingdom, these quarries became more prominent.

Evidence of use by 18th Dynasty rulers such as Hatshepsut, Thutmosis III, Amenhotep III and Akhenaten now litter this ancient quarryscape, predominantly in the form of inscriptions, either official stela recording royal missions or more informal graffiti left behind by the quarrymen themselves. A plethora of rock-cut shrines, mostly dedicated to the local deity, the crocodile god Sobek, were also installed by the New Kingdom pharaohs who sent expeditions onto Sobek's territory and naturally wished to appease such a ferocious god. The most notable structure on the West Bank of the quarries is the Speos of Horemheb,[15] a much grander rock-cut chapel carved into a hillside. The high-quality decoration of the Speos was not finished during Horemheb's lifetime and the structure became a curious amalgam of royal attention, with various Ramesside rulers, including Seti himself, adding their cartouches to the unfinished decorative scheme. Ramesses II even went so far as to add an entire relief to Horemheb's chapel which celebrated four anniversaries of his reign; his thirtieth, thirty-fourth, thirty-seventh and fortieth year in charge of the Two Lands.

Seti's expeditionary force landed on the West Bank, close to the quarries already opened by earlier New Kingdom rulers and immediately south of a series of Ramesside funerary chapels. There, the artists who accompanied the workforce carved two large stela into the side of the sandstone massif.[16] Both are wholly rhetorical and contain little pertinent information about the composition of the workforce or their day-to-day activities. Where textual sources fail, archaeology can present an alternative source of facts, and it is possible to reconstruct the method of extraction from material remains. The relatively soft sandstone which lay openly exposed could be quarried with heavy bronze chisels, the blocks loaded onto wooden sledges and pulled on rollers the short distance to the river bank. Along the bank are remains of both high- and low-water loading ramps that allowed the blocks to be manhandled down to the required level and shifted onto large wooden barges. From there, they could be shipped easily throughout Egypt. A harbour basin was also cut into the bedrock,[17] measuring over 100m in length, and with a short canal it permitted passage of a ship from the river. Anchoring holes were carved into the sides of the basin, so that the transport barges could be securely held in place and the quarried blocks moved on board via one of several long transport ramps.

Seti's aim in sending a quarrying expedition to Gebel Silsila so early in his reign is clear. Among his first priorities after taking power was the construction of the Karnak Hypostyle Hall and – crucially – the sandstone walls surrounding it. It was upon these walls that artists would carve the extensive war relief commemorating Seti's campaigns abroad. The majority of the blocks quarried during this expedition at Gebel el-Silsila were therefore most likely shipped the 180km north to the sprawling construction sites ringing the Karnak Temple.

By Year 6 of his reign, following his initial spat with the Hittite Empire and in the same year that he took action against the Libyan nomads in Tjemeh-Land, Seti sent another workforce south to Gebel el-Silsila. This time the expedition worked in the quarries on the East Bank, and again, a dedicatory stela commemorating Seti and his works was carved into the sandstone by the side of the quarry road. This text is more illuminating than the wholly rhetorical texts written four years before on the opposite bank, and even includes a comprehensive list of foodstuffs given to the members of the quarrying expedition by the benevolent king:

'On this day His Majesty Life-Prosperity-Health, was in Thebes doing what pleased him and his father Amen-Re, King of the Gods, spending the night awake, seeking blessings for all the gods of the land. When dawn came and the next day appeared, His Majesty Life-Prosperity-Health, commanded that an envoy of the king Life-Prosperity-Health together with a troop of 1,000 soldiers be gathered [...] to ferry monuments for his father Amun-Re and Osiris together with his retinue of gods [...] Every man among them received 20 *deben* of bread every day, bundles of vegetables, roasted meat and two sacks of grain every month.'[18]

Housing and feeding such an extensive cohort no doubt presented an intense administrative task and required extensive infrastructure. The primary archaeological evidence of this kind of infrastructure takes the form of workmen's huts; simple round or oval shelters built from drystone and thatched with reeds.[19] Vast conglomerations of pottery near these structures dating from multiple periods may indicate rubbish heaps. But there has, as yet, been little targeted investigation of the subsistence strategies and production methods that were used to feed the hungry quarrymen, scribes, soldiers and various officials. Twenty *deben* of bread, roughly 1.8kg in modern metric terminology, is a substantial amount, providing more than 5,000 calories; nearly twice what was given to other corvee labourers on state projects.[20] It is not clear why the workers at Gebel Silsila were so comparatively well-fed, although as is common with royal monumental inscriptions from Egypt, it is possible that the text simply exaggerates the actual types and variety of foods given to the workers.

A private inscription from the Year 6 mission to Gebel Silsila[21] provides us with a testimony from one of the leaders of the work gang: Hapy, the Superintendent of the Expedition and also the Chief of Retainers. On a small rock stela dedicated to the Lord of Silsila (possibly Sobek), Hapy proudly describes how he himself was praised by his king and entrusted with the responsibility of supervising this crucial mission which would bring building material to the many construction sites throughout Egypt. The destination of the sandstone from the Year 6 expedition is unclear; sandstone was widely used in multiple temples during Seti's reign. It is, however, tempting to guess that the lion's share was intended for Seti's own mortuary temple on the Theban West Bank which was beginning to rise out of the surrounding desert sand to stand as an eternal testament to the king's soul and his glorious reign.

With these two expeditions to Gebel Silsila, Seti had ensured a steady supply of the basic building material which, together with limestone of varying quality from several different quarries, would be used to raise and repair temples in his name. As the years passed and many of these temple projects neared completion, however, the time came to begin filling these holy structures with colossal images of the king and great obelisks carved from imperishable granite.

* * *

Year 9 found Seti in the south, this time to commemorate the opening of operations in the granite quarries on the West Bank of the Nile near modern-day Aswan. In a small stela inscribed directly into the granitic bedrock during his reign, Seti claims to have: 'Found a new quarry for great statues of black granite.'[22] This claim is somewhat unlikely. In fact, Seti was merely returning to the Aswan quarries after an apparent eighty-year hiatus since the reign of Amenhotep III, the very king whom Seti wished to emulate.[23] Going back to the Old Kingdom, state-sponsored expeditions were sent to quarry the granodiorite and rose granite which rises from the surrounding Nubian sandstone around Aswan and on the islands of Sehel, Saluga and Elephantine, and some of the most notable pieces of sculpture from ancient Egypt – including the Memnon Colossi and Rosetta Stone – are carved from this hard rock.

Unlike the softer sandstone or limestone, granite could not be extracted using metal chisels. Instead, heavy granite and dolerite pounders of varying shapes were used to strip the weathered crust off suitable boulders and painstakingly carve out the rough shape of the desired object. Secondary processes like dressing the surface would most likely also be conducted at the quarry before the final carving and polishing was undertaken at temple workshops throughout Egypt. For larger objects such as colossal statues, obelisks and shrines the quarrymen could choose to enlarge existing fractures in the bedrock in a process known as 'wedging', or alternatively use rapid heating and cooling of the rock surface with fire to induce fracturing. In Roman times, a process of driving wedges into natural or man-made fractures, thereby splitting away large chunks of rock, was also used extensively at Aswan.

The process used for the quarrying of granite for obelisks was more simplistic. When a suitable area of granite bedrock was identified, the ground was roughly flattened using simple stone hammers, and the rough outline of the obelisk traced. Channels were then carved in the rock around the shape of the obelisk before it was separated from the bedrock entirely by carving under its bulk. Once the obelisk was removed, it was even possible to continue the channels further down and quarry a second obelisk from the new face of the granite bedrock exposed by the removal of the first.

Seti's ambitions at Aswan are remarkably clearly spelt out in the two stelae which were carved into the rock face at the quarry in commemoration of the monarch's visit:

'His Majesty Life-Prosperity-Health decreed a multitude of works: to make great obelisks and statues great and wonderous upon the name of His Majesty Life-Prosperity-Health. He built great barges for ferrying them with crews within them, ferrying them from the quarry with courtiers and workmen [...] And his first-born son was before them, doing service beneficial to his Majesty.'[24]

This inscription goes beyond the customary laudations of royal might one expects of Egyptian monumental inscriptions, and alludes to the complex infrastructure required to transport the immense pieces of granite. Archaeological evidence from around the West Bank quarries used by Seti's quarrymen adds to the textual descriptions and shows that the expedition constructed slipways, ramps and a 2m-wide paved road leading to the river. The granite monuments could in this way be dragged on wooden sledges, most likely set atop rollers, from the quarry to the river-bank. There, they would be loaded onto unwieldly barges and (painstakingly slowly, one might imagine) be transported to their varied destinations throughout Egypt's major temples and cities. A unique relief and accompanying inscription in the mortuary temple of Seti's predecessor, Hatshepsut, at Deir el-Bahri[25] shows two of the great granite obelisks Hatshepsut raised at Karnak being transported down the Nile in this fashion. The two obelisks – each 30.7m long – are depicted lying base to base on a 63m-long barge, which is in turn is being towed by dozens of smaller craft. A linesman stands near the prow of the leading tow vessel, using a pole to gauge the depth of the river and alert the flotilla to the presence of sandbanks or other obstacles. Even aided by the current going downstream, it must have represented both an exceedingly complex – and also dangerous – operation, and an astounding feat of engineering. The great barges described by Seti in his inscription were no doubt intended to function in a similar manner.

The most pressing question in relation to Seti's operations at the granite quarries in Aswan is: where are the 'multitude of works' the king decreed? At Aswan itself, only the tip of a small 12m obelisk remains, most likely abandoned due to a flaw in the stone which became apparent during the carving of the decoration. Aside from this paltry piece of sculpture, and a handful of smaller statues of the king carved from black granite, the only truly grandiose granite monument which can with certainty be ascribed to Seti is the so-called Flaminian Obelisk.

Quarried at Aswan and decorated on three sides during the reign of Seti I, this 23m-tall obelisk was intended for the temple of the sun god Re-Horakhty at Heliopolis. It is likely that Seti himself had died by the time the three sides were finished, as the inscriptions on the fourth side were carved on the orders of his son, Ramesses II.[26] The obelisk adorned the temple at Heliopolis for nearly 1,000 years, until Egypt was invaded by the Persian ruler Cambyses II (559–530 BCE), who, according to the Roman author Strabo, 'sought to outrage the temples, mutilating them and burning them on every side, just as he did with the obelisks'.[27] Strabo goes on to describe how two of the obelisks survived Cambyses' fury and were brought to Rome. One of these was the obelisk quarried during the reign of Seti. Ammianus Marcellinus in his *Rerum Gestarum* describes how the Roman Emperor Augustus (63 BCE–AD 14), 'brought over two obelisks from the city of Heliopolis in Egypt, one of which was set up in the Circus Maximus, the other in the Campus Martius'.[28]

The Heliopolis obelisk of Seti was the first to make the perilous journey across the Mediterranean. On Emperor Augustus' orders, the obelisk was shipped from Heliopolis to Alexandria in a similar fashion to its original journey 1,200 years before from the quarries of Aswan. The details of its transport across the Mediterranean are not known, although Augustus ordered the construction of a special ship for the purpose. The ship itself is not preserved, nor is any drawing or detailed description. In his *Natural History*, the Roman author Pliny the Elder (AD 23–79) merely states that, 'the late Emperor Augustus consecrated the one [e.g. the ship] which brought over the first obelisk, as a lasting memorial of this marvellous undertaking, in the docks at Puteoli; but it was destroyed by fire'.[29] In Rome, Augustus' craftsmen added an inscription to the base of the obelisk praising their emperor's links to the divine Julius Caesar, and memorializing Augustus' accomplishment of bringing Egypt under Roman control.[30]

From Aswan to Heliopolis in 1281 BCE, from Heliopolis to Alexandria and from Alexandria to Rome more than 1,200 years later, this multinational monument was now raised at the Circus Maximus. It stood as a silent spectator to centuries of *ludi*: chariot races, religious processions and – until the construction of the nearby Colosseum in the late first century AD – gladiatorial combat. As Christianity rose to prominence and became the official state religion of the Roman Empire, the *ludi* fell out of favour and the Circus Maximus fell into decay. Flooding eventually toppled the obelisk and it was gradually buried in alluvial soil, lying undiscovered for nearly 1,000 years until it was unearthed at the height of the Italian renaissance in 1587. On the orders of the obelisk-obsessed Pope Sixtus V (1521–1590), the monument was re-erected by the Italian architect and sculptor Domenico Fontana (1543–1607)[31] as the centrepiece of the Piazza del Popolo, where it remains to this day, encircled by street vendors and tourists soaking up the Italian sun.

A few broken fragments of granite and sandstone obelisks which once stood at the Temple of Heliopolis have also been found off the coast of Alexandria.[32] They were most likely moved from their original location in a similar fashion to the Flaminian Obelisk during the Graeco-Roman period, and used to decorate one of several cities which once lay along the Delta's northern coast before coastal erosion and rising sea levels flooded them.

However, some fragments of obelisk and a handful of life-size statues does not account for the 'multitude of works' which Seti decreed should be made during his reign. So where are the other granite monuments? Some scholars[33] have suggested that the relative brevity of Seti's reign explains the paucity of granite monuments attributed to him. Seti reigned for eleven years, but the quarrying operations in Aswan were not begun until Year 9, two years prior to his death. The decoration of the Flaminian Obelisk was finished in the reign of his son, and it is reasonable to assume that other half-finished monuments were among his inheritance. Ramesses, who is particularly notable for his dedicated usurpation of the monuments of earlier rulers, was unlikely to have ordered such heirlooms finished in the image of his deceased father.

Particularly convincing examples of this usurpation of Seti's legacy by his son are the two colossal statues of Ramesses II seated at the entrance to the Luxor Temple.[34] Both statues are carved from black Aswan granite, but with a curious unique feature: a vein of rose red granite has been employed to carve the crowns of both figures. This particular use of a natural vein of red stone is evidently deliberate and mirrors an order issued by Seti I in the Lesser Aswan Stela that colossal statues should be carved 'of black granite whose crowns were to be made of red stone from the Red Mountain'.[35] The similarity is hardly a coincidence and suggests that the two colossal statues, traditionally ascribed to Ramesses II, were in fact quarried – but not finished – during Seti's reign. As is so often the case, the deeds of Ramesses II helped to obscure the deeds and accomplishments of his father.

* * *

Merely building the temples themselves and decorating them with obelisks, stelae and statues was not, however, enough. Temples were complex economic institutions in their own right; they owned land, villages and fleets, merchants, mining rights and a vast array of resources secured by the king from foreign lands in the form of tribute or the spoils of war. Some of this extensive wealth enriched and empowered the priesthood, and some was used in a more direct way, as adornments for the images of the gods and goddesses held in the temple *naos*, or shrine. Gold was of course prominently used for this embellishment, as were precious stones like turquoise.

Yellow gold in particular is intrinsically linked to ancient Egypt in the modern psyche, no doubt due to the discoveries of many fine gold objects currently on display in museums throughout the world. But Egypt's association with gold goes back far longer than Howard Carter's famous description of the opening of the tomb of Tutankhamun in 1922: '[A]s my eyes grew accustomed to the light, details of the room within emerged slowly from the mist, strange animals, statues, and gold – everywhere the glint of gold.' Already in the twelfth century BC, King Ashur-Uballit of Assyria remarked upon the widespread usage of gold in Egypt in a letter he sent to Pharaoh Amenhotep III:

'I send as your greeting-gift a beautiful royal chariot outfitted for me, and 2 white horses, also outfitted for me, 1 chariot not outfitted and 1 seal of genuine lapis lazuli. Is such a present that of a Great King? Gold in your country is dirt; one simply gathers it up. Why are you so sparing of it? I am engaged in building a new palace. Send me as much gold as is needed for its completion.'[36]

The peeved Assyrian ruler rather overstates the ease with which gold was mined in Egypt, although he was correct in his surmise that gold is not an uncommon mineral to find in Egypt's eastern desert in particular. Gold is formed deep underground and forced to the surface encased in crystalline rock, usually quartz. By quarrying and crushing this matrix, the so-called 'vein gold' can be extracted, although time and water often eases the task by eroding the quartz matrix and leaving the more durable gold as small flecks in rivers or – crucially in Egypt's eastern desert – where rivers used to run. The gold can then be collected by panning, a process whereby sediment is washed – or panned – to separate the lighter gravel and sand, leaving behind the heavier gold. Gold panning is made easier still by running the gold-bearing sediment across a sloping washing table overlain by a sheep's fleece or similar fabric. Gravity and water will again wash away the lighter sedimentary elements, leaving the gold behind, caught in the folds of material or hair.

The Egyptians themselves recognized three sources of gold: the gold of Koptos, exploited primarily in and around Wadi Hammamat, Wadi Umm Awad and Wadi Mia in the eastern desert; the gold of Wawat, from Wadi Allaqi in Lower Nubia; and the gold of Kush, from Upper Nubia. While the Egyptians focused their energies and resources primarily on attaining control of the gold of Wawat during the Middle Kingdom, the New Kingdom pharaohs shifted much of their production back to the gold-rich *wadis* in the eastern desert near Koptos.

The mining operation itself was led by officials from specific temples, and manned by temple personnel, such as gold-washers and prospectors. Some evidence suggests that the backbreaking labour of crushing the gold-bearing quartz was conducted by prisoners-of-war or other captives, including women and children.[37] Once the gold was separated from the surrounding matrix by panning, it could be refined through melting in a crucible to remove impurities and then cast into gold rings for ease of transport. Raw gold from the eastern desert has a high level of naturally occurring copper and silver, which could not be effectively removed by the relatively crude refining practised by the Egyptians. This impurity of the gold caused, at least on one occasion, a diplomatic quarrel when King Burna-Buriash II of Babylon decided to test a gift of some 11.5kg of gold, which he received as a token of friendship from the Egyptian Pharaoh Akhenaten. After refining the gold by melting it (alongside other, presumably more sophisticated methods than those employed by the Egyptians), Burna-Buriash was informed by his smelters that the actual amount of gold was less than 3kg – the remainder of the weight having been made up of various impurities – causing him to pen a missive, steeped in barely concealed fury, to the Egyptians demanding an explanation.[38]

Like many kings before him, Seti eagerly despatched mining expeditions into the eastern desert in order to secure gold for his temples and royal estates. One of these expeditions travelled east from the ancient city of Koptos along the Wadi Hammamat, although its composition or the date of its departure are not known. Only small rock carvings in the wadi listing Seti's cartouches and showing the king presenting offerings to the gods Min and Amun remain as a testament to their passing. More extensive evidence for mining operations during Seti's reign can be found at Wadi Mia, a southern gold-mining area located east of the city of Edfu.

During the ninth year of his reign, Seti himself followed the track from Edfu in the company of the Overseer of Royal Workmen, a Troop Commander for Gold by the name of Anena and an officer from a ship named *Appearing in Truth* by the name of Nebseny,[39] alongside a company of stonemasons and – even though they are not specifically listed – no doubt assorted gold washers, prospectors and other workmen. As Seti traversed the parched desert landscape, he claims to have discovered and addressed an obvious provisioning issue:

'His Majesty had gone back and forth across a great distance. Then he stopped upon the road to plan together with his heart. Then he spoke: "How difficult is a road with no water created in it. How can travellers soothe their parched throats? Who can quench their thirst? The homeland is far away and the desert wide! Woe to any man who thirsts in the wasteland."'[40]

The expedition no doubt carried water containers on carts, but Seti did not consider this solution sufficient to support the kind of plans he had for the area, which included intensified mining activity and the construction of a settlement and temple. He scouted the land and summoned the sailor Nebseny, charging him with overseeing the construction of an artesian well, sunk directly into the bedrock. The well itself, which is preserved to this day, consists of a 49m-deep shaft near the modern goldmine of Barramiya in Qesm Marsa Alam.[41]

In order to commemorate his operations in the area, Seti ordered the construction of a rock-cut chapel, the Kanais Temple,[42] close to the newly founded (most likely semi-permanent) settlement which housed the miners. The temple consists of a pillared outer portico which leads to three shrines. The central shrine was adorned with a statue of the king himself seated between the major deities to whom the temple was dedicated: Amun and Horus of Edfu. Other gods, including Osiris, Ptah and Re-Horakhty, adorn the secondary statue niches to the right and left. Isolated and protected from the weather and human vandalism, the temple decoration has survived astoundingly well, with the original colour still preserved on many of the reliefs and texts. The texts themselves comprise not merely an account of Seti's visit to the site, his founding of the temple, the digging of a well and the foundation of a settlement, but also policy statements regarding the use to which the mined gold should be put:

'I have spoken thus about the organizing of the transport ship crews for the gold-washers at my Temple: They must give/deliver to my Temple [in Abydos, for the transporting of gold] for my temple.'[43]

The statement is clear; all the gold mined at Wadi Mia was to be delivered to Seti's new temple at Abydos, which was – towards the end of his reign

– nearing completion, with only portions of the decorative scheme left to be finished. After the king's command follows a long list of the horrifying punishments to befall any official who dared to contravene his orders, as well as a warning to future rulers who wished to tinker with his programme.

* * *

As Seti was preparing to go on his inspection tour of the gold mines in the eastern desert, another expedition had already set off from Egypt under the command of a royal envoy and troop commander named Asha-Hebused[44] bound for the Sinai Peninsula. It is likely that this officer led his crew, consisting of miners, soldiers and officials, through the Wadi Hammamat to the Red Sea before crossing the narrow strait to the Sinai Peninsula. Making their way across the el-Markha Plain, ascending onto the desolate el-Tih Limestone Plateau, the expedition arrived at one of the most isolated Egyptian outposts, the turquoise mines at Serabit el-Khadim.

The sight that greets a modern visitor is very similar to that which would have met Asha-Hebused and his men: a large, elongated temple ending in a sacred cave dedicated to Hathor and surrounded by hundreds of stela and rock-carved inscriptions listing the offerings brought by successive expeditions to the fickle goddess in order to court her favour. Asha-Hebused undoubtedly brought similar offerings with him: faience throw-sticks, feline and other animal figurines, pot stands and sistrums. The blue and green faience mimicked the more valuable turquoise and was thought to please the goddess, who was – after all – the patron of this stone, the 'Mistress of Turquoise'. When the Hathor Temple was excavated by Flinders Petrie in the twentieth century, he recorded 2,792 whole or fragmented faience offerings, many decorated with the cartouches of New Kingdom rulers who sponsored missions to the site.

It was not only turquoise that attracted the Egyptian state to this remote outpost of its empire. Crucial deposits of copper – the core ingredient in bronze and other copper-alloys used to manufacture tools – were also found nearby at Wadi Maghara. A series of forts were already constructed on the el-Markha Plains from the Old Kingdom onwards[45] to secure the routes from the sea into the mountains, and to support and protect mining expeditions.

Local nomadic communities exploited the rich mineral deposits before the Egyptians, and evidence from the Old Kingdom in particular suggests that the Egyptian attempts to monopolize the mines – rather than purchase the material from the nomads – caused unrest and even resulted in attacks on Egyptian garrisons in Sinai, prompting retaliatory raids by representatives of the Egyptian state. Aside from ventures at Serabit el-Khadim, Seti also sent expeditions to the copper mining camp at Timna[46] on the east coast of the Sinai Peninsula, although the evidence for this expedition is extremely limited. It may be that, due to the commonality of copper deposits along Egypt's eastern desert, Seti did not consider it necessary to undertake the cost of sending large-scale expeditions to such a remote area.

* * *

Sandstone, granite, gold, turquoise and copper: the bones of the ancient Egyptian construction industry. During his reign, Seti either led or despatched missions to a wide-ranging selection of quarries and mines. However, despite the apparent disparate nature of the missions, a clear purpose lurks behind the edifice. The earliest expeditions, to the vast sandstone quarries at Gebel el-Silsila, were conducted by the second year of Seti's reign. Given Seti's desire to remove any remaining trace of the Amarna Period, and to a lesser extent the undignified political pushing and shoving that preceded it, one might imagine that Seti's focus during the first years of his reign were on removing any offending monuments, along with the restoration of temples and chapels fallen into disuse.

After this first push for regeneration, and after winning his first victories in the Levant and putting the ancient world on notice that Egypt was once more ascendant, the next step was to begin the construction of his own legacy: at Karnak, Luxor, Heliopolis, Memphis and, in particular, at Abydos. This required raw building material, and it was for this purpose that the missions to Gebel el-Silsila, and also to other sandstone and limestone quarries throughout the land, were despatched. While the feverish building programme continued throughout his reign (evidenced for instance by the second mission to Gebel el-Silsila in Year 6 of his reign), other projects had entered a second phase: the shells of their buildings were completed, and the artists and stonemasons were now going to work on the decorations which would adorn them. For those, the artists needed, and the king demanded, the Aswan granite. This was secured by Year 9 of his reign, and the work began on the manufacture of stela, obelisks and colossal statues, sadly curtailed by Seti's untimely death two years later.

It is tempting to see the expeditions to Serabit el-Khadim, Wadi Hammamat and Wadi Mia within this framework. These missions for turquoise and gold were also undertaken later in Seti's reign, and their purpose was surely both to secure material for the manufacture of cultic equipment for the new temple institutions, and also – along with the spoils of war Seti brought back from his Levantine adventures against Amurru and the Hittites – to enrich the priesthood and the state. Missions to copper mines, along with the import of copper from Cyprus, were certainly a constant throughout Seti's reign, given the amount of tools required for his ambitious building programme, which came to cover the length of the Nile Valley.

* * *

Among the multiplicity of religious structures which benefitted from royal patronage during Seti's reign, none is more awe-inspiring than the Karnak Temple located near the modern town of Luxor in Middle Egypt. Known as *Ipet Sut* ('Holiest-of-places') to the ancient Egyptians, this vast complex was a focal point for the worship of Amun and his Triad during the New Kingdom. Given Amun's de facto role as 'chief god' at this time in Egyptian history, expanding and decorating his temple became a keystone policy for most New Kingdom rulers. At the time of Seti's ascension, the Karnak religious complex was composed of three individual temples; the Precinct of Amun and the smaller temples dedicated to his mistress, Mut, and his son, Khonsu. Covering more than 250,000m², the Precinct of Amun alone is large enough to contain St Peter's Basilica in Rome more than seven times over.

The Karnak complex came from humble origins. During the Old Kingdom, possibly as early as the 3rd Dynasty,[47] the city of Thebes was merely a regional capital. Its peripheral position changed with the decentralization of the First Intermediate Period and it gradually rose to prominence as one of two power centres in Egypt: Herakleopolis in the north and Thebes in the south. As part of the expansion of the settlement under the local ruler Intef II, a small mud-brick chapel decorated with inscribed sandstone columns was built to honour the local god Amun.[48] When Intef II's grandson, Nebheptetre Mentuhotep II, reunified Egypt, this local Theban deity attained national status. After the death of Mentuhotep IV, his successors Amenemhat I and his son Senwosret I lavished more attention on the Temple of Amun at Thebes in an attempt to legitimise their reign by demonstrating a connection to the Theban royal family. Loyalty to the old family's deity of choice became an effective substitute for an actual connection by blood. Senwosret I ordered the construction of a small chapel in white limestone, inscribed with scenes showing himself being crowned by some of the most prominent deities in the Egyptian pantheon: Amun, Min, Horus and Ptah. The chapel was unceremoniously demolished 600 years later by Amenhotep III and the fragments used as construction fill for the Third Pylon. In the late 1920s, the pieces were carefully excavated by archaeologists and the chapel was reassembled and opened to the public.[49]

The arrival of the Hyksos in northern Egypt sparked the Second Intermediate Period and Thebes again became the headquarters of the Egyptian culture and the royal family. After the expulsion of the Hyksos, the early New Kingdom rulers credited Amun with granting them victory against their enemies and embarked on one of the most expansive and far-reaching construction projects in world history. As a direct result of the importance these pharaohs ascribed to Amun and his temple, almost every ruler until the Roman invasion of Egypt more than 1,400 years later would in some way, great or small, endow or expand the Karnak complex in general and the Precinct of Amun in particular.

Amenhotep I, Thutmosis I and Thutmosis II all added to the structure, and when Hatshepsut ascended to the Horus Throne of the Living, it was fronted by two large mud-brick pylons, clad in inscribed and decorated limestone. Hatshepsut continued her predecessors' building activity at the site, raising obelisks, ordering the construction of an additional pylon and constructing a barque shrine in red quartzite, commonly known as the *Chapelle Rouge*. The shrine served as a rest stop during the Festival of Opet when the cult images of Amun, his consort Mut and son Khonsu journeyed on sacred barges to the nearby Luxor Temple and back along an avenue of sphinxes. In an act of *damnatio memoriae*, Hatshepsut's son, Thutmosis III, would see most of her contributions to the architectural landscape at Karnak either usurped or destroyed.[50]

The long and prosperous reign of Amenhotep III saw even more royal attention and resources lavished upon the Karnak Temple and its priesthood. The king not only expanded the Precincts of Mut and Khonsu, but also finished an additional pylon (the fourth pylon), begun by Thutmosis II and Thutmosis IV but left unfinished. In a somewhat curious reversal of objectives, he ordered this pylon torn down later in his reign, the building materials instead used to build a brand-new pylon (the third pylon). Amenhotep also raised a colossal quartzite statue of himself standing 20m tall.

With the ascension of Amenhotep IV, and in particular when he elected to eschew the name of Amun from his own and change it to Akhenaten, the Karnak Temple fell out of royal favour. Rather than build to glorify Amun and his sacred triad, Akhenaten constructed the Gem-Pa-Aten,[51] a temple dedicated exclusively to the Aten sun-disk immediately north of the Karnak enclosure. With the end of the Amarna Period and the reigns of Tutankhamun, Ay and Horemheb, this structure was comprehensively destroyed and these restoration pharaohs returned to adding new architectural features to the Karnak Temple and resuming the donations of resources and manpower to the Amun priesthood. Horemheb, for instance, added two more pylons (the second and ninth pylon) during his reign. As Seti took over from Ramesses I, the Karnak Temple comprised seven pylons, several decorated courts, including the so-called 'Wadjet Hall' constructed during the reign of Hatshepsut, and a separate temple for the Theban god of war, Montu, built on the orders of Amenhotep III.

Seti, however, had more ostentatious visions for Karnak than just adding yet another pylon. Early in his reign, possibly as early as Year 1, he began planning for the grandest of all his architectural legacies. In between the third pylon of the temple, built during the reign of Amenhotep III, and the second pylon, begun by Horemheb but finished by Ramesses I, he ordered the construction of a vast hypostyle hall. In architectural terminology, a hypostyle merely describes a room with a roof supported by columns. This rather clinical definition hardly conveys the overwhelming splendour of the Great Hypostyle Hall at Karnak.[52] An area of more than 5,000m² inbetween the second and third pylon was covered with a wooden roof. The roof was supported by 134 carved and inscribed limestone columns, the largest of which are 10m in circumference and stand 24m tall. The hypostyle hall can be entered from four points; either through the mud-brick and limestone pylons or via gateways in the north and south walls of the hall.

Early scholarly opinion[53] held that Seti did not conceive of the hypostyle hall himself, but merely finished work already begun by Amenhotep III and interrupted by the reign of Akhenaten and the chaotic aftermath of the Amarna Period. The primary evidence in favour of this argument – that a foundation level of sand under the third pylon built by Amenhotep III extended under parts of the hypostyle hall – was, however, more recently shown to be erroneous.[54]

While the Karnak complex was undoubtedly the most important religious structure at Thebes, it was not the only one. Luxor Temple, which lies 2km south of Karnak, was an integral part of the sacred landscape of the settlement, especially during the Opet Festival when the semi-divine kingship of pharaoh was reaffirmed in the innermost sanctums of the temple. While most of Seti's new construction activity focused on Karnak, he also embarked on a campaign of restoration of monuments at Luxor soon after his ascension.[55] Amenhotep III had left substantial architectural and decorative elements unfinished there upon his death, including a colonnade hall, the hypostyle hall and several stelae and offering tables. Many of these monuments had not only been left to fall into disrepair, but had been actively attacked and defaced during the Amarna Period. Feeble attempts at restoration by Tutankhamun, Ay and Horemheb had not done much to alleviate this wretched state of affairs. Instead, it was left to Seti to finish the decoration of the colonnade hall. Several smaller pieces of sculpture made on the orders of Amenhotep III and defaced by Akhenaten's followers were also delicately restored, their carvings reproduced along their original lines.

Upon Seti's death, his son Ramesses continued his father's legacy at the Karnak Temple. He completed the last of the columns in the Great Hypostyle Hall and ordered several of the war reliefs recarved, inserting himself into scenes where he was not originally found. But while the hypostyle hall arguably represented one of Seti's most striking architectural visions, it was far from the only one.

* * *

Located 12km north of Tahrir Square in central Cairo is the cramped neighbourhood of El Matareya. Standing vigil above the crowded streets, with fruit-sellers offering their wares from the back of pick-up trucks, and shouting to be heard above the near-constant car horns, is the red granite obelisk of the Middle Kingdom ruler, Senwosret I. Under the feet of the pedestrians, buried deep under layers of modern concrete, sherds of glazed Ottoman pottery and Roman marble lies the remains of the ancient city and temple of Heliopolis, home to the cult of the sun god Re from the Old Kingdom onwards. What remains of the temple enclosure is increasingly under threat from encroachment of modern rubbish deposits and the spread of urban architecture onto the archaeological site.[56] These destructive factors have rendered much of the evidence from the site fragmented and difficult to interpret. Little remains now, aside from the so-called 'High Sands of Heliopolis', a large mound which lay at the centre of the mud-brick enclosure that made up the temple. Recent excavations in this area have confirmed the presence of monumental architecture, including a red granite statue of a king and a lintel of Ramesses II. Along with Amun at Karnak, Re (or Re-Horakhty) of Heliopolis was a crucial deity, and intrinsically linked to royalty and the power of the king. Heliopolis was also home to a temple dedicated to Atum, one of the original creators of the world.

According to the Heliopolitan Cosmogony, or creation story, Atum was present within the primeval waters of Nu, where he caused a pyramid-shaped mound of sand called *benben* to rise from the waters and, using his hermaphroditic characteristics, Atum masturbated and 'birthed' the god of the air, Shu, and his sister Tefnut. They mated and produced the earth god Geb and his sister, the sky goddess Nut, who in their turn created the world. Geb and Nut produced four children Osiris, Isis, Seth and Nephthys who populated the world with gods and people alike. The mound which lay within the temple enclosure at Heliopolis was believed to be a representation of the *benben*, and therefore the very place where the world began. Re, the sun god, was also instrumental in the creation of the world, and at Heliopolis, Re and Atum were intrinsically linked, sometimes even referred to as a single deity: Re-Atum.

Given the religious significance of Heliopolis, Seti was naturally keen to lavish attention upon the temple. Seti codified his vow on the Flaminian Obelisk in Rome, where the king is described as one 'who fills Helioplis with obelisks like shining rays, with whose beauty the Domain of Re is overflowing'.[57] As discussed elsewhere in this chapter, the granite and sandstone obelisks which Seti raised at Heliopolis are no longer found *in situ*. Through the actions of the Roman governors and emperors of Egypt, they were scattered, some to Alexandria and onwards to Rome, others to a long rest on the bottom of sea near the fifteenth-century Citadel of Qaitbay in Alexandria.

While nothing of Seti's renovations and various building projects at Heliopolis remain visible today, a model of the temple gateway at Heliopolis[58] nonetheless provides a useful clue for how it would have appeared. The model was found by local farmers at the site of Tell el-Yahudiyah in the Nile Delta before the first archaeological excavations of the area were conducted by Edouard Naville in 1890. The model was bought by the Charles Edwin Wilbour Fund and gifted to the Brooklyn Museum in New York, where it resides today. Carved in red quartzite, the model shows a rough approximation of the entrance pylon to the temple of Heliopolis during the reign of Seti I. Holes in the stone show where small-scale models of additional architectural elements could be placed, although these have long since vanished. However, noted Egyptologist Alexander Badawy[59] studied the remains of the model and reverse-engineered a reconstruction of how it would have appeared when it was deposited, most likely as a ritual offering, in the ground either at the Ramesside Temple at Tell el-Yahudiyah or at Heliopolis itself. His reconstruction shows the pylon fronted by two large black granite obelisks, one of which was almost certainly the Flaminian Obelisk now in Rome. It also shows three sphinxes, similarly carved from black granite, fronting the causeway leading to the temple gates, as well as a colossal statue. Aside from the Flaminian Obelisk, it is not known where the sphinxes or the colossal statue can be found today, but it is possible that they still lie undiscovered under the pavements of El Matareya. Another possibility is that Ramesses

II usurped his father's monuments, or that – like the colossal statues at the Luxor Temple – he inherited half-finished statuary and ordered it inscribed with his own name rather than that of his father.

Heliopolis was not the only site where Seti's contributions to the sacred landscape have been lost. Immediately to the south, at the site of Mit Rahinah near modern Cairo, Seti ordered the construction of both a new temple dedicated to Ptah, the patron of Memphis, and a smaller limestone chapel similarly dedicated to Ptah, accompanied by Mennefer and Tjesemet, two goddesses who personified the city of Memphis itself.[60] Due to stone quarrying in antiquity, agricultural and urban encroachment, along with a lengthy campaign of antiquity looting, only a few scattered sculptural fragments of Seti's Memphite legacy remain to be seen today.

* * *

Few sites in Egypt, even the great Karnak complex, have as significant a place as a cultic centre for the duration of the Pharaonic civilization as the site of Abydos in Middle Egypt. Located near the modern village of el-'Araba, occupation of the area dates far back into Prehistory, with the site already holding significant importance as a royal burial ground by the Early Dynastic Period. The rulers of the 1st and 2nd Dynasties were buried at Umm el-Qa'ab, their tombs accompanied by the construction of mortuary temples surrounded by large enclosure walls, known as 'forts'. During the Old Kingdom, a settlement and associated religious structures grew at nearby Kom es-Sultan[61] and the site developed even greater importance as local god, Khentimentiu, the 'Foremost of the Westerners', became associated with the deceased king. By the early Middle Kingdom, Khentimentiu had become linked to Osiris, the Ruler of the Underworld, and this link more than anything cemented the significance of Abydos. The first ruler of Egypt during the Middle Kingdom, Mentuhotep II, entirely rebuilt the Great Osiris Temple at the site, and this structure was further expanded by the first ruler of the 12th Dynasty, Senwosret I, and by many subsequent kings.

One of the most significant rituals associated with the worship of Osiris at Abydos was the 'Osiris Mysteries'. These took the form of an annual festival where an image of the god was carried on a gilded barge from his temple at

Abydos itself into the desert at Umm el-Qa'ab. There, the 1st Dynasty tomb of King Djer (known as *Ta Peqer* or 'Sacred Land') had become confused for the tomb of Osiris himself in the Egyptian collective memory. The specifics of the Mysteries are not clear, but a stylized battle against the enemies of Osiris, led by his brother Seth, took place before the statue was returned to the temple. While the rituals in the desert were hidden from profane eyes, the procession itself was most likely a public spectacle, with the inhabitants of the nearby towns[62] and dignitaries from the court lining the processional route. The procession became so significant in the minds of the Egyptians that thousands upon thousands of cenotaphs were constructed along the processional route, where stela and statues of deceased family members could be placed so that, even in death, they would still be able to view the Mysteries and benefit from the offering cult managed by the Osiride priests.

Given the significance of Abydos as a centre of the Osiris cult, and the status of Osiris himself as Ruler of the Underworld, it is little wonder that Seti chose to lavish attention upon the site for the entire duration of his reign. Seti's most significant contribution to the sacred landscape at the site is undoubtedly the great temple,[63] dedicated to Osiris, which he constructed south of the Great Osiris Temple that had stood, in various incarnations, since at least the Old Kingdom. The purpose of Seti's temple was not so much to honour Osiris; rather it functioned as a memorial temple for Seti himself, and also for the pharaohs who had gone before him. In this way, the function of the structure has more in common with the mortuary temples built by New Kingdom kings on the Theban West Bank than with structures such as the Precinct of Amun at Karnak.

It is not known precisely when Seti ordered the construction of the temple to begin, but it was most likely in the early part of his reign. By Year 4, the structure was sufficiently complete to begin its function; it was (partially) equipped with priests and donations,[64] although construction work certainly continued. A visitor to the temple at the time of Seti's death would have been greeted by a monumental pylon, which was yet to be decorated. This task was undertaken later in the reign of Seti's son, Ramesses. The gateway through the pylon led to an outer court, which contained two artesian wells sunk into the limestone bedrock, their water most likely used for ritual cleansing and the pouring of libations within the temple. A portico which had been roofed but not yet fully decorated led to a second court, which in turn led to two hypostyle halls. While not as impressive as the Great Hypostyle Hall in Karnak, the walls themselves were decorated with unsurpassed raised relief showing the pious king prostrate in front of a variety of deities, along with scenes showing the foundation of the temple itself and others related to the proper function and progression of kingship; the latter is a theme which is recurrent through the structure. This is understandable, given the non-royal birth of Seti and his need to legitimize his rule.

Seven smaller chapels lead off from the hypostyle halls, the central one of which is dedicated to Amun-Re. The first shrine in the sequence was naturally dedicated to Seti himself, with the gods Ptah, Re-Horakhty, Osiris, Isis and Horus representing the remaining five shrines. The decoration in the hypostyle halls and the shrines is interlinked and related to the proper conduct of the daily ritual for each of the individual gods, along with the conduct of their religious processions. South of the chapels is an annexe which contains one of the most significant historical documents from Seti's reign: the 'Gallery of Lists'. On the walls of this narrow corridor, Seti ordered a comprehensive list of all rulers of Egypt to be preserved for eternity. The list has some obvious failings; it is not an unbiased account, and rulers whom Seti did not think were worthy were simply left off. There is no Akhenaten, no Hatshepsut,[65] nor even Ay or Tutankhamun. The entire Amarna Period was effectively airbrushed out of history. The gallery is also notable for its depiction of Seti's successor, Prince Ramesses, shown as a young boy standing behind his father. This relief was carved during Seti's lifetime and shows that Ramesses was already then held in high regard, understandable given that he was Seti's eldest son. The two are also seen together lassoing a wild ox, a symbol of Egyptian kingship, in the nearby Bull Corridor.

The most extensive memorialization of a royal ancestor built by Seti at Abydos was the small Chapel of Ramesses I.[66] Standing within its own small enclosure, this limestone chapel was dedicated exclusively to the memory of Ramesses and contains some of the most exquisite reliefs of Seti's reign. Many of them show Ramesses and Seti together, offering to the gods of Abydos, Osiris, Isis and Horus, along with extensively detailed scenes of bearers carrying offerings for the *ka* of the deceased Ramesses. The texts inscribed on the chapel walls take the form of a dialogue in which Seti lists the actions he has taken as a dutiful son to his father, and Ramesses answers by assuring his son that the gods have ordained his right to rule: 'I have heard their speech; they have decreed the throne of Atum and the years of Horus, as protector. They give to you this land by testament, and the Nine Bows are captured for you.'[67]

In an accompanying inscription carved on a large dedicatory stela, Seti relates how his father ascended to the throne after being directly chosen by Amun-Re, the Lord-of-All. The text goes on to describe how Seti was nurtured and taught by his father's example: 'It was he, indeed, who created my beauty; he made great my family in (people's) minds. He gave me his counsels as my safeguard, and his teaching was like a rampart in my heart.'[68] While the inscriptions doubtlessly had a political function, it is nonetheless tempting to see true emotion in those words and the beauty of the accompanying inscriptions, especially considering the paltry tomb Seti was forced to bury his father in due to Ramesses' short reign.

Adjoining the Temple of Seti is a series of mud-brick magazines, used for the storage of offerings, as well as a small palace to house the king and his officials when he visited. Behind the temple, by the western enclosure wall, is a curious structure known as the Osireion. It comprises a simple stone hall with a raised platform and square pillars. Built at a lower level than the rest of the structures, the Osireion is prone to flooding, which has made significant archaeological work troublesome. While the common belief is that the Osireion functioned as the tomb or grave of Osiris, a far more realistic explanation is that it was in effect a cenotaph for Seti I, or perhaps Seti-Osiris, that is the king in his form as the Ruler of the Dead. Egyptian royalty had built cenotaphs at Abydos for millennia, so that while their bodies were buried at Saqqara, Dashur or the Valley of the Kings, their spirits had a home in Abydos and could receive nourishment from the daily offering rituals conducted by groups of priests dedicated specifically to the maintenance of the royal *ka*.

The Osireion, and the temple structure as a whole, was built from limestone brought from a nearby quarry, first overland and later by boat through a canal. The Osireion also contains elements of sandstone, almost certainly from the quarries at Gebel el-Silsila. Discovered by Flinders Petrie during his work at Abydos in the early twentieth century, the Osireion was both excavated and published by a trail-blazer in the field of archaeology, Margaret Alice Murray (1863–1963).[69] Working as one of the first female excavators in Egypt, Murray expertly recorded the Osireion after training with Petrie himself. She published her findings as *The Osireion of Abydos*, a book which has greatly informed much of the later work at the site.

When the temple was fully operational, it commanded an army of human resources, from the High Priest to fowlers, herdsmen, farmers and the crews of merchant ships. The wealth generated by the temple was channelled into the offering cults conducted at the site, including the memorial cult of Seti I himself. It was therefore much in the king's interest to ensure that no one tinkered with the economic endowments he had granted to his new temple. To combat such back-sliding, Seti ordered a large decree carved in Nubia near the town of Nauri, north of Dongola in modern-day Sudan. The decree contains the customary laudations for Seti himself, his piety, his great acts in war and his predestined right to rule, but the text also provides a detailed list of the appropriate punishments for various acts of vandalism or criminal activity against Seti's Temple at Abydos, its staff or resources. It bans anyone, including high officials and members of the military, from attempting to forcibly recruit or conscript any man or woman who works for the temple, on pain of being beaten with 200 blows and given five open wounds as punishment. The punishment for tampering with field boundaries is even harsher: the forced amputation of both nose and ears and demotion to field labourer.

The resources invested in its construction and maintenance, along with the harsh rhetoric of the Nauri Decree, shows the significance Seti ascribed to his temple at Abydos. As a memorial temple, it would function in tandem with his planned mortuary temple at Qurnah in Thebes and ensure that his *ka* was provided for in perpetuity, so that the king could experience an eternal, happy afterlife in the Fields of Reeds, in the realm of Osiris. Seti would not, however, live to see his great work finished. The honour of completing the monument was left, as was the case with so many of Seti's architectural contributions to Egypt's sacred landscape, to his son, Ramesses II.

Excursus: Piety or Politics?

Expanding and enriching the sanctuaries of the gods was a paramount duty of the Egyptian pharaoh. Along with defeating and conquering Egypt's foreign enemies, the construction of great temples was seen as a sign of the proper running of the world. Destruction or abandonment of temples was not simply a sin, but a sign that the world had turned upside down and that proper societal rules had been suspended. This sense of the correct order was the cause of the immediate restoration work undertaken by the successors of Akhenaten: Tutankhamun, Ay and Horemheb. They were desperate to reverse the centralization of their predecessor and his neglect of the various centres of traditional worship throughout Egypt, in particular the great Karnak Temple in Thebes. While Horemheb in particular successfully undertook much restoration and construction during his reign, the scale of Seti's construction ambitions were unrivalled since the reign of Amenhotep III.

Seti's obsession with construction and endowments of temples led scholars to construct an image of Seti as a man of 'admirable piety',[70] a king possessed of both grace and humility in the face of the divine. An artistic change in the representation of the figure of the king in reliefs during his reign further contributed to this image: rather than standing upright in front of the gods, an equal in every way, Seti is often shown humbling himself, kneeling or even prostrating before the gods in a show of abject humility. Only Amenhotep III was shown as frequently in a similarly bowed position, in particular during the latter part of his reign.[71] Seti was clearly inspired by these expressions of piety shown by his successor, although he greatly extended their use. At the end of his reign, the kneeling and prostrate positions were abandoned by Ramesses II, who seemingly felt that he had no need to show such humility.[72]

So should the large-scale temple construction and the depictions of Seti humbling himself before the gods be taken as a sign of his pious nature? Not necessarily. As Gardiner[73] noted, the construction of temples was an intensely political undertaking. By linking himself to the grand constructions of Amenhotep III, the last ruler before the Amarna heresy, Seti propagated the notion of a direct link between himself and the greatest ruler of the previous dynasty, even though no blood ties whatsoever existed. It cannot, however, be completely discounted that the time of religious turmoil and confusion in which the king grew up had an effect on his personality, and that as a result he was filled with a type of religious fervour, but there is little in the way of evidence to support this notion. The most sensible interpretation is perhaps that politics and personality combined as motives in the mind of the king, and together instigated one of the most extensive construction projects in Pharaonic history. From Nubia in the south to the Delta in the north, Seti's architectural legacy spans the length of the Nile Valley, and – had it not been for the uncommonly long reign of his son, and the advantages Ramesses gained from Seti's legacy – he would undoubtedly have been remembered as one of the greatest builders in human history.

Chapter 5

The Supporting Cast

In William Shakespeare's 1599 play *As You Like It*, the melancholy Jaques asserts that 'All the world's a stage, and all the men and women merely players' (2.7.139–140). And while Seti was undoubtedly the leading man in his own lifetime, he was no strolling player standing upon a stage alone. Like all supreme monarchs, he was supported firstly by a vast bureaucracy and royal administration, and secondly by the industry of his subjects. So while it may be tempting to look only at the character and the person of the king himself, it is equally important to investigate those men and women, from the most favoured courtiers to the lowliest workmen, who inhabited the king's milieu and aided his reign. It is from these people, and the administrative documents they often appear in, that we can gain a better understanding of Seti's policies and his actual management of the country, beyond the idealism of the ostentatious monumental inscriptions in Thebes and Memphis.

Even a supreme monarch requires counsellors and courtiers. Chief among all of pharaoh's advisers stood the vizier, a term imported into English from the Arabic term *wazier*, meaning 'viceroy'. In Egyptology, the term is used to denote pharaoh's first minister, who carried the Egyptian title *Tjati*. Rather than employing only a single vizier, the Egyptian king generally had two – a Vizier of the South and Vizier of the North – reflecting both the cultural and geographical division of Egypt into the Two Lands of Upper and Lower Egypt. While letters and administrative documents can provide us with a glimpse of the influence and role of the vizierate during different periods of Egyptian history, a single textual source, known as *Duties of the Vizier*,[1] provides far more comprehensive and detailed insight. This text is commonly found in tombs and tomb chapels of 18th and 19th Dynasty viziers, pre-eminent among these an almost complete example from the tomb chapel of the Vizier Rekhmire who served Thutmosis III. The text takes the form of a lengthy instruction in the duties, responsibilities and correct behaviour of a vizier and covers a dizzying array of policy areas over which the vizier held autonomy. Chief among these was the establishment of an administrative office or bureau, the 'Office of the Vizier', which employed scribes and archivists to aid the minister in his tasks. Initially the text details ceremonial positions which the vizier should take while holding audiences, instructing him to be seated on a stool, wearing a specific type of linen garment, flanked by the two overseers of his office. His scribes should be arrayed, most likely in order of seniority, before him. In an unusual show of egalitarianism, the text also underlines the equal nature of all petitioners to the vizier despite their status in life or the state hierarchy:

'One is heard after his equal, but one who is lower is not heard before one who is higher. However, if one of high status says: "No one shall be heard before me!" then he is to be seized by the representative of the Vizier.'[2]

It is unclear what the punishment for line-cutting was; presumably any presumptuous official was simply removed from the vizier's presence. The text goes on to describe what might be considered a type of strategy or policy meeting which would ideally take place every morning between the king and the vizier in either Memphis or Thebes, dependent on where the king was in residence. It does not provides details of how these meetings were structured, but once completed, the vizier was to go and meet the treasurer and report on the affairs of state with the words:

'All your affairs are whole and secure; every storeroom of the Residence is whole and secure. I have reported the closing and opening of the fortresses by every authority.'[3]

The treasurer would similarly give a general verbal report on the state of the kingdom, after which it was the duty of the vizier to go and oversee the opening of the gates to the palace so that petitioners and other officials could gain entry. Aside from these daily meetings, the vizier had overall responsibility for such disparate policy areas as agriculture, land boundaries, cattle counts, the state of fortifications, mining expeditions, taxation, various royal construction works, appointment of mayors and governors and – perhaps most importantly – the pursuit of corruption and disloyal behaviour among the officialdom.

With such a wide-ranging portfolio, it is surprising that the king had any duties left to attend to at all. However, the vizier functioned only as the king's representative, and while he was no doubt an immensely powerful figure, the frequent contact with the king (even though, given the transient nature of the king in ancient Egypt, it seems unlikely that they truly met on a daily basis) suggests that the king could, if he so desired, take a much more hands-on approach to the day-to-day running of his country.

So whom did the young King Seti trust enough to place in such an important administrative position? One might imagine that an ideal vizier should be competent, but not of a character disposition that might see him attempt to wrest power away from the king or indulge in more than the usual levels of corruption and skulduggery, which might be expected in any such hierarchy. Seti arguably had a far more detailed understanding of the role of the vizier than many kings, as he himself had served as a vizier to his father, Ramesses I, before his death.

In reality, it seems that Seti did not immediately choose a vizier, but rather maintained a man by the name of Nebamun in this position as Vizier of the North. Nebamun[4] had first served Horemheb and must have been of fairly advanced age by the time Seti became king. He is not well-attested, and his tomb still remains to be discovered. His age may have been viewed as a benefit by Seti: as an untried ruler, an old cunning administrator with lengthy experience of the state hierarchy could be a valuable asset, in particular if his loyalty to Seti was assured – and it seems very unlikely that Nebamun would have maintained his position if it was not.

But while we do not know much about Nebamun, the Vizier of the North, the Vizier of the South is far better attested. When Seti was crowned, he promoted a young official by the name of Paser,[5] the son of the High Priest of Amun, to companion in the palace and Chief Chamberlain. Both positions held great prestige as they guaranteed a level of access to the king which was not afforded to many. No doubt impressed by the young man, Seti eventually promoted him to Vizier of the South and governor of the city of Thebes. It seems that Seti made the right choice. Paser proved to be a prolific vizier, known from many statues, graffiti and administrative documents[6] not only from the reign of Seti himself, but well into the reign of his son, Ramesses II. Paser seems in particular to have lavished attention on the construction of royal monuments, an important responsibility given Seti's extensive building programme. In the biography carved into his beautifully decorated tomb in Thebes, Paser even records one of his inspection tours of the royal workshops at Karnak and the – somewhat sycophantic – compliments paid to the vizier by the officials overseeing the work:

> 'You are the eyes of the King of Upper Egypt and the ears of the King of Lower [Egypt] [...] You know of every decree and your teaching circulates in the workshop.'[7]

With Paser and his colleague in the north effectively in control of the day-to-day administration of the country, Seti's 'civil service' was in safe hands.

From a series of administrative texts known as the Palace Accounts,[8] which originate from Seti's palace in Memphis, we can as modern observers catch a glimpse of the bureaucratic bustle that followed Seti's rise to the throne and the first few years of the energetic young king's reign. Most of these accounts are dry even by the standards of a state bureaucracy. They detail the precise weight of flour arriving every day from the royal granaries to the palace bakeries, which were managed by Neferhotep, the Mayor of Memphis, and the weight of the finished bread. Meticulously, the scribe has then calculated the wastage of grain during the milling and baking processes. The accounts even list the names of individual bakers on duty and the division of bread sent to different parts of the royal court. The accounts are not only invaluable documents when studying subsistence, production and supply chains in early Ramesside society; they can also help us to partially reconstruct Seti's movements during his first few years in power, as the baking accounts in particular often mention the king's location in the country at a given time.

During Year 2 of Seti's reign, the accounts note the king's comings and goings between July and November. In early July, Seti stayed at the Palace of Thutmosis I in Memphis. A week later, he left Memphis, heading to the Delta, either to the city of Pi-Ramesses or alternatively to oversee preparations for further military campaigns into Canaan along Egypt's eastern frontier. He remained in the north for less than two weeks before travelling back to Memphis and from there to Thebes, possibly to oversee the initial stages of the construction of his tomb in the Valley of the Kings. The accounts suggest that he remained in Thebes for several weeks, possibly as long as a month, before travelling back north to the Delta for the end of the year. Considering that he had spent the early year locked in conflict in the Levant and establishing offerings for temples in Memphis and Thebes, the accounts contribute to an image of a highly itinerant and active king, travelling throughout his kingdom to secure his powerbase and personally oversee the new national foundations he was attempting to create after the chaotic post-Amarna interlude.

Aside from the extensive baking records, the Palace Accounts also include details of what appears to be a city-wide census of timber.[9] Contemporarily with his travels around Egypt in his second regnal year, Seti despatched envoys to the estates of officials throughout the Egyptian capital to create lists of, and probably requisition, large quantities of lumber. Given the rarity of good straight baulks of wood in Egypt, and the value of the cedar tree from Lebanon, such a requisition makes good financial sense. Most of the timber listed in the Accounts was already worked, and most seem to be ship components. We learn for instance that the Royal Scribe Ruru had in his possession one wooden mast of 11m in length made from the coniferous Lebanon pine. Ruia, a soldier who served on-board the warship *Djoserkare is a Star*, evidently owned another beam made from Lebanese timber, though this one is only 4.5m long. Additional components such as stern posts, ribs and planking owned by standard-bearers, gardeners, charioteers, royal estates and temples throughout Memphis give the impression that an entire disassembled fleet lay ready in the capital for the king to command. This curious hoarding of timber does not appear to have been confined to the occupants of Memphis: a contemporary will[10] from the workmen's village at Deir el-Medina specifically states that the workman Pashedu had in his possession two timber mooring posts which he ordered bequeathed to his son, Hehnekhu, upon his own death.

The timber count conducted in Memphis was a large-scale undertaking, and one naturally wonders why the young king felt the need to know the precise amounts of timber in his capital. The reason most likely lies in the type of timber counted and requisitioned: timber of a type and quality of use to shipwrights constructing larger vessels capable of sailing the Mediterranean. The primary objectives of Seti's first campaign in the Levant during his first few years in office were to reassert Egyptian control over Lebanon and – crucially – secure continued access to the valuable Lebanese cedar forests. Could it be that Seti was gathering what resources he had on hand to build a fleet capable of sailing to Byblos and claim even more timber? It seems likely, particularly in light of Seti's ambitious construction programme. Tall, straight and dense baulks of timber were not merely required by the shipwrights, but also by builders, quarrymen and sculptors. They were used as levers when breaking out basalts and granite from the rock-face, to build scaffolding for those who carved intricate temple reliefs and as roofing beams and flagpoles for the finished temples. Whether destined for the shipyard or the building site, the young king needed timber. And his subjects were compelled to comply.

With his capital and major cities in the hands of his officials and their representatives, Seti was free to travel through his kingdom. His reach was not only concentrated in the cities: a great deal of royal power was held in the provinces in the form of various royal estates and palaces, and it is likely that Seti occasionally visited these, even though they too were under the day-to-day management of lower-ranking officials. An ancient Egyptian king could donate land to various temple institutions, and along with the land came farming communities to work it. They then transferred some of their harvest in the form of taxes to the temple hierarchy, who could use this excess for trade or for consumption. But the king, or perhaps the state and the crown, also owned vast amounts of land in a similar system. These royal estates, called *Per-Nesut* (literally 'king's house'), were commonly named after specific rulers – presumably those who founded them: Seti's father, Ramesses I, had founded at least one estate, or at least renamed an older one as 'The Estate of Ramesses I'.[11] Some royal estates specialized in the production of specific materials or substances. The tomb of Tutankhamun, for instance, contained several wine amphora with the labels 'Year 5, Wine of the Estate of Tutankhamun, Ruler of Thebes, in the Western River, chief vintner Khaa' and 'Year 9, Wine of the Estate of Aten in the Western River, chief vintner Sennufe'.[12]

Other estates, most likely those in the fertile Nile Delta, held herds of cattle. From the New Kingdom biography of Kenamun,[13] a steward of Amenhotep II, we learn that officials occasionally took a census of this cattle, copies of which were despatched to the capital so that scribes could compile a complete list of the king's domain. The rearing of cattle on royal estates dates back as far as the Old Kingdom, and one of the primary reasons was to create a staple and high-protein food source for the men working on royal building projects. Zooarchaeological evidence from the Giza workmen's village, which housed the men who built the Great Pyramid of Khufu, has demonstrated that they subsisted on a diet high in beef, most likely from cattle reared at a royal estate in or near the Delta site of Kom el-Hisn.[14]

While officials, such as stewards and high stewards of the king, managed these estates, who conducted the actual work involved in their production? One likely source of workmen was the army. Granting soldiers plots of land where they could work in peacetime and even settle with their families was used widely during the latter part of the New Kingdom and Third Intermediate Period (*c.* 1070–712 BCE), as evidenced by land registers such as the Papyrus Wilbour[15] and Papyrus Reinhardt.[16] Other workers were prisoners-of-war, forcibly settled on royal or temple estates after being defeated and captured in battle. Ramesses III in particular settled huge population groups of Libyan captives in the eastern Delta after his defeat of a vast Libyan invasion. With time, this proved to be a misjudged policy, as the large and culturally separate units of Libyans banded together and formed a powerful political faction which eventually seized power in Lower Egypt during the Third Intermediate Period.

Few archaeological remains now survive to bear witness to the daily life of the many villages and settlements which clustered along the fertile riverbank and in the Delta marshes during Seti's reign, and whose inhabitants worked on the royal estates. It is also uncertain how many of these Seti visited during his reign, but from the Palace Accounts we can clearly see that the king spent a great deal of his time in Thebes and in the eastern Nile Delta. In both these places there are well-preserved settlements which can inform about the daily life and daily grind in Seti's Egypt: Deir el-Medina in Thebes and Pi-Ramesses in the Nile Delta.

The history of settlement at Deir el–Medina is intrinsically linked to a change in the royal burial practices between the Middle and New Kingdoms. Possibly the most notable Egyptian monument is the Great Pyramid of Khufu, dating to the Old Kingdom. This pyramid is the grandest of a large quantity of pyramids built from the 3rd Dynasty onwards at Giza, Dahshur, Hawara, Lisht and el–Lahun. While the great Giza pyramids were built from limestone, later examples from the Middle Kingdom were built from mud-brick and many have survived only as barely recognizable heaps of degraded silt. Their associated mortuary temples and the settlements which staffed them have fared somewhat better; most famously the 12th Dynasty settlement of el-Lahun in the Fayum region of Egypt, which housed the workmen and priests associated with the mortuary cult of Senwosret II, whose pyramid and mortuary temple lay nearby. Far more humble royal burials were predominant during the turbulent years of the Second Intermediate Period, with the royal burials at Abydos amounting to little more than a few subterranean limestone chambers with painted relief and texts.

By the early New Kingdom, and the shift in royal power from Memphis to Thebes, the burial of royals in the north came to an end. Instead, the early New Kingdom royals sought inspiration for their own tombs in the burial places of their ancestors: rock–cut tombs in difficult-to-reach valleys on the West Bank. Amenhotep I was the first king to be buried in a location whose very name evokes the grandeur of ancient Egypt: the Valley of the Kings. He hired an architect named Ineni and charged him with supervising the construction of a royal tomb with a separated mortuary temple whose location could not draw the attention of tomb robbers. In his biography, Ineni describes the construction process of Amenhotep I's tomb:

'I witnessed the excavation of the tomb of his Majesty in solitude, no one saw and no one heard [...] My mind was vigilant as I sought to be useful. I created fields of clay to hide their tombs in the necropolis. Works like these had not been done before.'[17]

Ineni evidently did his job well. The tomb of Amenhotep I has still to be identified with certainty by archaeologists, although some believe it to be

KV 39,[18] an empty and poorly preserved burial site in the Valley of the Kings. The mummy of the king himself was moved in antiquity and found – together with Seti I and many other royals – in a cache of mummies at Deir el-Bahri.

By Seti's reign, the tradition of burying the deceased pharaoh in sumptuously decorated rock-cut tombs in the Valley of the Kings had been firmly established. However, the constant construction of royal tombs meant that a full-time crew of skilled workmen had to be at hand. The early rulers of the 18th Dynasty had solved this problem of manpower by founding the settlement of Deir el-Medina, the workmen's village, close to the Valley of the Kings on the Theban West Bank.

Deir el-Medina[19] was founded during the reign of Thutmosis I, at least according to the archaeological material found at the site. Several mud-bricks in the earliest levels of the low wall which enclosed the village bear this pharaoh's cartouche, providing an excellent *terminus post quem* for his reign. The villagers themselves had a different notion, however, worshipping a deified Amenhotep I as the founder of their village, possibly because he was the first ruler to be buried in the Valley of the Kings, their workplace. The village was a fluid construct, expanding and contracting based on the number of inhabitants. At its height, it contained some eighty houses, and in theory eighty nuclear families consisting of a workman, his wife, children and additional relatives. The total number of inhabitants during this period may have ranged to as many as 500 within the village itself.

The houses[20] were built from sun-dried mud-brick and many followed a similar design. From the street, a visitor or occupant would take a few steps down into an entrance hall. Most of these contained an enigmatic structure known to archaeologists as a *lit clos*, a raised mud-brick platform whose function may have been as furniture – such as a bench or bed – or it may have been a household altar. A door led from the entrance hall into the dwelling's main hall, where wooden tables and chairs were found, along with religious equipment such as ancestor busts or statuettes. In some houses, a staircase led from the main room to a storage cellar. Others had separate bedrooms, although it is likely that occupants mostly slept on reed mats on the floor of the main hall. At the back of the house was a small kitchen with a hearth and bread-oven, only partially roofed to allow the smoke to escape.

Additional living space may have been afforded by using the roof for cooking and sleeping. Livestock, such as sheep, may even have been kept in the open air on the roof.

Working as they did on the tombs in the Valley of the Kings, the workmen could not be expected to farm and provide for their families in the customary manner. Aside from the lack of manpower, Deir el-Medina was located far from the fertile strip of soil along the Nile banks, in a rocky valley where farming was not possible. Instead, the inhabitants were provided with the necessary victuals by the state. Fortunately, written evidence of the bureaucracy involved in the daily provisioning of the workmen has to a great extent been preserved. Lists and records were kept on ostraca, flakes of limestone or pottery, which are far more durable than papyrus. Many of these were found in rubbish dumps by archaeologists working in or exploring the settlement. These ostraca, along also with fragments of papyrus, provide an enviable overview of the organization of the village. From these texts we know that the villagers were catered for by groups of associated workers, a type of support staff, who ranged from potters to fishermen, coppersmiths, wood-cutters and basket-makers.

A group of ostraca[21] dated to the second, third and fourth years of Seti's reign preserve some of the deliveries of goods to the village. Firewood, pottery of various types, bundles of vegetables, bread loaves and even animal dung for fuel was brought every tenth day in vast quantities to the community. Other documents record the delivery of vegetables, herbs, bread and beer. Further texts describe the delivery of rations in the form of sacks of grain, distributed according to the placement of a worker within the internal hierarchy: the chief workmen getting the lion's share of two sacks of emmer wheat and five-and-a-half of barley, a much lowlier maidservant getting only one-and-a-half sacks of each.[22] More rarely, on occasions of religious festivals for instance, the workers received luxury food and items directly from the king, foodstuffs such as honey, oils and cream and fine cloth.[23]

The vizier was – at least in theory – directly responsible for the village. Indeed, Seti's vizier, Paser, is well-evidenced at the site, and it seems he took a personal interest in the reorganization of the village and the work of its inhabitants.[24] Under the vizier were the two foremen who controlled the work gangs, one for the 'left' gang and one for the 'right'. These terms mirror the Egyptian terms for a ship's crew, which was divided into who rowed on the port and starboard side of a vessel. Another leading figure in the village was the Scribe of the Tomb, who was concerned with administration and record-keeping. Each foreman occasionally had a deputy foreman, usually their oldest son, who would follow in their footsteps when they died. The various skilled workmen, the stone-cutters, plasterers and painters came next in the hierarchy, followed by the outside personnel and the *Medjay* police who guarded both the village and the royal tombs.

While the men worked on the royal tomb, the women of the village produced the staples of the ancient Egyptian cuisine: beer brewed from barley, and wheat or barley bread. The brewing of beer seems to have been a popular activity, in particular for festivals, and work rotas kept by the scribe occasionally mention workmen who were allowed to stay home from work in order to help with the brewing of beer for a particular occasion, either a religious festival or even a private celebration.[25]

The payment of rations to the workers was an integral part of their survival. Any delays in payments naturally caused conflict. Possibly the earliest reference to an organized labour strike comes from Deir el-Medina. During the reign of Ramesses III, external factors – namely the wholesale collapse of the trade circuit in the eastern Mediterranean – and accompanying internal economic issues in Egypt caused long delays in the delivery of wheat to the village. As one of the major food staples, the workers and their families were naturally alarmed. According to the Turin Strike Papyrus, an account of the strike written by the scribe Amennakhte, on the eighteenth straight day without rations, the workers threw down their tools, left the village and went to the Temple of Thutmosis III, conducting a sit-down strike behind the temple. Quarrelling ensued with various officials who, to no avail, offered whatever slim rations they could gather. Angrily, the workmen told the officials:

'The prospect of hunger and thirst has driven us to this: there is no clothing, there is no [...], there is no fish, there are no vegetables. Send to Pharaoh, our good lord, about it, and send to the vizier, our superior, that we may be supplied with provisions.'[26]

The situation deteriorated further, to the point where the villagers began occupying the royal tomb, one of them even swearing – presumably in a fit of frustration – that if proper rations were not forthcoming, he would make plans to rob one of the royal tombs and simply buy his own food and supplies with the loot. The uneasy conditions continued; whenever rations were delayed, the workers would leave their village and blockade a temple on the West bank, even shouting at the Mayor of Thebes as he passed them. The mayor was so alarmed by the mob that he sent his gardener as an envoy to the striking workers, promising to give them fifty sacks of emmer wheat from the city's granaries until the king and the vizier could re-establish the village's supply chain.

When not striking, the workers would leave the village itself and walk up a tortuous path through the Theban hills to a small settlement they had constructed – consisting of little more than dry-stone huts and wind-shelters – on the path leading down into the Valley of the Kings itself. Many ostraca found in the village and in the valley preserve what amounts to work rotas or day books. On these chips of limestone, the Scribe of the Tomb took the register during the day, noting who was at work and who was absent – and in some cases providing a reason for their absence. Reasons could include illness; we know from an ostraca in the British Museum[27] dated to the fortieth regnal year of Ramesses II that a workman named Huynefer had a bout of illness and some type of eye infection, missing several days of work, while another, Simut, missed a day's work because of his wife's menstruation. A particularly unfortunate worker, Seba, was stung by a scorpion and – understandably – is listed as absent for several days afterwards.

Other reasons, such as brewing beer and performing religious offerings and libations, are also given. Among the most poignant is the perfunctory mention of Rahotep, who missed four days of work because he was wrapping the corpse of his son to prepare it for burial, and Amenemwia, who had to perform the same duty for his deceased mother. The level of detail which the written documentation has provided regarding the occupants of the village imbues them with a degree of familiarity. It is possible to trace entire families as they developed, as children were born and died, as marriage celebrations were held and offering feasts conducted.

Not all the documents found at Deir el-Medina are administrative. In 1927, a great library of literary texts written on papyrus was found near a private chapel. The collection of literary texts belonged to the scribe Qen-her-khepesh-ef and his family, and includes a great number of Middle Kingdom and New Kingdom stories and moral treatises, such as the *Satire of the Trades*, a Middle Kingdom composition wherein a father describes the horrors of every manual profession in order to scare his son into becoming a scribe. It also includes the *Maxims of Any*, a New Kingdom text which comprises lessons for proper conduct. The library also includes magical and religious texts, as well as private letters and wills. Aside from these drier documents, the library also contained love songs, popular during the New Kingdom and filled with flowery sentiments, and plentiful use of metaphors and similes.

Aside from making food, working in the valley, celebrating and – in some cases – reading or perhaps being told stories and tales, the workmen and their families also engaged in a complex economic machinery. This was based on barter trade, as the concept of currency was unknown in Egypt at the time. One ostraca records the price of an ox: two jars of fat, five flax-linen tunics, one kilt and one hide.[28] As skilled workmen, the inhabitants of the village also produced funerary equipment for the non-royal elite of Thebes. One of the carpenters for instance produced chairs, a bed, a coffin and a wooden statue for an official named Amennakhte.[29] Another carpenter was paid with grain, vegetables, fowl and a basket among other items for a wooden image of the god Seth.[30]

Occasionally these transactions between villagers could spark hostility, and some arguments might be brought before the village council, known as the *qenbet*, who would arbitrate. Many of these trials were summarized on ostraca or papyrus and can help us understand how justice was meted out within the tight-knit community. When the rulings of the *qenbet* was not enough and more divine authority needed, the villagers could ask the oracle for aid. The oracle was the statue of the deified Amenhotep I, the founder of the village. During religious festivals, the effigy would be carried around the village on the shoulders of eight priests. If questions were posed to the statue, it would answer by moving backwards for 'no' and forwards for 'yes'. Considering that the priests who carried the icon were temporarily recruited from among the local villagers, it is perhaps likely that answers were pre-agreed between the questioner and the priests, possibly even in exchange for some remuneration.

The villagers not only lived their lives in the proximity of the village, they were also buried nearby. Two large necropolises on the eastern and western side of the village have survived, with tombs in varying degrees of preservation from the 18th–20th dynasties. Among the most notable is TT1, the Tomb of Sennedjem,[31] which serves as a particularly dazzling example of an early Ramesside tomb at the site. Sennedjem was a simple workman in the community, most likely a mason, but his familial connections with the local cult of the goddess Hathor may have given him some primacy in the community, evidenced by the stunning array of high-quality funerary objects found in his tomb. He was a contemporary of Seti, but outlived the king, dying in the eleventh regnal year of Ramesses II. The tomb prepared for him also became the final resting place for most of his family; twenty bodies were found when the tomb was discovered in 1886 by the French Egyptologist Gaston Maspero.

Sennedjem spent his life as a workman at Deir el-Medina – his title being the common 'Servant in the Place of Truth' bestowed upon all the artisans working in the village. His profession was most likely that of a mason, a common vocation, and in the light of this commonality his tomb appears incongruous. He was not a scribe of the village, nor a foreman or particularly highly placed in the internal hierarchical structure of the society. Nevertheless, the decorations in his tomb, and the funerary equipment with which he was buried, are of a quality unparalleled except in the finest of noble and royal burials. The vaulted burial chamber is decorated with scenes showing Sennedjem and his wife, Iyneferti, harvesting wheat and flax in the fields of the afterlife. There is scripture from the Books of the Dead, and depictions of Sennedjem's extended family and the tomb-owner being led, hand in hand with Anubis, to the central figure of Osiris, the God of the Netherworld. In another panel, Anubis stands vigil over the mummified remains as it lies on a bed, with legs carved in the shape of a lion's paws. All the scenes are painted in vivid colours, with strong yellows and reds predominating. Among the funerary equipment found by Maspero and his colleagues in the tomb – and now held in museum collections across Egypt,

Europe and North America[32] – are blue-painted wine jars, a finely crafted and decorated cosmetic box and many exquisitely carved, painted and varnished anthropoid coffins, two of the finest – belonging to Sennedjem's son, Khonsu – currently held in the Metropolitan Museum of Art.[33]

Considering the Egyptian proclivity for building in stone, the job of mason must have been relatively common. Yet Sennedjem's burial assemblage seems almost excessively rich for a manual labourer. So what differentiated a mason at Deir el-Medina from a mason in Memphis? The obvious answer is twofold: resources and talent. Being a state-sponsored community, the villagers of Deir el-Medina were well-paid for their services and – in conjunction with their external work for the nobles of Thebes –were relatively wealthy individuals, controlling quantities and types of materials (such as luxury goods given on special occasions as gifts from the king) to which ordinary Egyptians had no access. Secondly, the artists and artisans at Deir el-Medina were also free to use their talent in painting and sculpting for the benefit of themselves, their families and friends. One ostracon[34] records how one workman paid his friend, who worked as a draughtsman in the village, some baskets, vegetables and sandals in exchange for decorating the burial chamber of his tomb. A few household goods in exchange for the services of an artist talented enough to work on the royal tombs in the Valley of the Kings was surely a bargain in anyone's money.

More nefarious methods were also allegedly used by certain villagers to ensure the wealth and splendour of their eternal homes. Papyrus Salt 124[35] contains a series of allegations against one of the foremen at Deir el-Medina during the later part of the Ramesside Period. The accuser, a workman and son of a former foreman by the name of Amennakht, writes to the vizier accusing the foreman Paneb, the adopted son of Amenakht's brother, Neferhotep, of a series of misdeeds. Some of these are moral; Amennakht accuses Paneb of conducting multiple affairs with married women in the village, including a mother and daughter, and also violent sexual assault. Other accusations relate to Paneb's corruption and misappropriation of labour and resources. According to Amennakht, Paneb stole stone from the royal tomb and ordered his men to fashion it into columns for his own personal burial chamber. He also allegedly stole various valuable commodities such as animal mummies from royal burials and even from the burial assemblages of his colleagues. It is difficult to be certain if Amennakht's accusations are entirely believable.[36] As a brother and son of two former foremen, Amennakht most likely expected the role of foreman to pass to him. However, he was ignored in favour of his brother Neferthotep's adopted son, Paneb. As such, Amennakht had much to gain from Paneb's downfall and every incentive to cast the new foreman in a villainous light.

Seti's interest in the village and the community at Deir el-Medina amounted to more than the occasional visit by his deputy, Paser. He also lavished more direct attention on the community by constructing a temple dedicated to Hathor at the site.[37] In addition to this new structure, the villagers' religious needs were catered to by the Temple of Amenhotep I, dedicated to the deified 'founder' of the village, as well as a series of private chapels. The temples formed an integral part of the religious and daily life, the chapels functioning sometimes as meeting places where affairs of the community could be discussed, and the workmen themselves serving as priests, on a rota basis, in the temples at the site. Religious processions and festivals were also an integral part of village life. The Temple of Hathor built by Seti for the inhabitants is modest by the scale of his grander works at Abydos, Luxor and Heliopolis, though it was still larger than the Temple of Amenhotep I which stood beside it. Today, little remains of this structure save for column bases and low walls. Later alterations by Ptolemaic rulers have also helped to obscure its original dimensions and scope.

The community at Deir el-Medina remains a fascinating source of study. The many written accounts, the well-preserved archaeology and, of course, the fruits of the villagers' labour at the royal tombs all combine to create a vision of a highly specialized community whose role in ancient Egyptian society and the cult of kingship was unparalleled. However, Deir el-Medina was hardly a typical example of an ancient Egyptian village or town, and its inhabitants not really representative of Seti's subjects as a whole. While Deir el-Medina and its citizens are a crucial thread in the tapestry of Seti's Egypt, another community – far larger – provides evidence for some of the different classes upon which Seti's throne rested.

* * *

Driving east from the sprawl and organized chaos of downtown Cairo along the Ismailia Desert Road, one is struck by the hostility of the landscape. Infrequent clusters of houses, white mosques with domed roofs glistening in the sun and clusters of palms and tamarisk shrubs are interspersed with broad swathes of featureless desert. Occasional villages along the road offer plastic bags of *ful* or *hawawshy*, a bread filled with minced lamb and onions, to the passing traveller. However, the quiet of the desert is immediately broken when one enters the labyrinthine roads of the eastern Nile Delta. Here, the landscape is green and fertile, the desert replaced by fields of wheat and rice, villages scattered throughout the landscape, standing atop the *tells* – turtleback mounds of degraded mud-brick and silt – where once Pharaonic, Greek and Roman communities lived. The Nile Delta is Egypt's bread basket, and has been since the early days of Pharaonic civilization, benefitting from the fertile silt that has been deposited by the river in the area for millennia.

Among the interchangeable hamlets lies the village of Qantir. Entering it by a bridge across a broad canal, there is little in its dirt roads and concrete houses that suggests any particular historical significance. Walking along the narrow irrigation trenches into the fields, a perceptive visitor will, however, note the thousands of pottery sherds which litter the ground, along with fragments of limestone and even the occasional pieces of faience. A pair of limestone feet stand lonely sentinel in one of these fields, one of the only aboveground signs that upon this soil once stood the capital of Pharaonic Egypt, one of the largest cities in the world at its time: Pi–Ramesses.

The story of the modern discovery of Pi–Ramesses begins in early 1884 with the eminent archaeologist, Flinders Petrie, and an outstanding case of mistaken identity. In a letter sent to his mother in England, Petrie describes his arduous journey by boat from the town of Faqus to San el-Hagar, an archaeological site which lies some 15km north of Qantir:

> 'The boatman had professedly been cleaning the boat; and perhaps it was as clean as a fish boat could be, well-scrubbed and cleared out; but of course the smell was irremovable.'[38]

Petrie soon set up camp and began his work from the morning of 6 February, the weather proving a serious obstacle to him, his tent being continuously blown down in storms and deluges of rain.[39] The sheer quantity of Ramesside sculpture found at the site led Petrie to the belief that he had identified the almost legendary capital of the Ramessides, Pi-Ramesses, which also has a passing mention in the Bible. However, Petrie was unable to find actual occupation layers dating to the Ramesside Period, and it was not until eighty years later that Egyptologists explained this curious absence.

Petrie had in fact been digging the Late Period capital of Tanis, which was built as Pi-Ramesses was abandoned due to the silting up of the Pelusiac branch of the Nile which had fed the capital of the Ramessides. The occupants moved enormous amounts of granite and limestone sculpture, structural components, stela and obelisks dated to the reigns of Seti I, Ramesses II and Merenptah, using it to construct their new capital further north. In this way, they effectively tricked Petrie into thinking he had identified a 19th and 20th Dynasty capital, when he had in fact been excavating a capital dated to the 21st Dynasty and later. Preliminary work by the Egyptian archaeologists Labib Habachi[40] and Mahmud Hamza[41] led other Egyptologists[42] to correctly surmise that the actual location of Pi-Ramesses was not at San el-Hagar, but instead, underneath the fields surrounding the modern village of Qantir, only 8km north of the old Hyksos capital, Avaris, at Tell el-Dab'a. The work by the Egyptian Ministry of Antiquities was followed in the 1980s by an Egypto-German mission led by Edgar Pusch and later Henning Franzmeier which continues to the present day.

After the expulsion of the Hyksos, the early 18th Dynasty rulers took over their capital at Avaris, building palaces and expanding the infrastructure. This ended during the 18th Dynasty after the centre of the settlement moved towards modern-day Qantir. The settlement which would later become Pi-Ramesses appears to have been founded during the reign of Horemheb, although its scope it still unknown. Some building work may also have been conducted during the reign of Ramesses I, who hailed from the eastern Delta and would have been familiar with the area. So by the time Seti ascended to the throne, Pi-Ramesses was little more than a provincial backwater. Seti would spend a great deal of resources expanding it and turning it into an urban centre. The reasons for the expansion are clear. Firstly, Seti's familial connections most likely led him to hold the area in special regard, and secondly, given the young king's prodigious foreign policy, settling at

Pi-Ramesses brought him closer to the border fortresses along the edge of the Delta where his armies were equipped and mustered.

Illegal excavations in the area during the early twentieth century allowed European and American scholars to amass vast collections of faience tiles from the site. One such collection, held in the Louvre Museum in Paris,[43] contains several faience inlays decorated with the cartouches of Seti I. Reconstructions have shown that these tiles most likely belonged to an imposing doorway. These tiles remain the only tangible evidence for a vast palace which Seti constructed at the site during his reign as he worked to transform the settlement into a royal residence. Other tiles from Seti's palace and the later buildings of Ramesses II were purchased by the American scholar William C. Hayes[44] from antiquities dealers in Cairo and gifted to the Metropolitan Museum of Art. During the archaeological work conducted by Mahmud Hamza[45] in 1928 at the site, excavators found thousands of ceramic moulds, dyeing material, faience tiles and blocks of calcite-alabaster cut into geometric shapes, ready to be placed as inlays in the faience tiles. On the basis of these discoveries, Hamza proposed that this was the area in which the plentiful faience tiles from the reigns of Seti I and Ramesses II were produced.

The most convincing evidence for Seti's expansion of the site into a fully-fledged production centre was uncovered by German archaeologists in an area designated QI. In the lower strata they identified evidence of large-scale metal working[46] in the form of melting channels and cross-shaped furnaces. Ceramic blasting pipes connected to foot-bellows channelled air continuously into the furnaces, allowing them to reach significant temperatures. The products of these melting shops are clear from the sheer amount of weaponry found at the site: arrow-heads of various types, spear-heads, daggers and axes were all found at the site – some even inscribed with the titular of Seti himself, weapons which most likely belonged to his private bodyguard. South of this armoury were other workshops dedicated to the production of goods in leather, wood and flint.[47] Here too, weapons predominate in the form of flint arrow-heads and lances. Together with the foundry, these workshops functioned as factories, mass-producing the weapons used to equip Seti's armies.

No Egyptian army would be complete without its charioteers, however. At some point during the reign of Seti, the foundry was shut down and its production most likely moved. Instead, a massive administrative building was constructed in its place. Hundreds of chariot components, such as horse-bits and wheel-hubs,[48] were found in this building, which must have been a chariot hall, a gathering or storage place for some of Seti's chariot regiments. Later, during the reign of his son, Ramesses II, the king augmented this chariot hall with a vast stable complex in an area designated QIV by modern excavators,[49] and by the reign of Seti's grandson, Merenptah, textual sources speak of Pi-Ramesses as the primary marshalling place of the Pharaonic chariot corps.[50]

With Seti's intervention, Pi-Ramesses developed from a simple settlement, to a royal residence and finally to a fully-formed metropolis. The frequent references in the Baking Accounts to the young king being away from Memphis on trips to the Nile Delta during the early days of his reign are undoubtedly related to his building work and expansions at Qantir.

Excursus: Seti's People

As is so often the case when history is written, it is the grand people who are remembered by the ages and future generations. We know much about Seti himself. We know something about his administration, courtiers and family. We know a little about the men who built his tomb, but we know almost nothing about the men who toiled in the foundries in Pi-Ramesses, fashioning the equipment which would allow the king and his armies to triumph across the Near East. By lucky chance, we may know the names of some of these lowest-ranked of individuals who lived in Seti's Egypt – the Palace Accounts after all preserve some tantalizing glimpses of the everyday humdrum of the royal residence and the people who populated it.

We learn that a man by the name of Huy worked as a sailor and delivered fowl to the palace kitchens during the summer of Seti's third year. We know that on a specific day during the first year of Seti's reign, a baker in the palace named Djadja produced 214 loaves of bread. We learn that a woman named Henut-Wedjebut was a slave or servant belonging to a charioteer by the name of Mery, and that she was given a shawl from a consignment of clothing brought to the palace. From rosters also included in these accounts, we learn the names of several Nubian prisoners-of-war, such as Khaemwaset

– no doubt an Egyptian name given to him by his captors – who belonged to a Chief Scribe named Nebmehyt.[51] But these dry accounts cannot help us to understand the personalities of these individuals; even less their ambitions or their concerns. From archaeological evidence, we can at best conclude how they spent their lives, how they worked, farmed, cut timber or baked bread.

But this great silent majority must always be borne in mind when history is written; it was after all on their labour and their lives that Seti and his administration rested.

Chapter 6

An Eternal Resting Place

'And so sepúlchred in such pomp dost lie,
That kings for such a tomb would wish to die.'
John Milton (1608–1674)

One group of characters is conspicuously absent throughout much of Seti's reign: his family. The role of the Great Royal Wife, the term used to describe the principal wife of the Egyptian pharaoh, was often subdued, so the almost complete absence of any reference to Seti's wife, Queen Tuya, during his reign is not in itself unusual. Their principal function, as base as it may appear to a modern observer, was one of promulgating the royal succession and ensuring the continuity of the dynasty. However, once, as was most common, the first-born son had ascended to the throne and her husband had died, the Great Royal Wife tended to become more active in the role of Dowager Queen, or King's Mother. So it went with Seti's wife. After Seti's death, Tuya suddenly burst onto the political scene during the reign of her son, appearing on monuments showing her conducting offerings together with her son, and as the model for royal statues. Politically, she even held a high enough status to correspond directly with the Hittite court after her son had entered into an uneasy peace with the traditional enemy after the twenty-first year of his reign. As for Seti's own mother, Sitre, the wife of Ramesses I, she is equally invisible during his reign. This is curious, as she might have been expected to hold the same importance to Seti as Tuya would later hold at the court of her own son.

While it was not unusual at this time in Egyptian history for the family of a ruling monarch to be very definitively consigned to the shadows, this was not always the case. The early and mid-18th Dynasty gave rise to several women who held immense power and influence: Ahhotep, the mother of the first New Kingdom pharaoh Ahmose I, may have ruled until he came of age and commanded the Theban armies in their war against the Hyksos. Ahmose's wife, Ahmose-Nefertari, similarly held great prominence during his reign. Hatshepsut, the guardian of Thutmosis III, attained enough influence to become a pharaoh in her own right, and both the mother and wife of Akhenaten, the Dowager Queen Tiye and the Great Royal Wife Nefertiti, were highly visible and influential members of the court during his reign. It may be, as Brand[1] has speculated, that the early 19th Dynasty pharaohs, including Seti, were uneasy about continuing to allow such power and influence to be seen to rest in the hands of the royal women, fearful perhaps of another Hatshepsut and eager to avoid the examples and precedence this situation had set. For that reason, the royal family may have been pushed into the background to ensure that similar circumstances, which were no doubt perceived as chaotic and inherently against the proper order of the country by Seti and his male contemporaries, could not arise again. Seti's children are equally absent, at least for the early part of his reign. His first-born son, Ramesses, was probably born before his own ascension. Two sisters, Tia and Henutmire, accompanied the young prince, but evidence for their existence almost exclusively stems from the reign of their brother.

A great deal of debate surrounds the role which Ramesses played in his father's administration.[2] From the Middle Kingdom onwards, there is occasional evidence that an Egyptian king might appoint his son not just as Crown Prince and Heir Apparent, but actually have him crowned as a full ruler and jointly govern the country in a co-regency. The most well-evidenced of these co-regencies is undoubtedly that between the Middle Kingdom kings Amenemhat I and his son Senwosret I. A stela[3] currently held in the Cairo Museum provides ample evidence for this arrangement: both kings are listed, their names in cartouches, and the text is 'double-dated' to Year 30 of Amenemhat's reign and Year 10 of Senwosret's, suggesting that Senwosret was crowned as king by his father in Year 20 of his reign. However, few other alleged co-regencies have provided similarly clear-cut and accessible evidence. The idea of a possible co-regency between Seti and Ramesses stems, as some modern scholars have noted, more from an inherent desire to exaggerate the role of Ramesses at the expense of his father than from actual evidence.

The inscriptional evidence from Seti's reign is fairly clear. Around Year 9 of Seti's reign, Ramesses appears on the public scene. He is placed in charge of supervising the king's excavations of granite in Aswan[4] as the Great Overseer of the Task Force, and holds the title King's Eldest Son and Hereditary Prince as well as Heir Apparent. These last titles are particularly significant as they mimic the titles Seti himself held during the reign of his father, Ramesses I, although Prince Ramesses is never promoted to Seti's vizier in the same manner Seti himself was. In *The Dedicatory Inscription*[5] composed during the early part of Ramesses II's reign, Ramesses claims to have been crowned by Seti while he was still a baby, held in his father's arms. Given the fact that this inscription was carved after Seti's death, it seems most likely that it is self-serving hyperbole on the part of the new ruler, eager to legitimize his reign to the best of his abilities. The inscriptions and depictions carved during Seti's reign contain no such suggestion; rather, Ramesses is consistently depicted in a manner which befits a Crown Prince, but not a fellow ruler. Most famously in the Gallery of Kings and the Bull Corridor in Seti's temple at Abydos, Ramesses is shown as a young child, wearing the side-lock of youth standing in front his father, and his title is given only as Hereditary Prince and King's Eldest Son of his Body.[6]

So if Prince Ramesses did not serve as his father's co-ruler, then what purpose and influence did he hold at court? Seti was most likely a relatively young man when he came to power, Prince Ramesses still a young boy. Nine years later, Ramesses may have reached his early to mid-teens and been of an age where Seti could begin to prepare him for the role of kingship that he would one day hold. It seems likely that Ramesses accompanied the army on campaign in Nubia during the eighth year of Seti's reign. Such a military endeavour might have represented the ideal training exercise for the Crown Prince: rather than going against a well-prepared and technologically equal enemy such as the Hittites, Seti was throwing Ramesses a 'soft ball', allowing him to deal with a band of Nubian rebels, no doubt backed up by a vastly superior Egyptian force. A year later, Ramesses was sent south to oversee the carving of the grand granite obelisks and statuary which would be lavished upon Seti's temple projects. In short, Ramesses was trained in the two most significant roles of the Egyptian kings – as a builder and a warrior.

Grooming Prince Ramesses for succession from around Year 9 of his reign seems an almost ominously prescient decision by Seti. In the summer of his eleventh regnal year, around 1279 BC, the king fell ill. The precise reasons for this illness remain unclear, despite extensive analysis of his mummified remains. Shortly after the inscription of the last monument of his reign, a stela from Gebel Barkal[7] in Nubia, Seti I, Menmaatre Seti-Merynptah, King of Upper and Lower Egypt, died. The death of another king, Amenemhat I, is described in poetic terms in the *Story of Sinuhe*:

'The god entered into his horizon, ascended to heaven and united with the sun, the divine body merging with him who created him. The residence was in silence, hearts were in mourning, the great double gate was shut, courtiers were grieving, princes were wailing.'[8]

No doubt a similar outpouring of grief pervaded the palaces in Memphis, Pi-Ramesses and Thebes when news of King Seti's death arrived. This was in particular the case due to the unexpected timing of the announcement: Seti does not appear to have been elderly, certainly not of an age comparable to that of his father or his son when they died – Ramesses II lived to be 89. Some scholars have suggested that Seti may have been as young as 39, with radiographic estimations of his age showing him to have been at the very least older than 35.[9] Assuming that he took the throne when he was well into his twenties and reigned for eleven years, these numbers seem realistic. With Ramesses being a young man between 16 and 19 when he came to power, Seti would have fathered him when he himself was in his late teens or very early twenties – again, a reasonable estimation. Extensive x-ray examination of Seti's mummy shows that he suffered from widespread arteriosclerosis[10] at the time of his death and that he, at some point during his life, had lost one of his molars, causing the neighbouring tooth to grow at a slightly crooked angle.

Seti's cause of death remains unclear. A nefarious deed seems excluded by the lack of any obvious physical damage to the body. While it is true that the head was separated from the body when it was discovered, this damage was done post-mortem and post-mummification, probably by particularly inconsiderate tomb robbers. Seti's heart was left in the chest cavity after embalming, as was common practice, but it was placed on the right, rather than the left side of the cavity. Some have interpreted this to mean that Seti died from complications arising from a coronary condition or a heart attack, and that the embalmers placed the heart in a different location in the hope of making it function better in the afterlife.[11] This interpretation seems shaky. Egyptian medicine was advanced by the standards of the Late Bronze Age world, but still crude. It is unlikely that the Egyptian doctors would have been able to definitively suggest a cause of death if the king died of a heart attack in his sleep for instance, or simply collapsed. A more likely explanation for the misplaced organ is that the embalmers simply made a careless mistake. It is of course possible that Seti did indeed die from some type of complication arising from his arteriosclerosis; a common effect of this condition can be coronary disease, including heart attacks.

Whatever ended Seti's life, the journey of his afterlife had only just begun as his body was taken to the Good House where the embalmers began their grisly work. His mummy is often considered the high-point of the art of mummification. His facial features appear tranquil, almost as if he simply sleeps deeply, the slightest hints of a smile playing around his lips. His head was shaved and slight creases in his forehead enforce the impression of serene cogitation. His hands were crossed on his chest, but not clenched. If a crook and flail, the ensigns of kingship, were placed with him in the coffin, they must have been simply laid on top of his body rather than – as was more customary – in the clenched fists of the deceased king. His mummy was unwrapped by Garston Maspero after its discovery in 1881, and Maspero noted that the skin was a dark brown, and that much of it was covered with resin-soaked bandages. Exposure to air over the decades has now turned the skin deep black.

Even though the body of the king was now preserved against the degradations of the ages, two further crucial elements were needed to ensure his safe passage to the afterlife: his mortuary temple and his tomb in the Valley of the Kings.

A key element of the Egyptian view of life and death was their belief that the human soul was composed of five individual elements: the *Ren*, which denoted a person's name; the *ba*, a more corporal component of the soul, capable of eating and drinking after death; the *sjeut*, a person's shadow;

the *ib*, the heart, which took on a separate existence in the afterlife; and – importantly – the *ka*, a designation which comes closest to our modern Western understanding of the 'soul', an individual's essence or life-force. Of these concepts, the *ka* is the most commonly described in texts. The extremely common *hetep-di-nesu*, or Offering Formula, which was written on stela, statuettes, offering tables and manifold other funerary objects throughout pharaonic history, focuses on the provision of voice offerings (offerings provided magically by speaking them aloud) to the *ka* of the deceased:

> 'An offering which the King gives to Osiris, Lord of Abydos, so that he may give bread and beer, oxen and fowl, alabaster and linen, for the *ka* of the Officer of the Ruler's Crew Seneb[tifi].'[12]

And just as any commoner's *ka* needed constant replenishment to survive in the afterlife, so the king's *ka* was of paramount importance and all rulers devoted considerable resource to its maintenance during their reign.

But for a pharaoh, a humble stela with an offering formula was hardly enough. From the Old Kingdom onwards, dedicated *ka*-chapels and mortuary temples were constructed close to the king's burial place. During the Old and Middle Kingdom, these temple structures were customarily located directly adjacent to the royal pyramid, and staffed by priests and workers from nearby state-sponsored towns. This arrangement changed from the early New Kingdom onwards. When the first royal tombs were built in the Valley of the Kings, security was paramount: the burial places had to remain hidden. Building a vast mortuary temple directly next to the hidden tomb somewhat negated the secrecy of its location, so the mortuary temples of the New Kingdom pharaohs were built on the West Bank at Thebes instead, on the edge of the desert, several kilometres from the tombs of the kings they served.

Seti too followed in the footsteps of his predecessors once he gained the throne, and it is likely that one of his first decisions as king was the placement and architectural layout of his mortuary temple. He chose a spot close to the modern village of Qurna. Today, it is an out-of-the-way and desolate location, the Theban hills tower over the sandstone structure and scattered palm trees cling to the stony soil. The location was not chosen at random, however. The temple was placed on a direct processional route which connected the Amun Precinct at Karnak with the mortuary temples of Mentuhotep and Hatshepsut at Deir el-Bahri. Every year, during the Beautiful Festival of the Valley, the sacred barque of the god Amun, accompanied by his consort Mut and son Khonsu, would appear from his precinct and be carried across the river to each of the royal mortuary temples. The inhabitants of Thebes followed behind, leaving votive offerings, food and flowers at the temples along the way, and also visiting the tombs and graves of their own ancestors. They held feasts in front of and even inside these tombs during the festival, eating, drinking and celebrating both life and death. By positioning his temple squarely on this processional route, Seti ensured that his *ka* would not be forgotten during the festivities, and that his eternal life would thereby be better ensured.

As construction began, Seti named his mortuary temple Seti Merienamun in the House of Amun, and also The Temple, Glorious is Seti Merenptah. The first name is identical to the name he gave to the Great Hypostyle Hall at Karnak built during his reign. The mortuary temple was also built to align with this structure, further emphasizing both the significance of the Amun Precinct to Seti, and perhaps his pride in this most extensive and impressive of his many construction projects.

The Qurna temple was surrounded by a vast enclosure wall, built from mud-bricks rather than stone. The wall was strengthened by towers and buttresses, which must have given the finished structure a fortress-like appearance. This was not innovative, but rather an archaizing trait.[13] In building such a heavily fortified enclosure wall, Seti was looking far back in Egyptian history, to the great funerary monuments of the early rulers of the 1st and 2nd Dynasty at Abydos and the deified Old Kingdom rulers, such as Snefru, the first pyramid builder. Even in making arrangements for his eternal life, Seti looked back and drew inspiration from an almost mythical time before the troubles and internal division of the late 18th Dynasty.

The entrance to the temple was fronted by two vast mud-brick pylons forming a processional route linking two courts. Adjacent to the first court, Seti's builders constructed a large limestone palace, no doubt a replica of the type of structure Seti inhabited during his lifetime. North of the palace, next to the second court, were a series of magazines, none of which survive to the present day. These magazines were used to store both cultic equipment for the rituals conducted within the temple, and also food and votive offerings intended for the king's cult. Similarly to his great temple at Abydos, Seti also incorporated a chapel dedicated to his father, Ramesses I, in his mortuary temple at Qurna. Due to his short reign, Ramesses I had not had time to build a mortuary temple of his own, so Seti built a smaller-scale temple to remedy this dearth and ensure that his father's *ka* was also provided for. The remainder of the temple comprised an open sun court, a hypostyle hall and the chapels and sanctuaries dedicated to the deified king, showing scenes of Seti receiving offerings or giving offerings to Amun. Other chapels are dedicated to the barque of Amun or to the four different manifestations of the god himself.

At the time of his death, the majority of the temple structure was complete – and certainly functional – although some of the decoration was finished during the reign of Seti's son, Ramesses II, who in time would build his own mortuary temple, the Ramesseum, further south between the existing structures built by Amenhotep II and Thutmosis IV.

Seti's temple at Qurna originally came to the attention of the European public due to the work of Napoleon's expedition of *savants*, scientists sent throughout Egypt with the mission of gathering information about history, geology, botany and other disciplines. They mistook the temple for a palace, and drew fanciful reconstructions of the colonnades and pylons found at the site. The notable Egyptologist John Gardiner Wilkinson visited the site in the 1830s, as did the 'father of hieroglyphs', Jean-Francois Champollion, working for a short while in the temple, copying and transcribing hieroglyphic inscriptions. Archaeological work in the area was first undertaken by Flinders Petrie in 1908–1909. Petrie not only excavated in the temple, but also at the nearby cemetery of Dra Abu el-Naga, finding a wealth of Middle and New Kingdom burials. Later work was undertaken by the Egyptian antiquities service, and reconstruction, restoration and excavation in the area has been conducted from the 1960s onwards by the German Archaeological Institute in Cairo.[14]

* * *

It was a scene repeated whenever a ruler of Egypt had ascended to heaven and the mummification of the royal body was completed. As Seti had walked with heavy steps in front of the funeral train bringing the casket containing his father's mummy to his humble tomb in the Valley of the Kings, so now did Ramesses II, newly proclaimed Lord of the Two Lands, King of Upper and Lower Egypt, son of Ra lead the train of attendants, priests and courtiers through the sweltering heat of the sacred valley. Their destination could not, however, have been more different from the one Seti walked towards eleven years earlier. The tomb of Ramesses I has all the hallmarks of a rush-job; understandable given the short duration of his reign. Seti had been prudent, and had no doubt ordered the construction work to begin on his own tomb the moment he took the throne, cogent of the ignominy of his royal father's final resting place – an embarrassment one cannot help but feel he had tried to compensate for during his reign, with the construction of beautiful chapels dedicated to his father at two of his major temples, Abydos and Qurna.

The work-gang at Deir el-Medina, well-provisioned by the state and under the watchful eye of Seti's vizier, Paser, had outdone themselves. Seti's tomb[15] was not only the largest and arguably most beautifully decorated at the time of his burial, it remained one of the biggest tombs built by any ruler in the valley. Stretching nearly 140m into the solid limestone rock of the valley, the tomb contains eleven chambers. From the entrance, the funeral cortege descended a short flight of stairs leading to three linked passages and to a pillared hall and side-chamber, possibly built to deceive tomb robbers into thinking that they had reached the burial chamber itself. In reality, these two rooms are barely halfway along the full length of the tomb. From a series of steps it continues further down into the earth to an antechamber and the burial chamber itself, surrounded by several auxiliary rooms, most likely intended to house some of the vast treasures buried with the ruler. The roof of the passages and chambers is vaulted and decorated with astronomical and religious scenes. Most crucially, from the point of view of Seti's afterlife, the walls are decorated with an unprecedented amount of funerary literature.

From the *Pyramid Texts* inscribed in the 5th Dynasty pyramids at Saqqara, to the *Coffin Texts* commonly found even in private burials during the Middle Kingdom and the dramatically named *Book of the Dead*, one of the most enduring corpuses of Egyptian literature is related to funerary and burial rites.[16] The Egyptian afterlife was an intensely complex creation, and the journey to the Field of Reeds exceptionally dangerous. To combat the dangers dreamed up by the priests and scribes throughout the ages, the Egyptians had at their disposal various sacred books, each containing advice and guidance on how to successfully pass from this life to the next. The first of these books encountered by the young King Ramesses as he entered his father's tomb was the *Book of Praying to Re in the West, Praying to the United One in the West*, a text known to Egyptologists by the more abbreviated title *The Litany of Re*. This composition invokes the seventy-five names of Re and praises the god who, at night, descends into the Netherworld, and describes the process by which the deceased pharaoh is deified and united with the sun god.

Descending further into the tomb, the walls carry scenes from *The Amduat* or the *Book of What is in the Underworld*, a crucial New Kingdom treatise which could almost be considered a road map to the afterlife. It is a narrative which describes how the deceased travels together with Re through the underworld as the sun god sets in the west. The underworld throughout which the barque of the sun god travels is divided into twelve hours of night, each corresponding to a realm or area of the Underworld. Some of these areas are intensely hostile, such as the seventh hour when the great enemy of the sun god, the snake Apophis who embodies chaos, discord and darkness ambushes the solar barque but is defeated by its divine passengers, including Isis and Seth.

As Seti's body was carried further into the tomb, it passed through passageways decorated with the 'Opening of the Mouth' ritual. The ritual was no doubt acted out by the new King Ramesses, maybe even in the antechamber which follows immediately after the decorated hallways. Seti's burial chamber is naturally the most heavily decorated part of the tomb. Further scenes from the *Amduat* can be found here, along with the *Book of Gates* and the – somewhat comically named – *Book of the Heavenly Cow*. The former is similar in content to the *Amduat* in that it contains a detailed description of the physical layout of the Underworld and the steps and spells necessary to guarantee safe passage to the final hour of the night where the deified king, now joined to the sun god, enters into the east to rise and live again. *The Book of the Heavenly Cow*, by contrast, concerns the early days of Egyptian history, a mythical time where the sun god Re ruled as pharaoh and there was little differentiation between deities and humanity. But humanity grew rebellious and arose against the sun god, who punished them by unleashing the goddess Hathor to destroy them, while Re withdrew to the sky, riding the heavenly cow, and began to build the Netherworld. However, as he looked down from his seat in the sky, Re saw the suffering of humanity at the hands of the murderous goddess and he pitied his former subjects. Unable to stop the bloodthirsty Hathor, Re decided to trick her. He took a jar of beer and dyed it the colour of blood. He then gifted it to Hathor who, thinking only of quenching her bloodthirst, drank the beer and fell into a drunken stupor, saving humanity from further punishment.

As Ramesses exited the tomb he may already have been planning his own policies. He had taken the throne names Usermaatre-Setepenre, 'the justice of Re is powerful, chosen of Re', and Ramessu-Meramun, 'Re bore him, beloved of Amun', names which would be copied by nine more rulers of Egypt until the New Kingdom finally collapsed after the reign of Ramesses XI. Ramesses' coronation was followed immediately by a flurry of building activity. He finished the decoration on the Great Hypostyle Hall in Karnak, and also completed the decoration on his father's temple at Abydos. He ordered the uninscribed colossal statues and obelisks carved from Aswan granite during the ninth year of his father's reign finished, inscribing them with his own name and titles. The decorative style he favoured was different from Seti's; gone were the delicate raised relief, replaced by the cruder – but more time-efficient – sunk relief, which would dominate the remainder of the Ramesside period.

Ramesses gives every impression of being a young ruler in a hurry to leave his mark. And leave his mark he did. He ruled for sixty-six years, longer than any other Egyptian pharaoh, and fathered over 100 known sons and daughters. He fought repeatedly in Syria against the Hittites, but failed to replicate his father's successes. Instead, he suffered at best a stalemate, and at worst a humiliating defeat, at Qadesh against the Hittite king Muwatalis and lost control of Amurru, the region Seti had secured during the early part of his own reign. Ramesses' enmity towards the Hittites marked the first half of his reign, and was not concluded until Year 21 when he signed a peace treaty with Muwatalis' successor, his brother, Hattusili III, in 1258 BC, a treaty which was further cemented by Ramesses' marriage to Hattusili's daughter, Maathorneferure, in 1246 BC.

Peace and stability during Ramesses' reign was guaranteed in no small measure by his longevity. He died aged 89 at the precipice of the most traumatizing event in the eastern Mediterranean for hundreds of years. Wars and environmental crisis had created a number of great migrations: Libyan tribesmen were moving towards Egypt, and groups of Ionian pirates, known as the Sea People, converged on the Hittite kingdom and the Lebanese city-states. The order which had existed, of great kings in Babylon, Egypt, Hatti, Mittani and Cyprus, was ended, and the international system of trade and diplomacy collapsed. The reigns of Ramesses II's successor, Merenptah, and later Ramesses III were marked by conflict and increasing economic turmoil, including labour strikes, rising grain prices and tomb robbery.

The reigns of the later Ramesside rulers Ramesses IV to Ramesses XI appear almost an early model for the latter days of the modern Soviet Union; interchangeable, aged and largely ineffective rulers desperately trying to keep their faltering country from falling apart. Eventually, with the death of Ramesses XI in 1077 BC, the country of Egypt effectively split in two, the northern half ruled by King Mendes from the city of Tanis, while the High Priest of Amun controlled the southern part of the country, effectively a pharaoh in all but name. Two-hundred years after Seti had been laid to rest in his tomb in the Valley of the Kings, bequeathing to his son an Egypt which was stronger and wealthier than the one he himself had received, the power of the land he had ruled was definitively broken. Egypt would suffer wave upon wave of invaders and occupiers – Libyans, Nubians, Persians, Greeks and Romans – until Cleopatra VII Philopator took her own life on 12 August 30 BCE while under siege in Alexandria, ending pharaonic rule of the Two Lands of Egypt for good.

* * *

In this, the final act of the story of Seti's life and legacy, another actor enters the stage. His name is Giovanni Battista Belzoni, a man who more than most would help to spread Seti's fame far beyond the shores of the king's native land. Judged by some historians as perhaps the most colourful man ever to rob an ancient Egyptian tomb[17] – and also humorously as *The Giant Archaeologists Love to Hate*[18] – Belzoni was born far from the desert and the Delta in the northern Italian town of Padua on 5 November 1778. He was the son of Giacomo Belzoni, a barber who desired little more than for his son to follow in his footsteps and become a barber himself. But the younger Belzoni had other ideas. At the age of 16, he left Padua and travelled to Rome, where he claimed to have studied hydraulic engineering.

However, his sojourn in Rome came to a dramatic end. Napoleon Bonaparte's invasion of Italy had been temporarily halted by Pope Pius VI, who sued for peace in early 1797. However, during a riot in Rome – instigated in part by Napoleon's brother Joseph Bonaparte – the French Brigadier General Mathurin-Léonard Duphot was shot and killed by troops from the Papal Army. The French took this as a breach of the peace treaty, and on 10 February 1798, French General Louis-Alexandre Berthier entered Rome unopposed and banished Pius VI, creating the Roman Republic. Belzoni was in a tricky position. Twenty years old and standing over two metres tall, the muscular young man seemed the perfect fit for a French infantryman's uniform. Seeking to avoid being press-ganged by the recruiting parties swarming the city, Belzoni left Rome with his brother Francesco, and in 1800 they arrived in Amsterdam, where they became petty merchants, selling trinkets such as rosaries and fake relics on the city streets.

In 1803, the two Paduan brothers crossed the English Channel and arrived in London, a place then steeped in poverty, riches and opportunities in equal measure. His immense strength and theatrical nature was welcomed, and Belzoni quickly found work in the many circuses and sideshows which entertained the citizens and visiting sailors, merchants and soldiers. He was employed by the renowned impresario Charles Dibdin Jr, who had become a shareholder in Sadler's Wells Theatre in 1802, to perform as a strongman at the Islington Theatre. Here he was billed as the 'Patagonian Sampson', famed throughout the city for his star performance, wherein he lifted twelve members of the theatre's company on a specially fabricated metal harness and carried them around the stage. Belzoni's proclivity for hydraulic engineering, in particular diverting and channelling water, was no doubt honed during his time on the stage. Dibdin made a series of dramatic alterations to the indoor stage, the most ambitious of which was the installation of a large water tank, 3ft deep and 90ft long, filled by water diverted from the New River. Upon this aquatic stage, the company – no doubt including Belzoni – performed such stirring patriotic plays as *A Fig for the French* and *The Siege of Gibraltar*, where an actual naval battle was performed in the water tank, complete with explosions, daring duels and drowning Spaniards:

> 'The ships, gun-boats, floating batteries etc. have been regularly constructed by professional men from His Majesty's dock yards, and float in a receptacle [...] representing the Siege of Gibraltar, concluding with the blowing up of the Spanish battering ships and an actual representation of saving the drowning Spaniards by Sir Roger Curtis.'[19]

Belzoni's strongman act was eventually embellished with various stage tricks involving water and hydraulics, skills he would later bring with him to Egypt and which would help to cement his position as one of the most successful tomb robbers of all time. While in London, Belzoni met a young woman, Sarah Banne, who was either from Ireland or Bristol, depending on the historical source consulted. They married and she became his companion for the rest of his life, outliving him by nearly fifty years. Sadly, the patriarchal world of the nineteenth century left little room in the annals of history for the role and voice of women, and much less is known about Sarah than about Belzoni himself, although she contributed greatly to his work. She also conducted her own research while in Egypt, travelling among Bedouin and Egyptians, studying the role of women in their societies, something no European man would have been permitted to properly investigate. She wrote about her experiences in her book *Mrs Belzoni's Trifling Account of the Women of Egypt, Nubia and Syria*, a title which betrays her wry sense of humour and perhaps also a prophetic acceptance of the limited impact of her work. The account is anything but trifling; Sarah's intelligence, perception and firm determination shine through the pages. In one instance, she describes visiting a headman at Aswan in his house, where she is offered coffee and a pipe of tobacco while the women of the house look on:

'I made a sign I wished them [the women of the house] to sit down, and in particular that the wife should take coffee with me: but he treated them very harshly, made me understand that coffee would be too good for them, and said water was good enough; at the same time he held the coffee-pot, pressing me to drink more: on my refusing, he locked it up in a small room, that the women might not drink it [...] After having smoked for some time, I laid it down; one of the women took it up, and began to smoke: on seeing such a horrid profanation, the man took it from her with violence, and was going to beat her, which I naturally prevented.'[20]

But Sarah's solitary journeying in Egypt and the Near East were still far into the future as the two of them lived in London in the early 1800s. Driven by Belzoni's insatiable wanderlust, probably a trait shared by Sarah, the couple travelled throughout Europe, seeking circus work wherever it presented itself. In 1815, while staying in Malta, the Belzonis encountered Ismael Gibraltar, the envoy of Muhammad Ali Pasha, the ruler of Egypt. Ismael told Belzoni of the extensive land reclamation and irrigation projects organized by the Pasha. Belzoni, intrigued, shared with Ismael his plans for a new type of waterwheel which could be powered by a single ox rather than many and would improve agricultural production throughout Egypt. Excited at the prospect, Ismael organized for Giovanni and Sarah to travel to Egypt with their Irish servant Henry James Curtin.

Arriving in Alexandria in June 1815, the Belzonis and Curtin were immediately ordered into quarantine, sheltering in a French house as an outbreak of plague swept over the city. As the plague lessened, Belzoni was introduced to the French consul-general, Bernardino Michele Maria Drovetti, who would later become Belzoni's nemesis and ardent competitor. Their first meeting, however, was wholly positive and the Belzonis travelled to Cairo with renewed optimism, preparing for Giovanni's audience with the pasha. In 1816, Belzoni demonstrated his new waterwheel to the pasha, who was impressed with the invention. The pasha's advisors and courtiers, however, were not. No doubt annoyed by the prospect of yet another European invention being foisted upon their countrymen, they asked if only oxen could power the wheel. Belzoni proclaimed that men could power it just as well, and the courtiers demanded a demonstration. A group of locals took up positions and began to turn the wheel. Curtin, Belzoni's servant, also joined in. Initially the machine worked equally well, but at a hidden signal from one of the advisors, all the locals jumped away from the machine, leaving the young Curtin holding the weight of the water. The wheel slammed back, flinging him across the room and breaking one of his legs. The pasha was outraged at what he perceived as an attempt to harm his people. Belzoni was told to take his machine and leave Muhammad Ali's presence.

Fortunately for Belzoni, just as his first Egyptian venture collapsed, another was just beginning. The arrival of Henry Salt, the British consul to Egypt, prompted a great rush for antiquities as Salt was an ardent collector. He hired the orientalist Johann Ludwig Burckhardt, who had recently rediscovered the ruins of the fabled city of Petra in Jordan, as his agent. Burckhardt travelled throughout Egypt locating artefacts and antiquities on behalf of Salt. At Luxor, he came across the head and shoulders of a colossal granite statue of Ramesses II. Weighing 7¼ tons, the statue fragment was too large and too far from the river to move onto a boat for shipment to Cairo by conventional means. To solve the conundrum of how to transport the head to Cairo, Burckhardt recommended Belzoni to Salt. Belzoni and Sarah travelled south and, over several weeks, Belzoni successfully moved the head with the help of hundreds of local workmen, transporting it on a sleigh set atop wooden rollers. When it reached the Nile, it was loaded onto a ship and sent to Cairo, where Salt greeted its arrival with glee.

Belzoni's success earned him permanent employment as Salt's agent throughout Egypt. He travelled to Abu Simbel and began the extensive work of clearing sand from the grand temple facade. He also worked at Giza and was the first European to enter the Great Pyramid of Khufu.

On 16 October 1817, Belzoni was in Thebes, this time working in the Valley of the Kings, or Beban el Malook as Belzoni referred to it. Less than a week before, he had found the paltry tomb of Ramesses I, which he wasted little time on. Instead, he told his workmen to focus their efforts on an area some 15ft from this tomb, an area Belzoni believed to be promising. He described his emotions at what followed with unusual philosophy:

'I may call this a fortunate day, one of the best perhaps of my life; I do not mean to say, that fortune has made me rich, for I do not consider all rich men fortunate; but she has given me that satisfaction, that extreme pleasure, which wealth cannot purchase; the pleasure of discovering what has been long sought in vain, and of presenting the world with a new and perfect monument of Egyptian antiquity, which can be recorded as superior to any other in point of grandeur, style and preservations, appearing as if just finished on the day we entered it; and what I found in it will show its great superiority to all others.'[21]

Belzoni and his men had uncovered the entrance to the tomb of Seti I. On the first day, they made it down the first passages until they reached a deep well. There appeared to be no way forwards, but a piece of plaster had been dislodged from the opposite wall and Belzoni realized that much of the wall opposite the pit was fake. It had been constructed to trick tomb robbers into thinking they had reached the end of the tomb. Belzoni was not fooled, however, and the next day he returned with beams, allowing him to traverse the pit and enter into the tomb itself. He wandered slowly through the passageways and chambers, the flickering of torchlight glinting off the perfectly preserved paintings and reliefs of the king and the gods who were responsible for helping him to the afterlife. Belzoni remarked often on how the tomb appeared as if it had just been finished, and indeed one of his first discoveries was a paint brush lying in the entrance corridor, where it had apparently been dropped by one of the workmen who had created and painted the false wall which sealed and hid the burial chamber.

In the chambers Belzoni found statues and hundreds of faience and wooden shabtis (figurines) which would serve the deceased king in his afterlife. He found the carcass of an embalmed bull and a stunning alabaster sarcophagus,[22] inscribed and decorated with scenes of the sun's journey through the Underworld. Belzoni did not, however, find any gold. The tomb had been robbed in antiquity, possibly through the small hole in the false wall which tipped off Belzoni to the existence of further chambers. The lid of the sarcophagus had been smashed to pieces as the feverish robbers tried to get at the golden jewels on the mummy. The lack of treasure did not, however, stop the rumour of great wealth from spreading through the local community. Shouts of jubilation rang out, and soon a party of horsemen thundered into the valley, led by a local headman, Hamid Aga, who joined

Belzoni in the tomb, immediately asking to see the 'large golden cock, filled with diamonds and pearls'[23] which he had been told about. Belzoni laughed and told him that there was no treasure of silver or gold in the tomb, and pointed to the stunning wall decorations, asking the headman whether they were not treasure enough. The headman looked them over and shrugged, telling Belzoni as he left the tomb: 'This would be a good place for a harem, as the women would have something to look at.'[24]

Three years after his momentous discoveries in the Valley of the Kings, Belzoni published his memoirs, *Narrative of the Operations and Recent Discoveries within the Pyramids, Temples, Tombs and Excavations, in Egypt and Nubia: and of a Journey to the Coast of the Red Sea, in Search of the Ancient Berenice; and Another to the Oasis of Jupiter Ammon*, to widespread acclaim. A year later, in 1821, Belzoni staged a vast display in The Egyptian Hall in Piccadilly, London, and recreated several rooms from the tomb of Seti I using plaster casts. The plaster casts were accompanied by a plethora of artefacts found by Belzoni, while the tall Italian himself, garbed in Arab dress, with his long black hair and beard flowing down his shoulders, acted as host, guide and storyteller: every inch the showman.

The end of Belzoni's life came in far less glamorous surroundings than his well-visited exhibition in London. He left Europe in 1823 to search for the source of the Niger River, travelling alone, Sarah opting to remain in England. In October 1823, Belzoni reached the kingdom of Benin and set off from the coast, reaching the village of Ughoton/Gwato where he died less than a week later. The cause of his death remains unclear; a likely explanation is that he developed dysentery, while other sources hold that the Italian strongman was robbed and murdered. The precise location of his grave and body remain unknown. Sarah, meanwhile, was forced to sell the collections of antiquities she had assembled with Giovanni in order to survive. Ignored by the public, the press and the scholarly community, Sarah vanished into obscurity, dying in relative poverty in St Helier on Jersey in 1870 at the age of 87.

Giovanni and Sarah both died without learning the solution to one of the greatest enigmas of the grand tomb of Seti they had discovered. They had found the shabtis, the statues, the sarcophagus and the decorations. But one crucial question remained unanswered: where was the king himself? Where was the mummy of Seti I?

Chapter 7

Rediscovering a Ruler

On a warm day sometime in the 1860s, a young man was tending to his goat herd on the craggy limestone hills near the mortuary temple of Hatshepsut at Deir el-Bahri. The man's name was Ahmed Abd el-Rassul,[1] one of three brothers belonging to an extended family who lived in the nearby community of Qurna. Spotting a small shrub some way from the rest of the herd, one of the goats began to meander down the slope of the cliffs. Cursing the wayward creature, Ahmed followed its bleating, which was suddenly cut off. He arrived to find that the goat had stumbled into a vertical shaft in the rock. Lighting a torch or candle, Ahmed followed a set of narrow steps cut into the rock and descended into the darkness. He paused at the foot of the steps as the flickering light of his flame played over dozens of varnished wooden coffins and glinted off gold. Most likely forgetting all about the prodigal caprine, Ahmed rushed home and told his brothers, Mohammed and Hussein, about his discovery. Eagerly, the brothers went to investigate and decided between them to keep their discovery secret from the other villagers and – especially –the antiquities authorities.

After French Egyptologist Auguste Mariette had brought the scale of illicit digging and smuggling of antiquities to the attention of authorities in Cairo in the 1850s, rules had been put in place to limit its scope. Potential archaeologists and treasure hunters were now required to obtain permission from the Antiquities Service to conduct excavations, and representatives of the Director-General of Excavations and Antiquities in Egypt, the French scholar Gaston Maspero (1846–1916), were present on digs. Yet by taking only small amounts of antiquities from their private cache, the Abd el-Rassul brothers could drip-feed them onto the market, in small enough quantities to prevent the authorities in Cairo from growing suspicious.

However, the brothers had grown bolder by the 1870s; now whole coffins, mummies and royal burial equipment were swamping the antiquities market. Maspero was made aware of the sudden influx of antiquities, and the shrewd archaeologist knew well that they did not come from any authorized excavation. Angrily, he despatched agents to Luxor to spy out the providers of the valuable artefacts, but to no avail. The local community – given that after so many years they must surely have been aware of the Abd el-Rassul brothers' private hoard – closed ranks and the agents were forced to return to Cairo without results.

The trail of illegal antiquities which pointed directly to Luxor continued to irk Maspero, who finally caught a break in 1881. He decided upon a sting operation, persuading wealthy American journalist and Egyptologist Charles Edwin Wilbour (1833–1896) to travel to Luxor and make it known that he wished to purchase antiquities – regardless of whether they had been discovered on legal or illicit excavations. Wilbour did not have to wait long. Shortly after his arrival, he was led to the village of Qurna and introduced to two of the brothers, Ahmed and Hussein Abd el-Rassul. They offered to sell him a (now sadly lost) king list of 18th Dynasty pharaohs inscribed on a piece of leather. Fobbing off his hosts with some excuse, Wilbour left the Abd el-Rassul household and immediately informed Maspero of his discovery. Jubilant at finally gaining traction in his case, Maspero ordered the two brothers arrested and interrogated under torture. Both, however, refused all knowledge of any illegal sales of antiquities and were eventually released.

Returning home, the brothers – marked by the rough interrogation and under immense stress and pressure – began to argue. Ahmed wanted a larger share of the treasure as compensation for the indignities he had suffered in prison, but the other brothers refused. The rift within the family grew, and eventually Mohammed betrayed his younger brothers. He went to the authorities and pledged to reveal everything, presumably in exchange for clemency. He told the story of Ahmed's lost goat and the initial discovery. He willingly took representatives of the antiquities service and the police to the location of the cache. Maspero's assistant, Emile Brugsch, was quickly summoned and in a matter of days, for the sake of security, he and his men cleared three dozen royal mummies and thousands of pieces of funerary equipment from the tomb.

Among the kings and queens of Egypt found jumbled together in the cramped chamber lay Seti I, along with his son, Ramesses II, and the empty coffin of his father, Ramesses I. An inked inscription on the mummy of Ramesses II reveals why these august personages had been so unceremoniously dumped together. It relates how the mummy of Ramesses II was taken from its tomb and moved to that of Seti I. Later on, both mummies were taken and placed together in the tomb of Ahmose Inhapy, the sister of the Second Intermediate Period king Seqenere-Tao. Later still, all three mummies (and many others) were moved together to what would be known as the 'Royal Cache', where they rested in obscurity until discovered by Ahmed Abd el-Rassul and his goat.

The question of course remains: why was the mummy of Seti, along with those of his predecessors and successors, not allowed to remain in peace in their tombs? One possibility is related to the safety of the royal mummy and the burial assemblage. A crashing economy and resultant famine during the latter part of the Ramesside period saw many of the citizens of Thebes – and also the workmen at Deir el-Medina – turn to tomb robbery as a means of raising material wealth to trade for grain, and also for personal enrichment.[2] The workers at Deir el-Medina in particular had an edge as their ancestors had worked on many of the royal tombs; it is likely that a list of their precise locations was still kept somewhere in the village. The priests at Karnak may have felt that the royal bodies would be safer if moved, protected from the possible destruction wrought by looters. This argument is given some weight by the previously mentioned inked text on the mummy of Ramesses II, which is signed in the name of Pinudjem, the High Priest of Karnak and *de facto* ruler of southern Egypt during the chaotic Third Intermediate Period.

Another possibility is that Pinudjem and other representatives of the state needed quick cash. It is likely that they stripped a great deal of gold – jewellery and other trappings – off the royal mummies and their coffins during the move; a move they probably justified by reference to a recent increase in tomb robbery. This argument is given particular weight both by the fact that many of the royal coffins had been meticulously stripped of their golden decorations and by the discovery of reused royal jewellery from the New Kingdom in the Third Intermediate Period and Late Period burials at Tanis.[3] Clearly, what came around went around.

In two short days, the cache had been emptied and Seti began his final journey. He was carried with his fellow monarchs to a waiting steamer ship. In what must have been a stirring sight, local women followed the royal convoy like mourners at a funeral, tearing their hair and clothes. As the steamer pulled into the current which would take it to Cairo, rifles were fired into the air in a final salute. Wherever the vessel passed, villagers lined up on the banks of the River Nile, silently paying their respects to the long-dead rulers of their land. After 3,000 years in Thebes, Seti was travelling north one final time.[4]

* * *

The story of Seti does not end with his death, burial and the indignities suffered by his corpse at the hands of tomb robbers and archaeologists. His place in the minds of historians – ancient as well as modern – and in the public perception are equally important to consider. History, like beauty – and far too often, truth – is in the eye of the beholder.

Some Classical historians, using as their source the fragmentary and somewhat dubious account of the Egyptian priest Manetho, ascribed Seti with a completely overstated reign of fifty-one or even fifty-five years. Josephus quotes Manetho in his *Contra Apionem*[5] and relates the story of a 19th Dynasty ruler by the name of 'Sethos', whom Manetho seems to have mistakenly considered the son of Harmesses Miamun, a king who had ruled for sixty-seven years (evidently Ramesses II, who ruled for sixty-six years). He claims that the power of Sethos lay in his cavalry and his fleet, and that he undertook many campaigns, including against Cyprus and the Lebanese city-states. He also claims that Sethos' nickname was Aegyptus, and that the land was named after him. This story is largely fantasy. It is clear that Manetho utterly misunderstood the ordering of the 19th Dynasty rulers, and also ascribed to Seti an unrealistically long reign, although his reference to the military prowess of Seti is curious, considering the prominent displays of Seti's campaigns on the Karnak Battle Reliefs. As a priest, Manetho may have had access to these and formed his opinions of Seti and his reign on their basis.

The Greek historian Herodotus of Halicarnassus (*c.* 484–425 BCE), known as the 'Father of History' (or occasionally, by exasperated Egyptologists, as the 'Father of Lies'), also describes a highly successful military ruler of Egypt, named 'Sesostris', who, he says, led an army as far as the coast of the Black Sea.[6] Scholars have proposed several pharaohs – Ramesses II, Seti I and the 12th Dynasty king Senwosret III – as possible inspirations for this entirely mythical character. Whether any one king was truly the inspiration remains unclear, in particular given the partially fictional nature of Herodotus' account. There is no existing evidence that any king of Egypt led an army further than the banks of the Euphrates River.

It was the discovery of KV17, Seti's tomb in the Valley of the Kings, which reintroduced Seti I to nineteenth-century scholars. They looked at the great monuments he had produced, the tomb in particular, and – after the discovery of his mummy in 1881 – the skill with which he had been embalmed. This led them to the conclusion that his was a reign of great prosperity and power, and of artistic brilliance. By the twentieth century, greater focus was on his military campaigns. In his seminal work *Egypt of the Pharaohs*, Sir Alan Gardiner on one hand declared him a great ruler, 'imbued with true affection and loyalty towards his father',[7] while on the other dismissing much of Seti's construction work as 'relatively unimportant'.[8] Instead, Gardiner and his contemporaries for much of the twentieth century focused on Seti's warlike exploits and his tendency towards religious and artistic orthodoxy, his piety and his conservatism. More modern scholars, notably Peter Brand, have noted the shadow which Ramesses II cast 'backwards' in history, effectively blotting out many of his father's accomplishments. Brand wrote: "[I]t was Seti I who laid a secure foundation for the Nineteenth Dynasty and re-established the principle of dynastic succession to the throne. His reign was a time of transition that saw the close of the turbulent post-Amarna and the dawn of the Ramesside age."[9] Slowly, Seti is beginning to emerge from the shadows cast by his illustrious successor.

Together with these scholarly and sombre treatments of Seti's person and reign, there are the more outlandish fictions. Among the earliest of these is the fantasy novel *Life of Sethos, Taken from Private Memoirs of the Ancient Egyptians*, published in 1731. It was written by the French priest Abbe Jean Terrasson and claims to tell the story of Seti's early life and upbringing by using 'ancient manuscripts' entrusted to the author. It follows Seti as he is inducted into the mysteries and rites of the ancient Egyptian religion, which

Terrasson mixed and merged with the arcana of Freemasonry. Despite the completely fictitious nature of the novel, Terrasson became accepted as a specialist in Egyptian religion and the novel eventually served as the inspiration for Wolfgang Amadeus Mozart's opera *Die Zauberflöte* (*The Magic Flute*), which premiered in 1791, sixty years after Terrasson penned his book.

Seti's links to Freemasonry were further explored by the American author and medical doctor John Adam Weisse, who wrote *The Obelisk and Freemasonry According to the Discoveries of Belzoni and Commander Gorringe; Also Egyptian Symbols Compared with Those Discovered in American Mounds* in 1880, a frankly perplexing work in which the author argues that Seti's tomb should be renamed 'The Masonic Temple of Seti I and Ramesses II' and claims that the kilts commonly worn by Egyptian pharaohs in sculptures and reliefs were in fact Masonic aprons. The book also includes a series of rather opaque calculations, which aim to numerically link the measurements of Egyptian obelisks to various stones found in or around Native American burial mounds. The author also relates several conversations he claims to have had with Sarah Belzoni, including one in which he alleges that she entrusted several mysterious documents to him. These were documents that she had inherited from Giovanni prior to his death, and which, very conveniently, supported Dr Weisse's outlandish theories.

It is difficult to unpick the precise purpose of Weisse's rambling dissertation, but it seems that his intention was to argue against the persecution of Freemasonry by the Catholic Church by claiming that many great men throughout history, including Seti I and Ramesses II, had been the very founders of Freemasonry, and that it had, in the author's words 'been the means of promoting civilisation, fostering the mechanical arts, and of holding together the more advanced minds for mutual protection and charity'.[10] Whatever his mission, considering other publications by the same publishing house – which include several treatises on the alleged ancient origins of Freemasonry and Rosicrucianism, alongside the notorious *Isis Unveiled* by the self-described psychic Madame Helena Blavatsky and a discourse on obscenities in the French language – one cannot dispute that Weisse's book was in thoroughly compatible company.

Conspiracy seems to dog Seti's inheritance even into the present day. His association with Freemasonry at the pens of Terrasson and Weisse have led modern conspiracy theorists to link him with everything from Satanism to extra-terrestrial intelligence, in particular in less salubrious sectors of the world wide web. One of the most enduring of these modern conspiracy theories concern Seti's great temple at Abydos: it holds that some of the signs and depictions carved into the walls are not hieroglyphs, but rather depictions of helicopters and alien spacecraft. The inscriptions in question were carved during the reign of Seti I, but later plastered over and recarved by his successor Ramesses II. The partial removal of some of the plaster has created optical illusions which some have interpreted as modern machinery depicted on ancient monuments. Several of the images purporting to show this phenomenon have also demonstrably been edited and retouched in order to make this effect more noticeable and trick the casual observer.

But Seti and his works have not only appeared in conspiracy theories on the dark side of the internet or in the minds of nineteenth-century occultists. The link between his son, Ramesses II, and the Biblical Exodus has made him a mainstay in Biblical movies, such as 1956's classic *The Ten Commandments*, where he is portrayed by the English actor Sir Cedric Hardwicke, and in *The Prince of Egypt* from 1998, where he is shown as the cruel pharaoh who orders the death of all male children of the Hebrew nation throughout his kingdom. He appears in the role of a conquering ruler in the 2014 movie *Exodus: Gods and Kings*, which begins with a fictionalized account of Seti's battles with Hittite troops. Seti also appears in the 1999 adventure film *The Mummy*, where he is advised by his vizier, Imhotep (an Old Kingdom architect who had been dead for 2,000 years when Seti took the throne), and engaged in what can only be described as a deeply unhealthy relationship with the handmaiden Ankhsunamun (the wife of Tutankhamun, who died several decades before Seti was born). In *The Mummy Returns* (2001), Seti is also revealed as the father of Princess Nefertiti. As the author, playwright and screenwriter William Goldman famously noted: 'In Hollywood, no one knows anything.'

* * *

A final character deserves to be mentioned as the story of Seti draws to a close. Her name was Dorothy Louise Eady, although she will be remembered by

Egyptologists as Omm Sety.[11] Born in 1904 in London, the young Dorothy suffered a serious head trauma as a child, developing the exceedingly rare foreign accent syndrome. Alongside her new accent, the young girl began to develop uncharacteristic behaviour. She became obsessed with ancient Egyptian religion, an obsession which resulted in her expulsion from school as she began to compare Egyptian mythology favourably to Christianity and refused to sing Christian hymns. When taken to visit the British Museum, the young girl became ecstatic, claiming in front of her bemused parents that she was now home, while pointing to a picture of Seti's temple at Abydos. She kissed the feet of the royal statues in the collection, and her vivid interest and vivacious personality soon drew the attention of the museum's curator, the eminent Egyptologist Sir Ernst Alfred Thompson Wallis Budge, who advised her to study hieroglyphs in order for her to properly understand the ancient Egyptian culture.

As a teenager she said she began to receive visitations from Seti I during the night. When she described these experiences, she was temporarily incarcerated behind the walls of a sanatorium. When she reached adulthood, the determined young woman moved to London, where she worked for an Egyptian magazine. There she met Egyptian student Eman Abdel Meguid, and in 1931 she travelled to Egypt to marry him. Upon arriving in Egypt, Dorothy's strange visitations and experiences increased, as did an inexplicable ability to charm snakes. Aside from Seti, she claimed to have received nightly visitations by a ghost named Hor-Ra, who told her the story of her previous life, which, in her mind, readily explained the curious affinity for and connection to Egypt she had felt from such an early age. She said that according to Hor-Ra, she had been a priestess named Bentreshyt in a previous life. Bentreshyt had been brought up in the Temple of Osiris at Abydos, and had been consecrated to the temple as a virgin. However, one day she had met the young King Seti and become his lover. When their affair was discovered, she was threatened with public exposure and execution. Unable to face the humiliation it would cause her family and the king, Bentreshyt took her own life.

During the 1940s and 1950s, after separating from her husband – with whom she had a son called Sety – Dorothy worked with archaeologists Selim Hasan and Ahmed Fakhry on excavations of pyramids in the vicinity of Cairo. She became known as an excellent draughtswoman and artist, and also helped to edit and proof-read the publications of her supervisors. At this stage in her life she took up the name Omm Sety, meaning 'mother of Sety'. In 1956, she moved to Abydos and worked as a draughtswoman in the very temple where she believed Bentreshyt had lived and died. From the moment she arrived, she displayed an uncanny knowledge of the area's layout and the various decorations found throughout the temple. She worked in one of the rooms of the temple and often brought food offerings and prayed to the gods. Her occasionally outlandish ways caused some comment in the local community, especially her decision to keep a cobra as a pet in her outdoor office. She was faced with retirement in 1964, but the Egyptian antiquities service made an exception to their rules and she was allowed to continue work.

When Dorothy Eady died in 1981, her final resting place became a source of some controversy. Because both Coptic Christians and local Muslims considered her a pagan, they refused to allow her to be buried in their cemeteries. Foreseeing this eventuality, she had built an underground tomb for herself near her home. But upon her death, the local authorities changed their minds, refusing to allow her body to rest in it. Instead, she was buried in the desert, just outside the boundaries of a Coptic cemetery.

Postscript: Who was Seti?

What can we truly claim to know about the personality of Seti? Not merely about the ambitions which drove him, the goals he wished to achieve in his life, but his moods, his attitude to life, his quirks and habits? The sad truth is that at a distance of 3,000 years, the echoes of such crucial components of an individual's nature have long since fallen silent. As historians, as Egyptologists and archaeologists, we are left with fragmented texts, scraps of papyrus, broken stones, pots and pieces of metal taken from trenches. From those we can piece together interpretations of function and usage, of chronological development and technological innovations. From the reliefs which decorate temples throughout Egypt, we can deduce how the royals and nobles of the land wished themselves portrayed. But everything we view is through a broken lens, a kaleidoscope of confusion caused by the passing of the ages, the selective survival of materials, the destruction of looters and the methodological oddities of archaeologists gone before us.

We can try to imagine how Seti felt when he was growing up, probably seeing his father Paramessu as a distant figure of authority, a larger-than-life character who filled Seti's world. Later, Paramessu would become an inspiration, a teacher to the young nobleman, taking his first tentative steps in the complex machinery of government. Then, with a stroke and the death of Horemheb, Seti the noble and Seti the soldier's son became Seti the heir apparent, Prince of Egypt. Seeing his father, feeble and aged, Seti must have realized that the day when the supreme authority and responsibility would pass onto him would not be long in coming. Maybe he faced the prospect with fear or trepidation, or maybe he looked forward to making an impact and leaving his mark on a society which had long needed a stable hand at the helm of state.

From his actions we can claim that he was a man haunted by great piety, an orthodox or religious conservative, even a fanatic, prostrating himself before the gods in abject displays of humility. Growing up during the religious upheaval of the post-Amarna period, one can hardly blame him if a deep-seated longing for the near-mythical stability of the Old and Middle Kingdoms, as well as the earlier 18th Dynasty, became ingrained in him from an early age. His choice to incorporate the names of Thutmosis III and Amenhotep III might be seen as further evidence of this nostalgia. But as with so many things in history, there are always alternative theories. Each of these actions, which some past authors used to determine Seti's character and personality, have distinct political overtones. Seti may simply have taken the names of his predecessors not out of personal nostalgia, but because they were well-remembered within Egyptian society. Or perhaps, as a northern noble born without royal blood, he simply wished to create an undeniable link between himself and the glory days of a dynasty long gone, to legitimize his own claim to the throne. Perhaps none of these interpretations are true; perhaps each has a grain of truth within it.

Seti's actions and his impact on ancient Egyptian society and history are much clearer, although neglected by posterity and overshadowed by the lengthy reign of his son. Seti was an active monarch, of that there can be little doubt. He was the *de facto* founder of the Ramesside Period and the 19th Dynasty, although the credit for many of its achievements would also fall to his son. His upbringing in a military family seemingly imbued him with a shrewdness and knowledge of strategy which enabled him to firmly re-establish Egypt's place as a power to be reckoned with in the Near East. His relentless quarrying and mining expeditions formed the basis not only for the great construction projects of his own reign, but also of those of his successor.

Ramesses II does not owe all his glory and achievements to Seti, and he rightfully deserves the moniker of 'Ramesses the Great' which history has bestowed upon him. But had it not been for Seti's short but effective reign, for his smart policy decisions, decisive military victories and extensive building programme, it is unlikely that Ramesses could have succeeded as much as he did. Any parent strives to create opportunities for their child; perhaps to gift more than what was given to them, to leave the world a better place, in little ways, than it once was. And Seti fathered the potential, the environment and the conditions in which the greatness of his son could truly flourish.

Abbreviations

Ä&L	*Ägypten und Levante*
ASAE	*Annales du Service des Antiquités de l'Egypte*
BIFAO	*Bulletin de l'Institut Français d'Archéologie Orientale*
BSFE	*Bulletin de la Société Française d'Égyptologie*
EA	*Egyptian Archaeology*
GM	*Göttinger Miszellen*
JAOS	*Journal of the American Oriental Society*
JARCE	*Journal of the American Research Center in Egypt*
JEA	*Journal of Egyptian Archaeology*
JNES	*Journal of Near Eastern Studies*
KRI I	K.A. Kitchen, *Ramesside Inscriptions Translated and Annotated: Translations I: Ramesses I, Sethos I and Contemporaries* (Blackwell: Oxford, 1993)
LEM	A.H. Gardiner, *Late Egyptian Mischellanies* (Brussels, 1937)
MDAIK	*Mitteilungen des Deutschen Archäologischen Instituts, Abteilung Kairo*
REE	*Revista de Estudios de Egiptologia*
SAK	*Studien zur Altägyptischen Kultur*
ZÄS	*Zeitschrift für Ägyptische Sprache und Altertumskunde*

Notes

Chapter 1

1. The Pharaonic Egyptian Civilization lasted for more than 3,500 years. Distilling so many events and societal details into a comprehensive overview for readers unfamiliar with Ancient Egypt is naturally difficult. Readers who desire additional information about the development of Egyptian civilization may wish to consult the following seminal tomes: B.J. Kemp, *Ancient Egypt: Anatomy of a Civilisation* (Routledge: London, 1989); K.A. Bard, *An Introduction to the Archaeology of Ancient Egypt* (Blackwell Publishing: Malden, Oxford and Carlton, 2008); and I. Shaw (ed.), *The Oxford History of Ancient Egypt* (Oxford University Press: Oxford, 2003).
2. Mariette's long career and impact on Egyptology has been discussed by many authors, but for an accessible overview, see among others B.M Fagan, *The Rape of the Nile: Tomb Robbers, Tourists and Archaeologists in Egypt* (3rd ed.) (Westview Press: Boulder, 2004), pp.181–90, and J. Thompson, *Wonderful Things: A History of Egyptology – 1: From Antiquity to 1881* (American University in Cairo Press: Cairo, 2015), pp.267–82.
3. For an overview of ancient Egyptian agrarian practices and rural economy, see for instance C. Eyre, 'The Village Economy in Pharaonic Egypt', in A. Bowman and E. Rogan (eds), *Agriculture in Egypt: From Pharaonic to Modern Times* (Oxford University Press: Oxford, 1999), pp.33–60.
4. For an excellent introductory overview of settlement types and layout in ancient Egypt, see S. Snape, *The Complete Towns and Cities of Ancient Egypt* (Thames & Hudson: London, 2014).
5. M. Lichtheim, *Ancient Egyptian Literature: The New Kingdom* (University of California Press: Berkeley, Los Angeles and London, 1976), p.173.
6. R.B. Gozzoli, *The Writing of History in Ancient Egypt during the First Millenium BC (ca. 1070–180 BC): Trends and Perspectives* (Golden House: London, 2006), pp.191–226.
7. T.A.H. Wilkinson, *Royal Annals of Ancient Egypt* (Columbia University Press: New York, 2000).
8. Such as seal impressions of King Den which records five kings and one queen who ruled during the 1st Dynasty: Narmer, Hor-Aha, Djer, Djet, Den and Den's mother and regent Merenith discovered at the site of Abydos in the 1980s.

9. M. el-Alfi, 'La Liste de Rois de Karnak', in *Discussions in Egyptology*, 19, 1991, pp.29–36.

10. M. el-Alfi, 'La Liste de Rois de Saqqarah', in *Discussions in Egyptology*, 26, 1993, pp.7–12.

11. K. Ryholt, 'The Turin King-List', in *Ägypten und Levante*, 14, 2004, pp.135–55.

12. F. Wendorf (ed.), *Holocene Settlement of the Egyptian Sahara* (Kluwer Academic/Plenum Publishers: London & New York, 2001–2002).

13. Although the usually so astute archaeologist used his discoveries at the site as a foundation for his discredited 'Dynastic Race Theory', which held in essence that ancient Egyptian civilization was brought from Mesopotamia during this period through the conquest of the country by a non-African elite. For Petrie's excavation results from his work at Naqada, see W.M.F. Petrie, *Naqada and Ballas 1895* (Bernard Quaritch: London, 1896).

14. T.A.H. Wilkinson, *Early Dynastic Egypt* (Routledge: London, 1999).

15. P. Der Manuelian and T. Schneider (eds), *Towards a New History for the Egyptian Old Kingdom: Perspectives on the Pyramids Age* (Brill: Leiden, 2015). N. Strudwick and H. Strudwick (eds), *Old Kingdom, New Perspectives: Egyptian Art and Archaeology* (Oxbow: London, 2011).

16. Author's translation based on epigraphic reproduction of the text by J. Vandier, *Mo'alla: La tombe d'Ankhtifi et la tombe de Sebekhotep* (IFAO: Cairo, 1950), pp.161–242.

17. M. Bietak, *Avaris, the Capital of the Hyksos: Recent Excavations at Tell el-Dab'a* (British Museum Press: London, 1996).

18. Manetho, quoted by Josephus Flavius, *Against Apion*, Book 1.73.

19. Author's translation based on epigraphic reproduction of the text by A. H. Gardiner. 1916. 'The Defeat of the Hyksos by Kamose: The Carnarvon Tablet, no. I' in *Journal of Egyptian Archaeology* 3, 95–110.

20. For a translation see: G. Boas, *The Hieroglyphics of Horapollo* (Pantheon Books: New York, 1950).

21. J. D. Ray, *The Rosetta Stone and the Rebirth of Ancient Egypt* (Profile: London, 2007).

22. J. Champollion, *Lettre à M. Dacier ... : relative a l'alphabet des hiéroglyphes phonétiques* (Paris, 1822).

23. For the most comprehensive biography of Flinders Petrie and analysis of the impact of his legacy on the field of Egyptology, see M.S. Drower, *Flinders Petrie: A Life in Archaeology* (University of Wisconsin Press: Wisconsin, 1995).

Chapter 2

1. For a detailed description of the circumstances in which the Amarna Letters were found, see A.H. Sayce, 'The Discovery of the Tel El-Amarna Tablets', in *The American Journal of Semitic Languages and Literatures*, 33/2, 1917, pp.89–90.

2. W.M.F. Petrie, *Syria and Egypt from the Tell el Amarna Letters* (London: Methuen & Co., 1898).
3. For an in-depth discussion of the contents of the Amarna Letter, as well as a modern translation with commentary, see W.L. Moran, *The Amarna Letters* John Hopkins University Press: Baltimore and London, 1992).
4. Amarna Letter EA 4, see Moran, *The Amarna Letters*, pp.8–9.
5. Amarna Letter EA 5, see Moran, *The Amarna Letters*, pp.10–11.
6. H. Smith, *The Fortress of Buhen: The Inscriptions* (Egypt Exploration Society: London, 1976), pl. LXXX.
7. Translation by H. Goedicke, 'The Thutmosis I Inscription Near Tomâs', in *Journal of Near Eastern Studies*, 55/3, 1996, pp.161–76.
8. D.B. Redford, *The Wars in Syris and Palestine of Thutmose III* (Brill: Leiden, 2003).
9. P. der Manuelian, *Studies in the Reign of Amenophis II* (Hildesheimer Ägyptologische Beiträge Verlag: Hildesheim, 1987), pp.45–89.
10. A. Kozloff and B. Bryan, *Egypt's Dazzling Sun: Amenhotep III and his World.* (Cleveland Museum of Art: Cleveland, 1992), no. 2.
11. A. Dodson and D. Hilton, *The Complete Royal Families of Ancient Egypt* (Thames & Hudson: London, 2004), p.154.
12. *The Epigraphic Survey*, OIP 102:The Tomb of Kheruef: Theban Tomb 192 (The Oriental Institute of the University of Chicago: Chicago, 1980).
13. B.M. Bryan,. 'The statue program for the mortuary temple of Amenhotep III', in S. Quirke (ed.), *The Temple in Ancient Egypt: New Discoveries and Recent Research* (British Museum Press: London, 1997), pp.57–81.
14. See descriptions of the Boundary Stela of Akhenaten in W.J. Murnane and C.C. van Siclen III, *The Boundary Stelae of Akhenaten* (Kegan Paul International: London and New York, 1993), and also B. Kemp, *The City of Akhenaten and Nefertiti: Amarna and its People* (Thames & Hudson: London, 2012), pp.32–35.
15. Kemp, *The City of Akhenaten*, pp.30–31.
16. See for instance a discussion of possible illnesses in C. Aldred, *Akhenaten, King of Egypt* (Thames & Hudson: London, 1988), and a rebuttal in D. Montserrat, *Akhenaten: History, Fantasy and ancient Egypt* (Routledge: New York, 2000).
17. J. van Dijk, 'The Amarna Period and the Later New Kingdom (*c.* 1352–1069 BC)', in I. Shaw (ed.), *The Oxford History of Ancient Egypt* (Oxford University Press: Oxford, 2000), pp.265–307 (esp. 276).
18. A. Stevens, *Private Religion at Amarna: The Material Evidence* (Archaeopress: Oxford, 2006).
19. Amarna Letter EA 27, see Moran, *The Amarna Letters*, pp.86–90.
20. V. Cordani, 'Aziru's Journey to Egypt and its Chronological Value', in J. Mynarova (ed.), *Egypt and the Near East: The Crossroads* (Czech Institute of Egyptology: Prague, 2011), pp.103–16.
21. W.J. Murnane, 'Overseer of the Northern foreign countries: reflections on the Upper administration of Egypt's empire in western Asia', in J. van Dijk

(ed.), *Essays on ancient Egypt in honour of Herman te Velde* (Groningen, 1997), pp.252–53.

22. Amarna Letter EA234, see Moran, *The Amarna Letters*, pp.292–93.

23. Amarna Letter EA288, see Moran, *The Amarna Letters*, pp.330–32.

24. See for instance discussions in W.M.F. Petrie, *A History of Egypt*, v. 3 (London, 1905), 1; W.F. Albright, 'Cuneiform Material for Egyptian Prosopography', in *Journal of Near Eastern Studies*, 5, 1946, pp.7–25; and E. Cruz-Uribe, 'The Father of Ramesses I: OI 11456', in *Journal of Near Eastern Studies*, 37/3, 1978, pp.237–244 (esp. 243–44).

25. Cruz-Uribe, 'The Father of Ramesses I'.

26. *Urk.* IV 2176:10.

27. A.V. de Perre, 'The Year 16 graffito of Akhenaten in Dayr Abu Ḥinnis: A contribution to the study of the later years of Nefertiti', in *Journal of Egyptian History*, 7, 2014, pp.67–108.

28. A. Dodson, *Amarna Sunset: Nefertiti, Tutankhamun, Ay, Horemheb, and the Egyptian Counter-Reformation* (The American University in Cairo Press: Cairo and New York, 2009).

29. J. Bennett, 'The Restoration Inscription of Tut'ankhamun', in *Journal of Egyptian Archaeology*, 25, 1939, pp.8–15.

30. Bennett, 'The Restoration Inscription', p.9.

31. Dodson, *Amarna Sunset*, pp.70–71.

32. Cruz-Uribe, 'The Father of Ramesses I'.

33. B.J. Kemp, *Ancient Egypt: Anatomy of a Civilisation* (Routledge: London and New York, 1991), pp.312–13.

34. A. Gardiner, 'The Coronation of King Haremhab', in *Journal of Egyptian Archaeology*, 39, 1953, pp.13–31.

35. M. Lichtheim, *Ancient Egyptian Literature: The New Kingdom* (University of California Press: Berkeley, Los Angeles and London, 1976), pp.12–15.

36. *Urk.* IV, pp.32–39.

37. See for instance Pap. Lansing 9.7–9.9, *LEM*, 108-3-9, Pap. Anastasi III, 5.6–9 and Pap. Anastasi IV, 9.5, *LEM* 44.10.

38. J. Kruchten, *Le décret d'Horemheb traduction, commentaire epigraphique, philologique et institutionnel* (Editions de l'Universite de Bruxelles: Brussels, 1981).

39. For a full publication of the tomb and the work of the Anglo-Dutch mission, see G.T. Martin, *The Memphite Tomb of Horemheb, Commander-in-Chief of Tut'ankhamûn* (EES: London, 1989); H.D. Schneider, *The Memphite Tomb of Horemheb, Commander-in-Chief of Tut'ankhamûn II: a Catalogue of the Finds* (Rijksmuseum van Oudheden Leiden and EES: Leiden and London, 1996); J.D. Bourriau, D.A. Aston, M.J. Raven and R. van Walsem, *The Memphite Tomb of Horemheb, Commander-in-Chief of Tut'ankhamûn III: the Pottery* (EES: London 2005); E. Strouhal, *The Memphite Tomb of Horemheb, Commander-in-Chief of Tut'ankhamûn IV: Human Skeletal Remains* (EES: London, 2008); and

M.J. Raven, V. Verschoor, M. Vugts and R. van Walsem, *The Memphite Tomb of Horemheb, Commander-in-Chief of Tutankhamun V: The Forecourt and the Area South of the Tomb, with Some Notes on the Tomb of Tia* (Brepols: Turnhout, 2011). See also an online resource on the excavations of the Tomb of Horemheb and other work at Saqqara by the same mission: http://www.saqqara.nl/excavations/tombs/horemheb.

40. For the original publication of this tomb after its discovery in 1908 by Edward Ayrton, see T.M. Davies, *The Tombs of Harmhabi and Touatânkhamanou* (London, 1912).

41. For a summary of the recent work at the site of the Tell el-Amarna Workmen's Village, see for instance B.J. Kemp, 'The Amarna Workmen's Village in Retrospect', in *JEA*, 73, 1987, pp.21–50.

42. For an extensive discussion of Egyptian queens, see for instance J. Tyldesley, *Chronicle of the Queens of Egypt: From Early Dynastic Times to the Death of Cleopatra* (Thames and Hudson: London, 2006).

43. British Museum BM EA 36.

44. G.T. Martin, 'Queen Mutnodjmet at Memphis and El-Amarna', in *L'Egyptologie en 1979*, II, 1982, pp.275–78.

45. Strouhal, *Human Skeletal Remains*, p.4.

46. P.J. Brand, *The Monuments of Seti I: Epigraphic, Historical and Art Historical Analysis* (Brill: Leiden, Boston, Cologne, 2000), pp.336–41.

47. *KRI* II, 287–288. See also an extensive discussion in W.J. Murnane, 'The Kingship of the Nineteenth Dynasty: A Study in the Resilience of an Institution', in D. O'Connor and D.P. Silverman (eds), *Ancient Egyptian Kingship* (Brill: Leiden, 1995), pp.185–220.

48. Brand, *The Monuments of Seti I*, p.339.

49. J. van Dijk, 'New evidence on the Length of the Reign of Horemheb', in *Journal of the American Research Centre in Egypt*, 44, 2008, pp.193–200.

50. Brussels Museum E. 2171, *KRI* I, 1:6–1:10.

51. *KRI* I, 1:6–1:10.

52. Cairo Museum JdE 38264, *KRI* I, 1:15–3:4.

53. *KRI* I, 4:6–4:8.

54. Abydos Dedicatory Stela of Seti I, *KRI* I, 110:15–114:18.

55. Author's translation based on transcription in *KRI* I, 111:3–111:4.

56. The status and lives of women in ancient Egypt has only comparatively recently received much direct scholarly attention. Several studies on the subject have now been published. See in particular: G. Robins, *Women in Ancient Egypt* (British Museum Press: London 1993); J. Tyldesley, *Daughters of Isis: Women of Ancient Egypt* (Viking: Harmondsworth, 1994) and B.A. Watterson, *Women in Ancient Egypt* (Thrupp: Wrens Park, 1998).

57. This particular example of a New Kingdom Love Poem is from Pap. Chester Beatty I; for a full translation see Lichtheim, *Ancient Egyptian Literature II*, pp.182–84.

58. Tia and Tia were buried together in a tomb at Saqqara; for a full publication of this tomb see G.T. Martin, *The Tomb of Tia and Tia: A Royal Monument of the Ramesside Period in the Memphite Necropolis* (EES: London, 1997).

59. J. von Beckerath, *Chronologie des Ägyptischen Pharaonischen* (Philip von Zabern: Mainz, 1997), p.190.

60. No description of the burial of Ramesses I has survived. This passage is based on information concerning royal mortuary rites shown in painted scenes in the Tomb of Tutankhamun (KV62). For a full publication of this tomb, see N. Reeves, *The Complete Tutankhamun: The King, the Tomb, the Royal Treasure* (Thames and Hudson: London, 1995). See also a detailed description of the tomb and its decorative scheme by the Theban Mapping Project: http://www.thebanmappingproject.com/sites/browse_tomb_876.html.

61. Ancient Egyptian mummification continues to fascinate modern observers, and as a result a vast body of literature exists concerning the precise techniques and processes involved. For an overview of the scholarly research into mummification practices, see R. David, 'Mummification', in I. Shaw and P. Nicholson (eds), *Ancient Egyptian Materials and Technology* (Cambridge University Press: Cambridge, 2000), pp.372–89.

62. KV16. For a description of this tomb see E. Hornung, 'The Tomb of Rameses I', in K.R. Weeks (ed.), *The Treasures of the Valley of the Kings: Tombs and Temples of the Theban West Bank at Luxor* (American University Press: Cairo, 2001), pp.19093; G.B. Johnson, 'KV 16: The Tomb of Rameses I in the Valley of the Kings', in *KMT: A Modern Journal of Ancient Egypt*, 11/4, 2001, pp.62–75; or consult the online Theban Mapping Project resource: http://www.thebanmappingproject.com/sites/browse_tomb_830.html.

63. The story of the rediscovery and repatriation of the mummy of Ramesses I is summed up by S. Ikram, 'Collecting and Repatriating Egypt's Past: Toward a New Nationalism', in H. Sil–verman (ed.), *Contested Cultural Heritage: Religion, Nationalism, Erasure, and Exclusion in a Global World* (Springer: New York, 2011), pp.141–54 (esp. 154).

64. *KRI* I, 111:5–111:6.

Chapter 3

1. For the full epigraphic record of these reliefs, see The Epigraphic Survey, *The Battle Reliefs of King Sety I* (The Oriental Institute: Chicago, 1986).

2. See for instance A.J. Spalinger, 'The Northern Wars of Seti I: An Integrative Study', in *JARCE* 16, 1979, pp.33–37; W.J. Murnane, *The Road to Kadesh: A Historical Interpretation of the Battle Reliefs of King Sety I at Karnak* (The University of Chicago: Chicago); and H. El-Saady, 'The Wars of Sety I at Karnak: A New Chronological Structure', in *SAK* 19, 1992, pp.28994. The chronological reconstruction of Year 1 of Seti's reign and the order of his campaigns given in this publication is based in part on the hypothetical reconstructions provided by Murnane, *The Road to Kadesh*, pp.40–43, 93–94, as well as Spalinger, 'The Northern Wars', p.43.

3. See translations of the relief texts along with other sources of Seti's campaigns in KRI I, 6–30.

4. For an overview of these excavations, see E.D. Oren 'The "Ways of Horus" in North Sinai', in A.F. Rainey (ed.), *Egypt, Israel, Sinai: Archaeological and Historical Relationships in the Biblical Period* (Tel Aviv University: Tel Aviv, 1987), pp.69–119; and E.D. Oren, 'The Establishment of Egyptian Imperial Administration of the "Ways of Horus": An Archaeological Perspective from North Sinai', in E. Czerny, I. Hein, H. Hunger, D. Melman and A. Schwab (eds), *Timelines: Studies in Honour of Manfred Bietak, II* (Peeters: Leuven, 2006), pp.279–92.

5. M.A. el-Maksoud, *Tell Heboua (1981–1991): Enquête Archéologique sur la Deuxième Période Intermédiaire et le Nouvel Empire à l'extrémité Orientale du Delta* (Ministère des Affaires Etrangères, Editions Recherche sur les Civilisations: Paris, 1998); and M.A. el-Maksoud and D. Valbelle, 'Tell Heboua-Tjarou: L'apport de L'Epigraphie', in *RdE* 56, 2005, pp.1–43.

6. Author's translation based on transcription in KRI I, 9:3–9:4.

7. Author's translation based on transcription in W. Helck, *Die Prophezeiung des Nfr.tj* (Wiesbaden, 1970).

8. Author's translation based on transcription in Helck, *Die Prophezeiung*.

9. For a comprehensive overview of the Shasu and their relationship with Egypt, see D.B. Redford, *Egypt, Canaan, and Israel in Ancient Times* (Princeton University Press: Princeton, 1992), pp.269–80.

10. Author's translation based on transcription in KRI I, 8:9–8:10.

11. Pap. Anastasi I, 23.7, Satirical Letter of Hori. Author's translation based on transcription in A.H. Gardiner, *Egyptian Hieratic Texts: Transcribed, Translated and Annutated* (J.C. Hinrichs'sche Buchhandlung: Leipzig, 1911), 23:5.

12. The hypothesis that Seti conducted his campaigns in the Levant directly after his defeat of the Shasu follows the hypothesis proposed by Spalinger, 'The Northern Wars', p.43, and contradicts the hypothetical reconstruction proposed by Murnane, *The Road to Kadesh*, pp.93–94. However, like Spalinger, I find it difficult to imagine that Seti and his entire army would return to Egypt following the defeat of a relatively weak enemy (the Shasu) on the borders of Egypt's sphere of influence. Instead, the Shasu campaign was more likely to have provided an easy start to Seti's campaign, rather than an overall strategic aim in itself.

13. Author's translation based on transcription in *Urk*. IV, 1310–1317.

14. Author's translation based on transcription in KRI I, 14:1–14:2.

15. Author's translation based on transcription in KRI I, 12:8–12:9.

16. Author's translation based on transcription in KRI I, 12:15.

17. A comprehensive discussion of the stratigraphy of Beth Shan, and in particular Level VIII (contemporary with Seti I), can be found in E.F. Morris, *The

Architecture of Imperialism: Military Bases and the Evolution of Foreign Policy in Egypt's New Kingdom (Brill: Leiden, 2004), pp.586–93.

18. For translations of the First and Second Beth Shan Stelas, see K*RI* I, 11:10–12:15 and 15:15–16:15.

19. Author's translation based on transcription in K*RI* I, 16:8–16:9.

20. See translation of the relevant section of The Taking of Joppa and discussion of the use of the Apiru in the story in C. Manassa, *Imagining the Past: Historical Fiction in New Kingdom Egypt* (Oxford University Press: Oxford, 2013), p.107.

21. Author's translation based on transcription in K*RI* I, 16:9–16:10.

22. The Epic of Gilgamesh, Tablet V, trans. by A. George, *The Epic of Gilgamesh: The Babylonian Epic Poem and Other Texts in Akkadian and Sumerian* (Penguin Books: London, 1999), pp.39–47.

23. E. Linder, 'The Khorsabad Wall Relief: A Mediterranean Seascape or River Transport of Timbers', in *JAOS*, 1986, pp.106–02, 273–81 (esp. 273–75).

24. Author's translation based on the transcription in P.E. Newberry, *Beni Hasan, Part I* (London, 1893).

25. Author's translation based on the transcription in A. De Buck, *Egyptian Readingbook* (Ares Publishers: Chicago, 1948), pp.56–63.

26. N. Strudwick, 'Report on the work of the University of Cambridge Theban Mission 1998', in *ASAE* 75, 2000, pp.133–51; and N. Strudwick, 'The Tomb of Senneferi at Thebes', in *EA* 18, 2001, pp.6–9.

27. For a full translation, see R.K. Ritner, *The Libyan Anarchy – Inscriptions from Egypt's Third Intermediate Period.* (Society of Biblical Literature: Atlanta, 2005), pp.87–99.

28. The importance of local labour in the felling and transportation of Lebanese cedar is also alluded to in *Kings* 5:5, when King Solomon requests that King Hiram's own men oversee the tree felling as 'there is not among us any that can skill to hew timber like unto the Sidonians'.

29. Stela BM 1189, K*RI* I, 38:1–38:14.

30. Author's translation based on transcription in K*RI* I, 41:1–41:2.

31. Spalinger, 'The Northern Wars', p.33.

32. Murnane, *The Road to Kadesh*, p.50.

33. See translation of the Biography of Weni in Lichtheim, *Ancient Egyptian Literature* 1, pp.18–22.

34. J.C. Darnell, 'The Rock Inscriptions of Tjehemau at Abisko' in *ZÄS* 130, 2003, pp.31–48.

35. *LEM*, 5.5–6. See also an extensive discussion of conscription by both A. Kadry, *Officers and Officials in the New Kingdom* (Studia Aegyptiaca: Budapest, 1982), p.148, and Spalinger, *War in Ancient Egypt*, p.266.

36. K*RI* IV, 78:14–81:14.

37. Cairo Museum CG 583 and 586. Author's translation based on transcription in *Urk.* IV, 1813–1826.

38. For an overview of the excavations of QIV at Qantir-Piramesses, see E.B. Pusch, 'Vorbereicht über die Abschluskampagne am Grabungsplatz Q IV 1997', in *Ä&L* 9, 1999, pp.17–37.
39. *LEM*, 27:7–14.
40. *LEM*, 126:8–127:14.
41. *LEM*, 69:14–70:10.
42. *LEM*, 133:10–136:3.
43. For a basic introduction to the Hittite civilization, see T.R. Bryce, *The Kingdom of the Hittites* (Oxford University Press: Oxford, 1998).
44. Translation of a fragment of the *Deeds of Shuppiliumash*, adapted from Dodson, *Amarna Sunset*, p.60.
45. Translation adapted from Murnane, *The Road to Kadesh*, pp.24–25.
46. Translation taken from Murnane, *The Road to Kadesh*, p.54, who adapted his English translation from C. *Kühne and* H. *Otten, Der Sausgamuwa-Vertrag* (Wiesbaden, 1971).
47. K*RI* I, 24:10–25:1.
48. K*RI* I, 25:5–25:9.
49. Murnane, *The Road to Kadesh*, p.53.
50. Translation by F. Dunand and C. Zivie-Coche, *Gods and Men in Egypt: 3000 BCE to 395 CE* (Cornell University Press: Ithaca, 2005), p.126.
51. Translation by R.K. Ritner, 'Execration Texts (1.32)', in *Contexts of Scripture Online*, W. Hallo (ed.). Consulted online on 4/10/2016, p.51.
52. Ritner, *Execration Texts*, p.52.
53. For descriptions of the development of Egypto-Libyan relations during the Pharaonic period, see in particular J. Osing, 'Libyen, Libyer', in W. Helck and W. Westendorf (eds), *Lexicon der Ägyptologie*, III (Harrassowitz: Wiesbaden, 1980), cols 10151033; D.T. O'Connor 'The Nature of Tjemhu (Libyan) Society in the later New Kingdom', in A. Leahy (ed.), *Libya and Egypt: 1300–750 BC* (University of London: London, 1990), pp29–114; and S. Snape, 'The Emergence of Libya on the Horizon of Egypt', in D.T. O'Connor and S. Quirke (eds), *Mysterious Lands* (UCL Press: London, 2003), pp.93–106.
54. L. Habachi, 'King Benhepetre Mentuhotep: His Monuments, Place in History, Deification and Unusual Representations in the Form of Gods', in *MDAIK* 19, 1963, pp.21–23.
55. K. Sethe, *Ägyptische Texte zum Gebrauch im akademischen Unterricht: Texte der mittleren Reiches* (Georg Olms: Hildesheim, 1929), pp.3–17.
56. R. Enmarch, *A World Upturned: Commentary on and Analysis of The Dialogue of Ipuwer and the Lord of All* (Oxford University Press: London, 2008), 14.13.
57. W.C. Hayes, 'Inscriptions from the Palace of Amenhotep III', in *JNES* 10, 1951, pp.35–242 (esp. 99).
58. *Urk*. IV, 1656.
59. K*RI* I, 22:5–22:6.

60. Murnane, *The Road to Kadesh*, pp.99–100.
61. E.F. Morris, *The Architecture of Imperialism: Military Bases and the Evolution of Foreign Policy in Egypt's New Kingdom* (Brill: Leiden, 2005), p.831.
62. For further information about the British Museum excavations of Kom Firin, see N. Spencer, *Kom Firin I: the Ramesside Temple and the Site Survey* (British Museum: London, 2008); and N. Spencer, *Kom Firin II: The Urban Fabric and Landscape* (British Museum Press: London, 2014).
63. For information about the recent excavations at Zawiyet Umm el-Rakham, see for instance S. Snape, 'The excavations of the Liverpool University mission to Zawiyet Umm el-Rakham 1994–2001', in *ASAE* 78, 2004, pp.149–60; S. Snape, 'Vor der Kaserne: External Supply and Self-Sufficiency at Zawiyet Umm el-Rakham', in M. Bietak, E. Czerny and I. Forstner-Müller (eds), *Cities and Urbanism in Ancient Egypt: Papers from a Workshop in November 2006 at the Austrian Academy of Sciences* (Verlag der Österreichischen Akademie der Wissenschaften: Wien, 2010), pp.271–88; and S. Snape, 'A Stroll Along the Corniche: Coastal Routes between the Nile Delta and Cyrenaica in the Late Bronze Age', in F. Förster and H. Riemer (eds), *Desert Road Archaeology in Ancient Egypt and Beyond* (Heinrich-Barth-Institut: Cologne, 2013), pp.439–54.
64. For a discussion of the levels of self-sufficiency at Zawiyet Umm el-Rakham, see N. Nielsen, *Subsistence Strategies and Craft Production at the Ramesside Site of Zawiyet Umm el-Rakham* (Unpublished Doctoral Thesis: University of Liverpool, 2016).
65. K*RI* I, 19:14.
66. Murnane, *The Road to Kadesh*, pp.58–65.
67. Spalinger, 'The Northern Wars of Seti I', p.35.
68. Spalinger, 'The Northern Wars of Seti I', p.35, contra Murnane, *The Road to Kadesh*, p.105, who suggested the Chief of Aleppo as an alternative candidate.
69. For an overview of the relations between Assyria and Hanigalbat during the Late Bronze Age, see A. Harrak, *Assyria and Hanigalbat: a historical reconstruction of bilateral relations from the middle of the fourteenth to the end of the twelfth centuries B.C.* (Olms: Hildesheim, 1987).
70. For an in-depth discussion of the Battle of Qadesh and its aftermath, see Spalinger, *War in Ancient Egypt*, pp.209–34.
71. A complete translation of the Biography of Harkuf can be found in Lichtheim, *Ancient Egyptian Literature* I, pp.23–27.
72. For an excellent introduction overview of Nubian culture and relations between Egypt and Nubia, see W.V. Davies (ed), *Egypt and Africa: Nubia from Prehistory to Islam* (British Museum Press: London, 1991).
73. Author's translation of Stela Berlin 14753 based on transcription in G. Meurer, *Nubier in Ägypten bis zum Beginn des Neuen Reiches. Zur Bedeutung der Stela Berlin 14753* (Achet Verlag: Berlin, 1996).

74. For Amenhotep III's policy in Nubia, see in particular D. O'Connor, 'Amenhotep III and Nubia', in D. O'Connor and E. Cline (eds), *Amenhotep III: Perspectives on His Reign* (University of Michigan Press: Ann Arbor, 2002), pp.261–70.

75. K. Spence and P. Rose, 'New Fieldwork at Sesebi', in *EA* 35, 2009, pp.21–24. See also the original field-reports by the Egypt Exploration Society mission to the site in the 1930s: A.M. Blackman, 'Preliminary Report on the Excavations at Sesebi, Northern Province, Anglo-Egyptian Sudan, 1936–37', in *JEA* 23, 1937, pp.145–51; and H.W. Fairman, 'Preliminary Report on the Excavations at Sesebi (Sudla) and Amarah West, Anglo-Egyptian Sudan, 1937–38', in *JEA* 24, 1938, pp.151–56.

76. For the Egypt Exploration Society excavations of Amara West, see in particular P. Spencer, *Amara West I* (Egypt Exploration Society: London, 1997). For the more recent British Museum excavations, see available bibliography including downloadable content on The British Museum Website and also a descriptive guidebook of the excavations, N. Spencer, A. Steven and M. Binder, *Amara West: Living in Egyptian Nubia* (British Museum Press: London, 2016).

77. For an overview of the Argentinian excavations of Aksha, see P. Fuscaldo, 'Aksha (Serra West): la Datación del Sitio', in *REE* 3, 1992, pp.53–4; and P. Fuscaldo, 'Some more on Aksha', in *REE* 5, 1994, pp.9–24.

78. Author's translation based on transcription in K*RI* 102:15–103:4.

79. Ibid.

80. K.A. Kitchen, 'Historical Observations on Ramesside Nubia', in E. Endesfelder, K. Priese, W. Reineke and S. Wenig (eds), *Ägypten und Kusch* (Akademie Verlag: Berlin, 1977), pp.213–26 (esp. 218).

81. J.C. Darnell, 'A Stela of Seti I from the Region Of Kurkur Oasis', in S. Snape and M. Collier (eds), *Ramesside Studies in Honour of K.A. Kitchen* (Rutherford Press: Bolton, 2011), pp.127–44 (esp. 135–36).

82. Author's translation based on transcription in K*RI* 102:15–103:4.

83. K*RI* I, 302:4–303:11.

84. Darnell, 'A Stela of Seti I', pp.139–44.

85. Some limited evidence, namely a relief fragment from the fortress of Akhsha in Nubia, may indicate that Ramesses II participated in the raid on Irem in Year 8 of Seti's reign; see A.J. Spalinger, 'Historical Observations on the Military Reliefs of Abu Simbel and other Ramesside Temples in Nubia', in *JEA* 66, 1980, pp.83–99 (esp. 98–99).

Chapter 4

1. R.J. Leprohon, *The Great Name: Ancient Egyptian Royal Titulary* (Society of Biblical Literature: Atlanta, 2013), p.19.

2. *Urk*. IV, 261.2–4. See also discussion by Lepohon, *The Great Name*, pp.9–11.

3. Author's translation based on the transcription in *Urk*. IV, 80:8–80:17.

4. BM EA854.

5. H. Sourouzian. 'Statues et représentations de statues royales sous Séthi I', in *MDAIK* 49, 1993, pp.239–58 (esp. 248).

6. See Brand, *The Monuments of Seti*, pp.374–76, for an overview of scholarly treatment of Seti's artistic record.

7. *PM* V, 47, and V. Solia, 'A Group of Royal Sculptures from Abydos', in *JARCE* 29, 1992, pp.107–22 (esp. 121), fig. 26.

8. See for instance Metropolitan Museum of Art 42.2.1 of Ramesses II, and Cairo Museum CG 42150 of Ramesses III and the statue of Nebre, the commander of the fortress at Zawiyet Umm el-Rakham during the reign of Ramesses II; see S. Snape, 'The Excavations of the Liverpool University Mission to Zawiyet Umm el-Rakham, 19942001', in *ASAE* 78, 2004, pp.149–160, fig. 14.

9. See discussion of the lappet wig in Brand, *The Monuments of Seti*, pp.19–22. See also examples of early Ramesside figures (most likely Seti himself) depicted in profile wearing this type of headwear on ostraca from Thebes, such as no. 7618 from Museo Archaeologico Nazionale in Florence.

10. Metropolitan Museum of Art, 22.2.21, Solia, 'A Group', fig. 7–10.

11. *Cf* Cairo CG 42073, a grey granite statue of Amenhotep II kneeling with an offering table, and Cairo JE 86059, an alabaster statuette of Thutmosis III kneeling holding two *nw* jars.

12. *KRI* I, 293:11–293:13

13. Author's translation, see Sethe, *Lesestucke*, pp.70–71.

14. For an overview of the current archaeological exploration of the Gebel Silsila quarries, see M. Nilsson, 'Surveying the Sandstone Quarries of Gebel el Silsila', in *KMT* 25/3, 2014, pp.34–43, and M. Nilsson and J. Ward, 'Update from the Field: Gebel el Silsila Project', in *Newsletter of the Society for the Study of Egyptian Antiquities* 2016/2, pp.2–4. See also www. gebelelsilsilaepigraphicsurveyproject.blogspot.co.uk/.

15. A. Thiem, *Speos von Gebel el-Silsileh: Analyse der Architektonischen und Ikonographischen Konzeption im Rahmen des Politischen und Legitimatorischen Programmes der Nacharmanazeit* (Harrassowitz: Wiesbaden, 2000).

16. *KRI* I, 86–80.

17. Klemm and Klemm, *Stones and Quarries*, pp.180–84, 186–87.

18. Author's translation based on the transcription in *KRI* I, 60:9–60:14.

19. For a discussion of the provisioning of the workmen at Gebel el-Silsila, see S.K. Doherty, 'Provisioning an Egyptian Quarry Force', in C. Alvarez, A. Belekdanian, A. Gill and S. Klein (eds), *Current Research in Egyptology 2015* (Casemate Publishers: Oxford, 2016), pp.34–49; and Klemm and Klemm, *Stones and Quarries*, p.185.

20. B. Menu, *Reserches sur l'historie juridique, economique et sociale de l'ancienne Egypte* (Versaille, 1982), pp.184–96.

21. K*RI* I, 61:10–61:15. See also R. Stadelmann, 'Konliche Votivstelen aus dem Toraum des Totentempels Sethos I in Gurna', in *MDAIK 44, 1988, pp.255–74, who discusses the use of the stone quarried from Gebel el-Silsila.*

22. Author's translation based on the transcription in K*RI* I, 73:10–73:15. L. Habachi, 'The Two Rock-Stelae of Sethos I in the Cataracts Area Speaking of Huge Statues and Obelisks', in *BIFAO 73, 1973, pp.113–25.*

23. T. Heldal, 'Constructing a Quarry Landscape from Empirical Data: General Perspectives and a Case Study at the Aswan West Bank, Egypt', in N. Abu-Jaber, E.G. Bloxam, P. Degryse and T. Heldal (eds), *QuarryScapes: Conservation of Ancient Stone Quarry Landscapes in the Eastern Mediterranean* (Geological Survey of Norway: Trondheim, 2009), pp.125–54 (esp. 132).

24. Author's translation based on the transcription in K*RI* I, 74:12–74:15.

25. S. Bergdoll, *The Temple of Deir el-Bahari* (Neopubli, 2013), pp.193–95 (reprint of E. Naville, *The Temple of Deir el Bahari*, III [London, 1898], Pl. CLIII and CLIV).

26. P. Brand, 'The "Lost" Obelisks and Colossi of Seti I', in *Journal of the American Research Center in Egypt* 34, 1997, pp.101–14 (esp. 110), who argues that the three 'available' sides were inscribed first while the monument was still horizontal, before it was raised and scaffolding put in place to decorate the final side. The location where this final decoration took place is still a subject of debate with Brand, 'The "Lost" Obelisks and Colossi', p. 236, arguing that it was conducted close to the destination of the obelisk by a temple workshop, contra L. Habachi, *The Obelisks of Egypt: Skyscrapers of the Past* (Charles Scribner's Sons: New York, 1977), p.32, and R. Klemm and D.D. Klemm, *Stones and Quarries in Ancient Egypt* (British Museum Press: London, 2008), p.236, who argue that the obelisks were decorated in the quarry before they were shipped to their destination.

27. Strabo, *Geography*, XVII.27.

28. Ammianus Marcellinus, *Rerum Gestarum*, XVII.4.12.

29. Pliny, *Natural History*, XXXVI.14.

30. B. Brier, *Cleopatra's Needles: The Lost Obelisks of Egypt* (Bloomsbury Publishing: London, 2016), p.34.

31. This architect also famously raised an Alexandrian uninscribed obelisk in Saint Peter's Square weighing more than 300 tons in 1586, restored the Lateran Obelisk found in 1587 and raised a year later in Piazza San Giovanni, and also raised a third obelisk, the Obelisco Esquilino, in front of Santa Maria Maggiore on Piazza del Quirinale. Among his published works is a detailed account of the operation to raise the obelisk in Saint Peter's Square: D. Fontana, *Della Transportatione dell' Obelisco Vaticano e delle Fabriche di Sisto V* (Rome, 1590).

32. Brand, *The Monuments of Seti I*, pp.134–35.

33. See in particular P. Brand, 'The "Lost" Obelisks and Colossi of Seti I', in *JARCE* 34, 1997, pp.101–14.

34. Brand, 'The "Lost" Obelisks and Colossi', pp.112–13.
35. Author's translation based on the transcription in K*RI* I, 73:13; Brand, 'The "Lost" Obelisks and Colossi', pp.112–13, contra Habachi, 'The Two Rock-Cut Stelae', p.124.
36. EA 16: Moran, *The Amarna Letters*, p.39.
37. J. Ogden, 'Metals', in P.T. Nicholson and I. Shaw (eds), *Ancient Egyptian Materials and Technology* (Cambridge University Press: Cambridge, 2000), pp.148–77 (esp. 162).
38. EA 10: Moran, *The Amarna Letters*, p.19.
39. K*RI* I, 72:1–72:10.
40. Author's translation based on transcription in K*RI* I, 66:2–66:4.
41. D. Klemm and R. Klemm, *Gold and Gold Mining in Ancient Egypt and Nubia/Sudan* (Springer Verlag: Heidelberg, 2013), p.193.
42. S. Schott, *Der Tempel Sehos I. im Wadi Mia* (Vandenhoeck & Ruprecht: Gottingen, 1961).
43. Author's translation based on the transcription in K*RI* I, 67:15–68:1.
44. K*RI* I, 53–55.
45. Such as the fortress of Ras Budhran, see G. Mumford and R. Hummel, 'Preliminary Findings at a Late Old Kingdom Fort in South Sinai, Including the Pottery, from the 2008 Season' in *Journal of Ancient Egyptian Interconnections* 7, 2015, pp. 52–82.
46. The evidence for expeditions despatched by Seti I to Timna is extremely limited, and still contended by scholars. It is, however, likely that at least one mining crew was despatched to the site during his reign, which as a result saw the construction of a small chapel dedicated to the goddess Hathor at the site; see R. Giveon, 'Amenmesse in Canaan', in *GM* 83, 1984, pp.27–30.
47. J. Lauffray, *Karnak d'Égypte: Domaine du Divin. Dix ans de Recherches Archéologiques* (Éditions du Centre National de la Recherche Scientifique: Paris, 1979).
48. M. Ullmann, 'Zur Lesung der Inschrift auf der Säule Antefs II. aus Karnak', in *ZÄS* 132/2, 2005, pp.166–72. See also L. Gabolde, 'Origines d'Amon et Origines de Karnak', in *Égypte, Afrique & Orient* 16, 2000, pp.3–12, and L. Morenz, 'Die Thebanischen Potentaten und ihr Gott: zur Konzeption des Gottes Amun und der (Vor-)Geschichte des Sakralzentrums Karnak in der XI. Dynastie', in *ZÄS* 130, 2003, pp.110–19.
49. P. Lacau and H. Chevrier, *Une chapelle de Sesostris 1er* (Service des Antiquities: Cairo, 1969).
50. See details concerning the construction of the Chapelle Rouge and Hatshepsut's additional construction activity at Karnak in J. Tyldesley, *Hatchepsut* (Penguin Books Ltd: London, 1996).
51. D. Redford, S. Redford and S. Shubert, 'East Karnak Excavations, 1987–1989', in *JARCE* 28, 1991, pp.75–106.

52. For an overview of the Great Hypostyle Hall and recent archaeological and epigraphic work in the area, see H.H. Nelson, *The Great Hypostyle Hall at Karnak* (The Oriental Institute: Chicago, 1981), W. Murnane, 'The Karnak Hypostyle Hall Project: 1992–2002', in Annales du Service des Antiquités de l'Égypte 78, 2004, pp.79–127 and http://history.memphis.edu/hypostyle/.

53. *Cf* R. Engelbach, 'The Origin of the Great Hypostyle Hall at Karnak', in *Ancient Egypt*, 1925, pp.65–71.

54. Brand, *The Monuments of Seti I*, pp.197–201.

55. Brand, *The Monuments of Seti I*, pp.89–102.

56. For an overview of the modern excavations at Heliopolis, see in particular M. Abd el-Gelil, A. Saadani and D. Raue, 'Some Inscriptions and Reliefs from Matariya', in *MDAIK* 52, 1996, pp.143–56; M. Abd el-Gelil, M. Shaker and D. Raue, 'Recent Excavations at Heliopolis', in Orientalia 65, 1996, pp.136–46; M. Abd el-Gelil, R. Suleiman, G. Faris and D. Raue, 'The Joint Egyptian-German Excavations at Heliopolis in Autumn 2005: Preliminary Report', in *MDAIK* 64, 2008, pp.1–9; and M. de Dapper, D. Raue and A. Ashmawy, 'The Temple of Heliopolis: Excavations 20122014', in *EA* 46, 2015, pp.8–11.

57. Author's translation based on the transcription in K*RI* I, 118:8.

58. Brooklyn Museum 49.183.

59. A. Badawy and E. Riefstahl, 'A Monumental Gateway of Sety I – An Ancient Model Restored', in *Miscellanea Wilbouriana* 1, 1972, pp.1–23.

60. M.J. Berlandini, 'La Chapelle de Séthi I: Nouvelles Découvertes', in *BSFE* 99, 1984, pp.28–52.

61. M.D. Adams, 'The Abydos Settlement Site Project: Investigation of a Major Provincial Town in the Old Kingdom and First Intermediate Period', in C. Eyre (ed.), *Proceedings of the Seventh International Congress of Egyptologists* (Peeters: Leuven, 1998), pp.19–30.

62. For a summary of the current work being conducted in the Middle Kingdom settlement of Wah-Sut (South Abydos), see J. Wegner, 'Excavations at the Town of *Enduring-are-the-Places-of-Khakhaure-Maakeru-in-Abydos*: A Preliminary Report on the 1994 and 1997 Seasons', in *JARCE* 35, 1998, pp.1–44, and J. Wegner, 'The Town of Wah-Sut at South Abydos: 1999 Excavations', in *MDAIK* 57, 2001, pp.281–308.

63. Multiple studies of this temple have been conducted, but for the most extensive see A.R. David, *Religious Ritual at Abydos (c. 1300 BC)* (Aris & Phillips Ltd: Warminster, 1973).

64. The Nauri Decree; see further details below, K*RI* I, 38–50.

65. Apart from leaving her out of the Abydos King-list, Seti also usurped one of the most notable monuments of Hatshepsut, the Speos Artemidos Temple located close to the Middle Kingdom necropolis of Beni Hasan near the modern town of el-Minya in Middle Egypt; see for instance A. Fakhry, 'A New Speos from the Reign of Hatshepsut and Thutmosis III at Beni-Hasan', in *ASAE* 39, 1939,

pp.709–23, and H. Goedicke, *The Speos Artemidos of Hatshepsut and Related Discussions* (HALGO: Oakville, 2004).

66. An overview of the reliefs from the Chapel of Ramesses I which were discovered by *sebakkhin* and acquired by the Metropolitan Museum of Art can be found in H.E. Winlock, *Bas-Reliefs from the Temple of Rameses I at Abydos* (Metropolitan Museum of Art: New York, 1921).

67. Author's translation based on transcription in K*RI* I, 110:5–110:6.

68. K*RI* I, 111:5–111:6.

69. M.A. Murray, *The Osireion at Abydos* (Egyptian Research Account: London, 1904).

70. J.H. Breasted, *A History of Egypt from the Earliest Times to the Persian Conquest* (Charles Scribner's Sons: New York, 1905), p.414.

71. M. El-Saghir, *The Discovery of the Statuary Cachette of Luxor Temple* (DAIK: Mainz, 1991), p.25.

72. Brand, *The Monuments of Seti I*, p.13.

73. A.H. Gardiner, *Egypt of the Pharaohs* (Oxford University Press: London, 1961), p.25.

Chapter 5

1. For an alternative translation and a thorough investigation of this text and its occurrence, see G. van den Boorn, *The Duties of the Vizier: Civil Administration in the Early New Kingdom* (Kegan Paul International: London, 1988).

2. Author's translation from N. de Garis Davies, *The Tomb of Rekh-Mi-Re at Thebes* (New York, 1935), pls 26–28.

3. Ibid.

4. Brand, *The Monuments of Seti I*, pp.340–41.

5. V.A. Donohue, 'The Vizier Paser', in *JEA* 74, 1988, pp.103–23. Paser also serves as the fictionalized protagonist in the popular series *The Judge of Egypt* by French Egyptologist and author Christian Jacq.

6. For a comprehensive list, see Donohue, 'The Vizier Paser', pp.103–23.

7. Author's translation based on the transcription in K*RI* I, 293:15.

8. K*RI* I, 207–230. W. Spiegelberg, *Rechnungen aus der Zeit Setis I, circa 1350 v. Chr. mit anderen Rechnungen des neuen Reiches* (Trubner: Strassburg, 1896). A. Spalinger, 'Baking during the Reign of Seti I', in *BIFAO* 86, 1986, pp.307–52.

9. K.A. Kitchen, 'Towards a Reconstruction of Ramesside Memphis', in E. Bleiberg and R. Freed (eds), *Fragments of a Shattered Visage: The Proceedings of the International Symposium of Ramesses the Great* (Memphis State University: Memphis, Tenn., 1991), pp.87–104.

10. O. DeM 108. K*RI* I, 409:9.

11. Papyrus Cairo 58057. K*RI* I, 204.

12. M.R.G. Jané, 'The Meaning of Wine in Egyptian Tombs: The Three Amphorae from Tutankhamun's Burial Chamber', in *Antiquity* 85 (329), 2011, pp.851–58 (esp. 853).

13. *Urk.* 1394: 3–4.
14. M. Moens and W. Wetterstrom, 'The Agricultural Economy of an Old Kingdom Town in Egypt's West Delta: Insights from the Plant Remains', in *JNES* 47/3, 1988, pp.159–73.
15. A.H. Gardiner, *The Wilbour Papyrus, Vol. III: Translation* (Oxford University Press: Oxford, 1941–1948).
16. S.P. Vleeming, *Papyrus Reinhardt: An Egyptian Land List from the Tenth Century BC* (Akademie Verlag: Berlin, 1993), and S.L.D. Katary, 'Land-tenure in the New Kingdom', in A.K. Bowman and E. Rogan (eds), *Agriculture in Egypt: From Pharaonic to Modern Times* (Oxford University Press: Oxford, 1999).
17. Author's translation from *Urk.* IV: 53–62.
18. J. Rose, *Tomb KV 39 in the Valley of the Kings: A Double Archaeological Enigma* (Western Academic & Specialist Press: Bristol, 2000).
19. Much has been written about the village of Deir el-Medina and its inhabitants, but for a general introduction to the daily life and excavation history of the village, see L.H. Lesko (ed.), *Pharaoh's Workers: The Villagers of Deir el Medina* (Cornell University Press: Ithaca and London, 1994).
20. L. Meskell, *Private Life in New Kingdom Egypt* (Princeton University Press: Princeton, 2002), pp.941–25.
21. O. DeM 128, K*RI* I, 300–304.
22. O. Cairo 25608 recto, A.G. McDowell, *Village Life in Ancient Egypt: Laundry Lists and Love Songs* (Oxford University Press: Oxford, 1999), pp.232–33.
23. O. Leipzig 2, McDowell, *Village Life*, pp.233–34.
24. Graffiti of Pharaonic Egypt, p.149
25. H. Jauhiainen, *'Do Not Celebrate Your Feast Without Your Neighbours': A Study of References to Feasts and Festivals in Non-Literary Documents from Ramesside Period Deir el-Medina* (Helsinki University, 2009).
26. Translation by P.J. Frandsen, 'Editing Reality: The Turin Strike Papyrus', in S. Israelit-Groll (ed.), *Studies in Egyptology: Presented to Miriam Lichtheim* (Magnes Press: Jerusalem, 1990), pp.166–99.
27. British Museum EA5634, J.J. Janssen, 'Absence from Work by the Necropolis Workmen of Thebes', in *SAK* 8, 1980, pp.127–52.
28. O. Turin 57456. McDowell, *Village Life*, pp.74–75.
29. O. DeM 146. McDowell, *Village Life*, p.80.
30. O. Brooklyn 37.1880. McDowell, *Village Life*, pp.84–85.
31. B. Bruyere, *La Tombe No. 1 de Sen-Nedjem a Deir el-Medineh* (IFAO: Cairo, 1959).
32. A. el-Qader Adel Mahmoud, *Catalogue of Funerary Objects from the Tomb of the Servant in the Place of Truth Sennedjem (TT1)* (IFAO: Cairo, 2011).
33. Metropolitan Museum of Art, 86.1.1–2.
34. O. DeM 198. McDowell, *Village Life*, p.69.
35. P. Vernus, *Affairs and Scandals in Ancient Egypt* (Cornell University Press: Ithaca, 2003).

36. M.L. Bierbrier, 'Paneb Rehabilitated?', in R.J. Demaree and A. Egberts (eds), *Deir el-medina in the Third Millenium ad* (Nederlands Instituut voor het Nabije Oosten: Leiden, 2000), pp.51–54.
37. L. Weiss, *Religious Practice at Deir el-Medina* (Peeters: Leuven, 2015).
38. M. Drower (ed.), *Letters from the Desert: The Correspondance of Flinders and Hilda Petrie* (Aris and Phillips: Oxford, 2004), p.48.
39. W.M. Flinders Petrie, *Ten Years' Digging in Egypt: 1881–1891* (The Religious Tract Society: London, 1893), p.30.
40. L. Habachi, 'Khata'na-Qantir: Importance', in *ASAE* 52, 1954, pp.443–562.
41. M. Hamza, 'Excavations of the Department of Antiquities at Qantir (Faqus District): Season May 21ˢᵗ Jly 7th, 1928', in *ASAE* 30, 1930, pp.31–68.
42. Eg. M. Bietak, 'Die Haupstadt der Hyksos und die Ramsesstadt', in *Antike Welt* 6, 1975, pp.28–43.
43. L. Habachi, 'Sethos I's Devotion to Seth and Avaris', in *ZÄS* 100, 1974, pp.95–102.
44. W.C. Hayes, *Glazed Tiles from the Palace of Ramesses II at Kantir* (New York, 1937).
45. Hamza, 'Excavations of the Department of Antiquities at Qantir', pp.51–52. H.W. Müller, 'Bemerkungen zu den Kacheln mit Inschriften aus Qantir und zu den Rekonstruktionen gekachelter Palasttore', in *MDAIK* 37, 1981, pp.339–57.
46. E. Pusch, 'Metallverarbeitende Werkstätten der frühen Ramessidenzeit in Qantir-Piramesse/Nord', in *Agypten und Levante*, 1, 1990, pp.76–113.
47. A. Tillmann, *Neolithikum in der Späten Bronzezeit Steingeräte des 2. Jahrtausend aus Auaris-Piramesse* (Philipp von Zabern: Mainz am Rhein, 2007).
48. A. Herold, 'Piramesses, The Northern Capital: Chariots, Horses and Foreign Gods', in *Capital Cities: Urban Planning and Spiritual Dimensions*, 1998, pp.129–46. A. Herold, *Streitwagentechnologie in der Ramses-Stadt: Bronze an Pferd und Wagen* (Philipp von Zabern: Mainz am Rhein, 1999).
49. E. Pusch, 'Recent Work at Northern Piramesse', in *Fragments of a Shattered Visage*, 1991, pp.199–220.
50. Pap. Anastasi III (7.2–7.10).
51. *KRI* I, 206–231.

Chapter 6

1. Brand, *The Monuments of Seti I*, pp.343–49.
2. *Cf* K.C. Seele, *The Coregency of Ramses II with Seti I and the Date of the Great Hypostyle Hall at Karnak* (Chicago, 1940). W.J. Murnane, 'The Earlier Reign of Ramesses II and his Coregency with Seti I', in *JNES* 34, 1975, pp.153–90, *contra* Murnane, *Road to Kadesh*, p.93. A.J. Spalinger, 'Traces of the Early Career of Ramesses II', in *JNES* 38, 1979, pp.271–86. Brand, *The Monuments of Seti I*, pp.312–32.
3. Cairo Museum CG 20516.

4. S. Seidlmayer, 'New Rock Inscriptions at Elephantine', in *Egyptian Archaeology* 14, 1999, pp.41–43.
5. K*RI* II, 327:12–328:4.
6. *Cf* Capart, 'Le Temple', Pl. XLVIII.
7. J. van Dijk, 'The Date of the Gebel Barkal Stela of Seti I', in D. Aston, B. Bader, C. Gallorini, P. Nicholson and S. Buckingham (eds), *Under the Potter's Tree: Studies on Ancient Egypt Presented to Janine Bourriau on the Occasion of her 70th Birthday* (Peeters: Leuven, 2011), pp.325–32.
8. Author's translation based on R. Koch, *Die Erzählung des Sinuhe* (Foundation Égyptologique Reine Elisabeth: Brussels, 1990).
9. J.E. Harris and E.F. Wente (eds), *An X-Ray Atlas of the Royal Mummies* (The University of Chicago Press: Chicago, 1980), pp.210–11.
10. Harris and Wente, *An X-Ray Atlas*, p.294.
11. C. Hobson, *Exploring the World of the Pharaohs: A Complete Guide to Ancient Egypt* (Thames & Hudson: London, 1993), p.97.
12. This inscription is drawn in black ink on a ceramic vessel datable to the 13th Dynasty, currently held in the Manchester Museum, acc. no. 3964.
13. R. Stadelmann, 'The Mortuary Temple of Seti I at Gurna: Excavation and Restoration', in E. Bleiberg and R. Freed (eds), *Fragments of a Shattered Visage: The Proceedings of the International Symposium on Ramesses the Great* (Memphis State University: Memphis, Tenn, 1991), pp.251–57 (esp. 253).
14. R. Stadelmann, 'Der Tempel Sethos' I. in Gurna', in *MDAIK* 28, 1972, pp.293–99. J. Osing, *Der Tempel Sethos' I. in Gurna: Die Reliefs und Inschriften* (Philipp von Zabern: Mainz, 1977). K. Mysliwiex, *Keramik und Kleinfunde aus der Grabung im Tempel Sethos' I. in Gurna* (Philipp von Zabern: Mainz, 1987). R. Stadelmann, *Der Tempel Sethos' I. in Gurna: Architektur und Deutung* (Philipp von Zabern: Mainz, 1988).
15. N. Reeves and R.H. Wilkinson, *The Complete Valley of the Kings* (Thames and Hudson: London, 1996), pp.137–39.
16. E. Hornung, *The Ancient Egyptian Books of the Afterlife* (Cornell University Press: Ithaca, 1999).
17. B.M. Fagan, *The Rape of the Nile: Tomb Robbers, Tourists and Archaeologists in Egypt* (3rd ed.) (Westview Press: Boulder and Oxford, 2004), p.65.
18. I.N. Hume, *Belzoni: The Giant Archaeologists Love to Hate* (University of Virginia Press: Charlottesville, 2011).
19. *The Times of London*, Saturday 12 May 1804.
20. A. Siliotti (ed.), *Belzoni's Travels: Narrative of the Operations and Recent Discoveries in Egypt and Nubia by Giovanni Belzoni* (British Museum Press: London, 2001), p.295.
21. Siliotti, *Belzoni's Travels*, p.201.
22. This sarcophagus is today housed in Sir John Soane's Museum in London. After being transported back to the United Kingdom, the sarcophagus was

initially housed in the British Museum storerooms, but the museum refused to pay the high price Belzoni and his investors demanded for it. Instead, it was bought by Sir John Soane, the noted architect, in 1824 and added to his private collection of Egyptian artefacts. For a useful in-depth study of this artefact, see John H. Taylor, *Sir John Soane's Greatest Treasure: The Sarcophagus of Seti I* (Pimpernel Press Ltd: London, 2017).

23. Siliotti, *Belzoni's Travels*, p.207.
24. Siliotti, *Belzoni's Travels*, p.208.

Chapter 7

1. Fagan, *The Rape of the Nile*, pp.195–98.
2. T.E. Peet, *The Great Tomb-Robberies of the Twentieth Egyptian Dynasty: Being a Critical Study, with Translation and Commentaries of the Papyri in Which These are Recorded* (Clarendon Press: Oxford, 1930).
3. A.P. Kozloff, 'The Decorative and Funerary Arts during the Reign of Amenhotep III', in D. O'Connor and E.H. Cline (eds), *Amenhotep III: Perspectives on his Reign* (University of Michigan Press: Ann Arbor, 2001), pp.95–124 (esp. 112).
4. The story of the Abd el-Rasul clan and the discovery of the Royal Cache in Tomb DB320 is the subject of one of the finest piece of Egyptian cinema, the 1969 film *The Night of Counting the Years*, directed by Shadi Abdel Salam (1930–1986).
5. Josephus, *Contra Apionem*, I.15–16.
6. Herodotus, *The Histories*, II.102–110.
7. Gardiner, *Egypt of the Pharaohs*, p.249.
8. Gardiner, *Egypt of the Pharaohs*, p.255.
9. Brand, *The Monuments of Seti I*, p.394.
10. J.A. Weisse, *The Obelisk and Freemasonry According to the Discoveries of Belzoni and Commander Gorringe; Also Egyptian Symbols Compared with Those Discovered in American Mounds* (J.W. Bouton: New York, 1880), p.174.
11. H. El-Zeini, *Omm Sety's Egypt: A Story of Ancient Mysteries, Secret Lives and the Lost History of the Pharaohs* (St. Lynn's Press: Pittsburgh, 2007). J. Cott, *The Search for Omm Sety* (Warner Books: New York, 1987).

Selected Sources

Badawy, A., and Riefstahl, E., 'A Monumental Gateway of Sety I – An Ancient Model Restored', in *Miscellanea Wilbouriana* 1, 1972, pp.1–23.

Bard, K.A., *An Introduction to the Archaeology of Ancient Egypt* (Blackwell Publishing: Malden, Oxford and Carlton, 2008).

Berlandini, M.J., 'La Chapelle de Séthi I: Nouvelles Découvertes', *in Bulletin de la Société Française d'égyptologie* 99, 1984, pp.28–52.

Bietak, M., 'Die Haupstadt der Hyksos und die Ramsesstadt', in *Antike Welt* 6, 1975, pp.28–43.

Bietak, M., *Avaris, the Capital of the Hyksos: Recent Excavations at Tell el-Dab'a* (British Museum Press: London, 1996).

van den Boorn, G.P.F., *The Duties of the Vizier: Civil Administration in the Early New Kingdom* (Kegan Paul International: London, 1988).

Brand, P., 'The "Lost" Obelisks and Colossi of Seti I', in *JARCE* 34, 1997, pp.101–14.

Brand, P.J., *The Monuments of Seti I: Epigraphic, Historical and Art Historical Analysis* (Brill: Leiden, 2000).

Brier, B., *Cleopatra's Needles: The Lost Obelisks of Egypt* (Bloomsbury Publishing: London, 2016).

Cott, J., *The Search for Omm Sety* (Warner Books: New York, 1987).

Cruz-Uribe, E., 'The Father of Ramesses I: OI 11456', in *JNES* 37/3, 1978, pp.237–44.

Davies, W.V. (ed.), *Egypt and Africa: Nubia from Prehistory to Islam* (British Museum Press: London, 1991).

de Dapper, M., D. Raue and A. Ashmawy. 'The Temple of Heliopolis: Excavations 2012-2014' in *EA* 46, 2015, 8-11.

Dodson, A., and Hilton, D., *The Complete Royal Families of Ancient Egypt* (Thames & Hudson: London, 2004).

Donohue, V.A., 'The Vizier Paser', in *JEA* 74, 1988, pp.103–23.

El-Maksoud, M.A., *Tell Heboua (1981–1991): Enquête Archéologique sur la Deuxième Période Intermédiaire et le Nouvel Empire à l'extrémité Orientale du Delta* (Ministère des Affaires Etrangères, Editions Recherche sur les Civilisations: Paris, 1998).

El-Saady, H., 'The Wars of Sety I at Karnak: A New Chronological Structure', in *SAK* 19, 1992, pp.289–94.

Enmarch, R., *A World Upturned: Commentary on and Analysis of The Dialogue of Ipuwer and the Lord of All* (Oxford University Press: London, 2008)

Fagan, B.M., *The Rape of the Nile: Tomb Robbers, Tourists and Archaeologists in Egypt* (3rd ed.) (Westview Press: Boulder, pp.181–90).

Habachi, L., 'The Two Rock-Stelae of Sethos I in the cataracts Area Speaking of Huge Statues and Obelisks', in *BIFAO* 73, 1973, pp.113–25.

Habachi, L., 'Sethos I's Devotion to Seth and Avaris', in *ZÄS* 100, 1974, pp.95–102.

Habachi, L., *The Obelisks of Egypt: Skyscrapers of the Past* (Charles Scribner's Sons: New York, 1977).

Harris, J.E., and Wente, E.F. (eds), *An X-Ray Atlas of the Royal Mummies* (The University of Chicago Press: Chicago, 1980).

Herold, A., *Streitenwagentechnologie in der Ramses-Stadt: Bronze an Pferd und Wagen* (Philipp von Zabern: Mainz am Rhein, 1999).

Hume, I.N., *Belzoni: The Giant Archaeologists Love to Hate* (University of Virginia Press: Charlottesville, 2011).

Kemp, B.J., *Ancient Egypt: Anatomy of a Civilisation* (Routledge: London, 1989).

Kitchen, K.A., 'The Arrival of the Libyans in Late New Kingdom Egypt', in A. Leahy (ed.), *Libya and Egypt: 1300–750 BC* (University of London: London, 1990), pp.15–27.

Kitchen, K.A., 'Towards a Reconstruction of Ramesside Memphis', in E. Bleiberg and R. Freed (eds), *Fragments of a Shattered Visage: The Proceedings of the International Symposium of Ramesses the Great* (Memphis State University: Memphis, Tenn., 1991), pp.87–104.

Klemm, D., and Klemm, R., *Gold and Gold Mining in Ancient Egypt and Nubia/Sudan* (Springer Verlag: Heidelberg, 2013).

Kruchten, J., *Le décret d'Horemheb traduction, commentaire epigraphique, philologique et institutionnel* (Editions de l'Universite de Bruxelles: Bruxelles, 1981).

Leprohon, R.J., *The Great Name: Ancient Egyptian Royal Titulary* (Society of Biblical Literature: Atlanta, 2013).

Lesko, L.H. (ed.), *Pharaoh's Workers: The Villagers of Deir el Medina* (Cornell University Press: Ithaca and London, 1994).

Manassa, C., *The Great Karnak inscription of Merneptah: Grand Strategy in the 13th Century BC* (Oxbow: Oxford, 2003).

Moran, W.L., *The Amarna Letters* (John Hopkins University Press: Baltimore and London, 1992).

Morris, E.F., *The Architecture of Imperialism: Military Bases and the Evolution of Foreign Policy in Egypt's New Kingdom* (Brill: Leiden, 2005).

Müller, H.W., 'Bemerkungen zu den Kacheln mit Inschriften aus Qantir und zu den Rekonstruktionen gekachelter Palasttore', in *MDAIK* 37, 1981, pp.339–57.

Murnane, W.J., 'The Earlier Reign of Ramesses II and his Coregency with Seti I', in *JNES* 34, 1975, pp.153–90.

Murnane, W.J., *The Road to Kadesh: A Historical Interpretation of the Battle Reliefs of King Sety I at Karnak* (The University of Chicago: Chicago, 1990).

Murnane, W.J., 'Overseer of the Northern foreign countries: reflections on the Upper administration of Egypt's empire in western Asia', in J. van Dijk (ed.), *Essays on ancient Egypt in honour of Herman te Velde* (Groningen, 1997).

O'Connor, D., *Abydos: Egypt's First Pharaohs and the Cult of Osiris* (Thames & Hudson: London, 2009).

Oren, E.D., 'The "Ways of Horus" in North Sinai', in A.F. Rainey (ed.), *Egypt, Israel, Sinai: Archaeological and Historical Relationships in the Biblical Period* (Tel Aviv University: Tel Aviv, 1987), pp.69–119.

Oren, E.D., 'The Establishment of Egyptian Imperial Administration of the "Ways of Horus": An Archaeological Perspective from North Sinai', in E. Czerny, I. Hein, H. Hunger, D. Melman and A. Schwab (eds), *Timelines: Studies in Honour of Manfred Bietak*, II. (Peeters: Leuven, 2006), pp.279–92.

Pusch, E., 'Metallverarbeitende Werkstätten der frühen Ramessidenzeit in Qantir-Piramesse/Nord', in *Ägypten und Levante* 1, 1990, pp.76–113.

Pusch, E.B., 'Vorbereicht über die Abschluskampagne am Grabungsplatz Q IV 1997', in *Ä&L* 9, 1999, pp.17–37

Ray, J.D., *The Rosetta Stone and the Rebirth of Ancient Egypt* (Profile: London, 2007).

Schott, S., *Der Tempel Sehos I. im Wadi Mia* (Vandenhoeck & Ruprecht: Gottingen, 1961).

Seele, K.C., *The Coregency of Ramses II with Seti I and the Date of the Great Hypostyle Hall at Karnak* (Chicago, 1940).

Shaw, I. (ed.), *The Oxford History of Ancient Egypt* (Oxford University Press: Oxford, 2003).

Siliotti, A. (ed.), *Belzoni's Travels: Narrative of the Operations and Recent Discoveries in Egypt and Nubia by Giovanni Belzoni* (British Museum Press: London, 2001).

Snape, S., *The Complete Towns and Cities of Ancient Egypt* (Thames & Hudson: London, 2014).

Solia, V., 'A Group of Royal Sculptures from Abydos', in *JARCE* 29, 1992, pp.107–22.

Sourouzian, H., 'Statues et représentations de statues royales sous Séthi I', in MDAIK 49, 1993, pp.239–58.

Spalinger, A., 'Baking during the Reign of Seti I', in *BIFAO* 86, 1986, pp.307–52.

Spalinger, A.J., 'The Northern Wars of Seti I: An Integrative Study', in *JARCE* 16, 1979, pp.33–37.

Spalinger, A.J., 'Traces of the Early Career of Ramesses II', in *JNES* 38, 1979, pp.271–86.

Spalinger, A.J., 'Historical Observations on the Military Reliefs of Abu Simbel and other Ramesside Temples in Nubia', in *JEA* 66, 1980, pp.83–99.

Spencer, N., Steven, A., and Binder, M., *Amara West: Living in Egyptian Nubia* (British Museum Press: London, 2016).

Spencer, N., *Kom Firin I: the Ramesside Temple and the Site Survey* (British Museum: London, 2008).

Spencer, N., *Kom Firin II: The Urban Fabric and Landscape* (British Museum Press: London, 2014).

Spiegelberg, W., *Rechnungen aus der Zeit Setis I, circa 1350 v. Chr. mit anderen Rechnungen des neuen Reiches* (Trubner: Strassburg, 1896).

Stadelmann, R., 'Konliche Votivstelen aus dem Toraum des Totentempels Sethos' I. in Guarna', in *MDAIK* 44, 1988, pp.255–74.

Stadelmann, R., 'The Mortuary Temple of Seti I at Gurna: Excavation and Restoration', in E. Bleiberg and R. Freed (eds), *Fragments of a Shattered Visage: The Proceedings of the International Symposium on Ramesses the Great* (Memphis State University: Memphis, Tenn, 1991), pp.251–57.

Thiem, A., *Speos von Gebel el-Silsileh: Analyse der Architektonischen und Ikonographischen Konzeption im Rahmen des Politischen und Legitimatorischen Programmes der Nacharmanazeit* (Harrassowitz: Wiesbaden, 2000).

Thompson, J., *Wonderful Things: A History of Egyptology – 1: From Antiquity to 1881* (American University in Cairo Press: Cairo, 2015), pp.267–82.

Tyldesley, J., *Daughters of Isis: Women of Ancient Egypt* (Viking: Harmondsworth, 1994).

Index